WORLD ETHICS

EDINBURGH STUDIES IN WORLD ETHICS

Other titles in the series:

WORLD ETHICS

THE NEW AGENDA

2nd Edition

Nigel Dower

EDINBURGH UNIVERSITY PRESS

© Nigel Dower, 1998, 2007

Edinburgh University Press
22 George Square, Edinburgh

First published 1998
This edition 2007

Typeset in Times
by Koinonia, and
printed and bound in Great Britain by
Antony Rowe Ltd, Chippenham, Wilts

A CIP record for this book is available
from the British Library

ISBN 978 0 7486 3270 1 (hardback)
ISBN 978 0 7486 3271 8 (paperback)

CONTENTS

PREFACE

A word about the origins of this book might be helpful. In the 1970s I became involved through the World Development Movement in aid and trade issues and this led to an interest in environmental problems as well as an involvement in the United Nations Association. By the beginning of the 1980s I felt the need to relate my philosophical interest in ethics to these practical concerns and this resulted in 1983 in a book entitled *World Poverty – Challenge and Response*. At that time an interest emerged amongst students, first in the Philosophy Department and later in the Politics and International Relations Department too, and this resulted in an honours course on 'ethics and international relations' which has run most years since then. This book is partly based on ideas and arguments used in that course. It is also an attempt to draw on materials which have appeared in various articles and chapters which have appeared mainly in the last ten years.

With this background it will be no surprise that this work is at one level a work of advocacy – a recommendation that we take seriously the idea of being world citizens and that we need to look critically at the dominant assumptions about the role and norms of the nation-state. It does not however attempt to give detailed prescriptions about particular cases, but rather sets out the case for an attitude or approach. This approach can be summed up as 'solidarity, pluralism and the way of peace': solidarity as responsibility for the well-being of fellow human beings generally, pluralism as the need to accept within limits diversity over the ways individuals and peoples understand the good, and the way of peace as the generally preferred way of tackling issues and conflicts, both intellectual and practical. Perhaps my belief in social responsibility, tolerance and the way of peace reflects my Quaker ideal of 'answering that of God in everyone', but I should stress that the kinds of arguments used are equally accessible to those with or without religious faith.

The advocacy of a form of cosmopolitanism is however for the most part very much in the background. The main purpose of the work is to

vii

set out as clearly as possible the various positions and the arguments for them which can be adopted towards the ethics of the relations of states and more generally ethical relations between people worldwide. This is important for two reasons: because the issues are important in themselves and contribute to the central issues in ethics, and because it is only if we uncover and understand the different starting points that we can appreciate why so often different groups come out with such different views about issues of foreign policy and so on.

This book then is an exercise in philosophical ethics. Although no doubt readers with some background knowledge of or interest in ethics will find it more immediately accessible, it is written in such a way that it should make sense to students who have not studied ethics as a course before and to the general reader with some interest in theoretical reflection. In a way it provides a rather unusual introduction to many of the central issues of ethics. Although it is a textbook, it is not merely an exposition of familiar material. Indeed one of its distinctive features is the attempt to organise ideas and arguments in a somewhat unfamiliar way. It is not a textbook in international relations, and a student wanting basic factual information about international relations or the dominant non-normative theories of international relations, must look elsewhere. Nor is it an attempt either to describe the present state of the world or to predict how the future will go. Any serious interest in ethics presupposes that the future is not determined, at least in the sense that we can make choices, individually and collectively, about what to do, and that what we choose to do is at least partly influenced by what we think ought to be done or is worth pursuing. Ethical reasoning can make a difference. One may be quite pessimistic about some of the trends in the world, as I confess to being about the environmental consequences of our continued commitment to affluence. But trends are not inevitabilities, and if trends can be checked through transformations of attitude and of ethical priority, it is worth all the argument. I was once described twenty years ago as a 'factual pessimist and a moral optimist'. It was an accurate description. It still is. I hope the reader can share this moral optimism in the face of an imperfect world.

This book is the first in a series of works in the Edinburgh Studies in World Ethics, of which I am the series editor. It would be artificial to provide a separate Preface from the series editor, but let me merely add that the idea of the series first formed four years ago when the then commissioning editor of Edinburgh University Press visited the Department of Philosophy in Aberdeen. The other books will be on more specific issues such as Aid and Trade and the Global Environment. The general guideline for books in the series is that they adopt a broadly cosmopolitan approach of the kind indicated above and consider critically alternative approaches to cosmopolitanism and alternative versions of cosmopolitanism.

My thanks go to Gayle Dower, Peter McCaffery, Michael Partridge and Dan Shaw for comments on earlier drafts, to Stephen Chadwick for extended discussion of themes, to members of the Department's Global Citizenship Project for general stimulus, to numerous students for the accumulation of ideas that later surface as 'my' thought, to Louise Gregory for proofreading, to Mary and Rudi Dower for their understanding and acceptance of my recent preoccupations, and to my mother Jean Dower for general encouragement and interest. Indeed, it was in my formative years that I first learnt from her and my father Arthur the ideas of world citizenship. This book is dedicated to the memory of my father, who, both by example and by precept, took the wider view.

Nigel Dower
Aberdeen, September 1997

PREFACE TO THE
SECOND EDITION

I am grateful to Edinburgh University Press for this chance to revise and update the first edition which I was working on some ten years ago. I have shortened some sections which now seem less important or interesting, added some new arguments and examples, and rewritten bits that now seem unclear. By and large the main arguments and language remain the same. If one were to write a new book altogether after such a time lapse, something rather different might well be written, but I do not disagree with any of my main theses.

It may be that in a few years time people will ask 'what was 9/11?' but the crashing of the planes into the Twin Towers on 11 September 2001 remains for now a defining moment in world affairs. The initial response was to attack Afghanistan as harbouring al-Qaida and then to pursue the 'war on terror'. This has tended to reinforce the influential perspective of Samuel Huntington of the 'clash of civilisations' with militant Islam cast in the role of the enemy (Huntington 1996). Meantime other areas of activity like the ever-expanding world economy, dominated at the present time by Western states and companies, proceeds as if Fukuyama's thesis of the 'End of History' were true (Fukuyama 1992). I refer to the relentless projection of a certain model of development – not just economic growth but the values of libertarianism and the free market coupled with the values of good governance – as if it were just a matter of time before these values are adopted universally or at least accepted in all parts of the world.

But these perspectives – the clash of civilisations and the spread of Western values – are both dangerous for different reasons. What we need is a frank recognition that we do indeed live in a diverse world, but also that we need to find areas of convergence in an agreed global ethic. This message was already at the heart of the first edition of this book but events since then have made the case even stronger. Bhikhu Parekh has put the challenge neatly when he said that we need to find a global ethic which we can both assent to and consent to; that is, an ethic which we each for our different intellectual reasons can assent to, but which is at the same time an ethic which many others can consent to through a process of global inter-cultural dialogue (Parekh 2005).

In various respects my emphases are different now. First, I now think we need to distinguish more carefully a global ethic from a cosmopolitan ethic. Or rather, we need to say that a cosmopolitan ethic is a strong form of a global ethic. The point at issue is that a global ethic in a weaker but I think commonly accepted form is the claim (against relativism) that there are or are to be accepted universal values – centrally ideas about human well being and the basic norms of social co-existence – that are common to all people. A cosmopolitan ethic is a global ethic which also includes significant claims about transnational obligations – obligations that go beyond mere tolerance or non-interference – and claims about membership of some kind of global moral community. This ethic is more opposed to communitarian claims that significant obligations extend as far as more limited established communities.

This second feature of cosmopolitanism of course relates to the discourse of global citizenship. To put the distinction between a global ethic and a cosmopolitan ethic another way: not everyone who accepts a global ethic as a universal ethic would accept the idea of global citizenship.

This distinction between a global ethic and a cosmopolitan ethic helps us to make sense of the idea that the internationalist 'morality of states' could be based on some form of global ethic – though of course it need not be either – without being a cosmopolitan approach. This is well illustrated in thinking about the rules of war which can, from an internationalist point of view, be based on the recognition of the common humanity of all, including the soldiers and civilians of an enemy state.

Second, when I was writing the book in 1995–7 I saw it as my main task to make a case for cosmopolitanism as such, in opposition to mainstream thinking which failed to adopt any cosmopolitan approach. Whilst I believe that much contemporary thinking about international and global affairs does still fail to embrace cosmopolitan thinking (even if it includes a global ethic in the weaker sense indicated above), the situation is actually more complicated. The issue is now rather more that there are rival cosmopolitanisms at work in the world. In Chapter 4 I had indicated three broad types of cosmopolitanism – dogmatic idealism, libertarian minimalism and solidarist pluralism – but more needs to be said about these different forms. First, dogmatic idealism is far more prevalent in the modern world than I had implied. We only need to consider the immense influence of both Christian and Muslim fundamentalism. In characterising libertarianism as minimalist I was setting it up as a contrast to solidarist pluralism, but in fact this contrast is too sharp. The dominant libertarian view insofar as it is cosmopolitan is not necessarily minimalist, nor is the view that I wish to promote one that is completely pluralist. Those who advocate liberty may well accept a significant trans-boundary obligation to promote liberty and the conditions under which it flourishes, and this often goes with the active promotion too of the values of good governance – democracy, human rights, accountability – seen as the conditions of development. Likewise, but with different agendas and priorities, advocates of social justice, socio-economic rights, the conditions of peace or measures adequate to protect the environment, may promote policies and measures which are not accepted by many others, either because they have different values or they have different views about how to implement them. So the real issue is not between minimalism and global responsibility to promote values or the conditions of living, but between different views about what is to be promoted and what is not be promoted – a specific religious world-view, liberty, democracy, social justice, etc. However I still think that solidarist pluralism captures more reasonably the right kind of cosmopolitanism.

Since I wrote the first edition, the NATO operation in Kosovo took place in 1999. This was interesting from a world ethics point of view because a significant motivation, if not the main motivation for it, was cosmopolitan – namely a humanitarian concern for Kosovans whose rights were being violated. Humanitarian intervention by military means may be done for a number of reasons, but insofar as it is from a genuine concern for ordinary people, the reasoning is cosmopolitan rather than internationalist, and comes into conflict with the internationalist assumptions underlying the UN Charter, especially article 2.7. That it was inspired by cosmopolitan considerations does not of course make it right, since one might have objections to it, both because the use of force is either wrong in itself or because it is wrong in being counter-productive. This illustrates an important dimension to cosmopolitan thinking which I did not adequately emphasise; namely, that even if a cosmopolitan has the right goals, there may be significant disagreements about the ethics of the means.

Three other developments since I last wrote should be mentioned here and will be commented on more fully later. First, in 2000 the UN adopted the millennium development goals (MDGs). This of course only confirms earlier commitments in international forums to measures to tackle global poverty, but it is symptomatic of an increasing acceptance of a cosmopolitan conception of global justice. In 1999 the International Criminal Court (ICC) came into existence. It underlines the fact that individuals do not merely have human rights but also obligations towards any other human beings, which are not merely moral but also legal. This is an important aspect of the development of global citizenship as having an institutional as well as ethical content. During the last ten years world leaders and many citizens in many countries have woken up to the serious challenges of global warming or what is now called climate change. If one of the motives for a cosmopolitan version of a global ethic which takes seriously our trans-boundary obligations towards one another is the recognition that our collective well-being or interests need a high degree of co-operation, then this issue alone may well prove the catalyst to a conversion in many people to a world ethic of the kind advanced in this book.

I am pleased to add that since the first edition of my book a number of other books have come out in the Edinburgh Studies in World Ethics – Robin Attfield's *Ethics of the Global Environment* (1999), Peter Brown's *Ethics, Economics and International Relations* (2000), Des Gasper's *Ethics of Development* and Iain Atack's *Ethics of Peace and War* (2005). Further books are in the pipeline or planned.

Whilst, as I explain in the introduction, there were particular reasons for calling my book 'World Ethics' and the series 'Edinburgh Studies in World Ethics', I realise that 'cosmopolitan ethics' and 'global ethics', given the surge of interest in the former and the way the latter has come to be understood, would have been just as appropriate. But the important thing is that increased critical engagement with ethical issues of a global kind takes place, whatever label is given to the ethics that informs it. Of course, not all perspectives in global ethics are equally valuable and some views may from one's own point of view be wrong, but – and this may of course be an article of faith – it seems reasonable to suppose that the more people who engage with these global ethical issues, the more likely it is that we will create a better world.

Nigel Dower
Aberdeen, November 2006

INTRODUCTION

I. WHAT IS WORLD ETHICS?

A. THE NATURALNESS OF ETHICAL STATEMENTS ABOUT WORLD AFFAIRS

Consider the following statements:

1. Governments in the rich countries ought to give more or better aid to the Third World.
2. It is morally disturbing that the global economy is destroying indigenous cultures in the Third World.
3. The Internet should not in general be subject to censorship or restrictive regulation.

1

4. Brazil ought not to cut down its rain forests and Northern transnationals should stop trading in hardwoods.

5. Iraq ought not to have invaded Kuwait in 1990.

6. It was a good thing that such a degree of consensus on the role of women was achieved at the Cairo Conference on Population in 1994.

7. Individuals in the rich countries ought to question their reliance on the private motor car.

8. The immense economic gap between the rich North and the poor South is unjust.

9. It was right to boycott French goods in the face of the resumption of their nuclear tests in 1995.

10. People have rights to freedom which are often not allowed by their government.

11. Intervention in another country to prevent the continuation of human rights violations is justified.

12. Britain should not export arms to Indonesia.

13. Economic sanctions against South Africa in order to help end apartheid were obligatory.

14. America was right to drop the atomic bomb on Hiroshima and Nagasaki in 1945.

If you the reader agree with any of those statements, you are expressing, whether or not you have thought of it in these terms before, some form of world ethic or a global ethic (see next section). The chances are that you will agree with some of them and disagree with others. But even if you disagree, you will recognise the statements you disagree with as statements which others might reasonably hold and your disagreement will probably be based on an alternative world ethic. You would not dismiss them as irrelevant or meaningless. First we need to make some initial distinctions.

B. A WORLD ETHIC AS A SET OF VALUES AND NORMS

A world ethic, then, is an ethical theory or approach which is or includes a set of norms and values to guide our relations with the rest of the world. These norms and values will have two components: a set of universal values applicable to all human beings and a set of obligations and responsibilities which are global in scope and link all human beings together. Between them these universal values and global responsibilities constitute the substantive normative content of a world ethic. Most people have a world ethic of some kind, even if it is poorly articulated, rarely thought about and largely implicit. They may not think of it as a world ethic, since the phrase is not common. It may merely be the natural expression of their ordinary ethical beliefs in certain contexts. If the approach includes a more or less worked-out or explicit understanding of why these values and responsibilities are accepted, then the approach can be called a theory.

Our ethical judgements naturally range over many areas and focus on what individuals should do as well as what states should do. These judgements are simply part of the range of judgements we make, given our basic moral beliefs. They are expressions of or applications of these beliefs.

C. WORLD ETHICS

Above I have referred to a 'world ethic', but the attentive reader may have noted that the book is called 'world ethics'. Is there a significant distinction between 'ethic' in the singular, and 'ethics' in the plural? Although natural language is fairly fluid, there is an important distinction to be drawn which can usually be marked by using these two terms in a slightly different way. In this context 'world ethics' is not meant to signify something parallel to what might be called 'world religions', that is a survey of the major ethical systems or 'ethic(s)' of the world. 'World' here refers primarily to the content of an ethical view – its assertion of universal values and global responsibilities.

World ethics, plural in form but grammatically singular, is the philosophical enquiry into the nature, extent and justification of the ethical claims which are made about human beings – either individually or in social groups, formal organisations or political units such as states – in their relations with individuals, groups, organisations and political units throughout the world.

Whereas an ethic may be the set of values of an individual, social group or professional body, ethics in the sense intended is sustained reflection *about* values. Many people, once they start thinking about values, perhaps because of a general questioning of what they were taught or because of a particular crisis or dilemma which pushes them into thinking critically about what they hold, become engaged in an activity of reflection. Perhaps they do not do this in very sustained way, but if it becomes sustained and rigorous, it moves into academic activity and often becomes what we call 'moral philosophy' or 'ethics'. This activity has many aspects to it: one is seeking to justify some set of values and norms, often by engaging with other views both from the past and in current thinking; another is the stepping back and asking wider questions like 'what is the nature of morality anyway?' or 'are moral values objective truths or are they reflections of social convention or personal preference?' These two areas of enquiry are both characterised by two features of the academic

examination of ethical issues: attention to clarity of meaning and defini-
tions; and to logical argument, that is to what follows from what and what
is consistent with what.[1]

In a sense there is a parallel between this field of enquiry and another
area of what is called 'applied ethics', namely medical ethics. In the latter
area people reflect on and apply their moral beliefs to particular life and
death issues such as abortion and euthanasia. Likewise someone interested in environmental problems considers and applies his or her moral
beliefs to an area of concern, and there is a large literature on what is
called 'environmental ethics'.

D. A WORLD ETHIC AS SOCIAL REALITY

In order to forestall a misunderstanding, I should note here another sense
of 'world ethic' which will emerge later on, namely a set of principles and
values about world relations which are in some sense established, accepted
and shared by a significant number of actors throughout the world. Here
the word 'world' signifies the fact that a certain set of values is accepted
by actors throughout the world, whereas in what I have discussed so
far, a world ethic signifies an ethic with a certain substantive normative
content, and world ethics signifies the intellectual, often philosophical,
exploration of ideas which have this content. It will turn out to be quite
important, if the arguments for a world ethic are well founded, that there
is a general acceptance of a set of values throughout the world. But that
issue needs to be taken up later on.

II. FURTHER INITIAL CONSIDERATIONS

A. DOES EVERYONE HAVE A WORLD ETHIC?

Not everyone will have a world ethic, even implicitly. This is part of
what makes the subject as an academic enquiry interesting and important. Those committed to ethical relativism – the view that moral values
vary from culture to culture – or to a radical form of communitarianism
– the view that moral relations are constituted by established community
and shared traditions – may hold that the ideas of universal values and
obligations across the world, which I shall call cosmopolitan obligations,
are incoherent. Likewise those in the field of international relations who
think that between states there is a moral vacuum in which power and
national interest simply determine policy, will deny the relevance of ethics
to international relations or see its role as marginal and as a servant of
prudence. Such thinkers could in a sense engage in world ethics as a
philosophical enquiry, but precisely with the aim of showing that a 'world
ethic' as a set of norms is problematic. Some of the discussion of this

book will be an engagement with those who challenge the possibility of a world ethic.

B. WORLD ETHICS, GLOBAL ETHICS AND INTERNATIONAL ETHICS

The phrase 'world ethics' was chosen deliberately both for this book and for the series of which it is part, precisely to straddle the two levels of interests which I have indicated – the individual and the state.[2] In recent years the phrases 'international ethics' and 'global ethics' have gained currency. Although much of what has been written under the title 'international ethics' falls comfortably within the field of what I call world ethics, there is a common presumption that 'international' refers to inter-state relations. This is certainly the sense in which it is used within the discipline of 'international relations', so although it can also mean 'global' generally (as when someone is described as a 'good internationalist'), it seems sensible to use a term which includes both the level of inter-state relations and the level of individuals and non-state bodies.

Conversely, the phrase 'global ethics' has the opposite association in many contexts, namely reference to individuals or informal groupings or movements rather than to states, and also sometimes has an implication that it is about idealism as opposed to hard practical decision making. It can also have connotations of what is currently called 'globalisation', processes in which economic relations, networks of communication and information and so on become global.[3] Nevertheless it has also come to be used to indicate the field of enquiry of this book (see e.g. Gerle 1995; Parekh 2005; Widdows 2005; Dower 2005). Little then depends on whether one refers to world ethics or to global ethics and in certain contexts I will use the word 'global' as well. This book attempts then to provide both a normative international relations theory and a defence of an ethic for individuals in which the global dimension of responsibility is significant. In the way I develop my argument, the ethical theory at bottom is the same for international and global relations.

C. IS WORLD ETHICS APPLIED ETHICS?

Earlier I characterised a person's global ethic as 'applied ethics', that is the expression or application of their basic moral values to issues in the area of global affairs, as in medical or environmental areas. In all these cases, however, the word 'apply' is misleading. It suggests that we have a well formed pre-set body of moral beliefs and we simply apply them to the area of concern and come out with our answers. But this is not in fact what generally happens. The very activity of thinking about an area of concern extends and clarifies our moral thinking, particularly if it brings us into critical contact with those who differ from us. Moral thinking is extended in the sense that we may either have to rethink our moral values generally or at least become clearer about what is fundamental to our beliefs. If for instance animal welfare matters, how different is human welfare and what kind of moral theory is needed to account for obligation to non-humans? What do concerns about abortion and euthanasia tell us about the value of human life?

The concerns relevant to world ethics raise many such wider issues. If I have obligations to help alleviate world poverty, as many would hold, what does' that tell us about the nature of morality? It would seem to conflict with a common view of morality that duties relate to members of one's own 'community'. If the world as a whole is a community, in what sense? If we need to respect the diversity of cultures in the world, what does that tell us about the commonly clamed 'universality' of moral values? If governments are in their foreign policies subject to ethical critique, how is this to be done? Do the moral standards applicable to governments, either in practice or in theory, differ from those seen as appropriate to individuals?

A world ethic then is both an application of one's moral beliefs to global issues and a part of one's overall ethical approach or theory – a significant part insofar as its presence in one's thought informs the general character of that ethic.[4]

III. A NEW AGENDA?

In one sense the enterprise of world ethics is a new agenda, but in another sense it is not. I am not claiming that the idea of a world ethic is a new one, only now thought up in the late twentieth century. The idea that individuals belonged to a world moral community, to the brotherhood of humankind for instance, goes back to the ancient world, and similarly the idea that states are to be guided in their foreign policies by ethical considerations, for example about the rules of war, has a long intellectual history.

A. OUR GLOBAL PREDICAMENT

The agenda is new in the sense that, although the theory of world ethics has been around for a long time, there is a need to reapply it in a more active and vigorous form. For instance the idea that we are morally citizens of the world may have been accepted by many over the centuries, but its implications in the modern world, for example in the field of North–South relations or environmental protection, are quite new. There is now a need for individuals to be far more conscious of their ethical responsibilities as world citizens than in the past. Similarly whilst the ethical norms governing the relations of states have been well established in the last few hundred years and were grounded in the global thinking of writers like Grotius, there is a need to reapply and rethink these ground rules for state conduct. We need both to make them adequate for the late twentieth century when they are not currently adequate for it, and to re-establish their grounding in a world ethic, as opposed to what has often come to be thought of as an autonomous 'morality of states' which endorses the status quo by keeping the concept of sovereignty central.[5]

The theoretical understanding of ethics and of the nature of morality as global was available to thinkers over many centuries, and in any case is quite independent of any current conditions in which humans may find themselves. The ethical principles do not depend for their validity upon any of the following conditions: being accepted generally by others; being established in practices, institutions or laws; or being what is needed if we are to avoid collective calamity. Even as the world is now, neither of the first two is the case, though arguably the third condition is the case, even if it is not perceived to be so by many. Indeed part of my argument will be that since the third condition is the case, we need the first two to be the case. That is, we need the establishment and acceptance of a world ethic, or more precisely, anticipating a later argument, a consensus on global ethical principles which may stem from a number of different 'world ethic' sources. We also need these established in practices, institutions and laws.

What makes it a new agenda is the logic of our current world situation. But it does so in two rather different ways. First, the problems of the world, such as absolute poverty, conflict, environmental degradation, climate change, refugees and human rights abuses, require of individuals and states a new sense of global responsibility. In the past, it was somewhat easier to think of individuals in practice having duties towards their own citizens, especially those immediately around them, whatever theoretically might have been the case about caring for others in other parts of the world. The opportunity for effective action was rarely there, unless it was actively sought out, and it was easy enough for states to be morally satisfied with themselves if they did not engage in aggression towards other states, and if they abided by the rules of war and honoured contracts and treaties.

But arguably all that has changed. Individuals have active responsibilities, responsibilities in practice not merely in theory, towards people in other parts of the world. These include duties of giving aid and opposing practices which undermine well-being, but also, perhaps even more significantly, duties not to be beneficiaries of economic processes which either exploit the poor elsewhere or damage the environment. Likewise states

can be seen as having in practice responsibility for human beings everywhere, and responsibility not to continue practices which either damage
the environment elsewhere or contribute to negative global impacts on
the environment. A 'world ethic' then involves a re-evaluation of what
individuals and states ought to do. This would be the case even if collectively it was not in our interests to do these things.

But second, the world situation is such that not only is it right or one's
duty to do these things, but also if we do not generally do these things,
then we are storing up trouble on a global scale. If, as some might argue,
a morality is a set of rules and norms the function of which is to protect
the collective interests of the group, there is indeed plenty of evidence to
suggest that we need a world ethic, a set of global principles generally
accepted, established and acted on, for our collective well-being and even
survival.

The case for a world ethic should not however rest on this 'collective prudence' argument alone, though it is valid as far as it goes. The
theory that we have obligations towards all human beings does not,
and cannot, simply rest on an argument to do with collective prudence,
and may require of us actions as members of a world moral community
which are not necessarily underpinned by such concerns. For instance,
my being obliged to respond to world poverty is the case, whether or not
our responding generally to this problem is in our collective interests for
the sake of future stability and peace in the world.

B. RELATIONSHIP TO INTERNATIONAL RELATIONS AS AN ACADEMIC DISCIPLINE

It should now be clear that the programme of this book is quite different
from that adopted by many writers interested in international relations,
particularly those within the academic discipline called 'international
relations'. The 'realist' temper of mind is very common in international
relations, and even though 'realism' does not mean one single thing in
international relations, its approach in any form is markedly different
from that adopted here. It might be, for instance, 'sceptical realism'
which denies that ethics applies to international relations at all. It might
be an approach which focuses on the 'reality' of international relations,
that is on the real mechanics and motivations which shape or determine
foreign policy, where ethical norms may be seen as applicable but largely
redundant from an explanatory point of view. Or realism might be an
'internationalist' theory which sees ethics as having a role as shown in
customary norms and respect for international law, but accepts ethics as
relevant only to the extent that it is already there in the 'reality' of international relations, namely in the actual norms accepted, established in

custom and law, acted on, or constituting the motivations of international actors.

International relations as a separate academic discipline is of very recent origin in the twentieth century. Indeed it has only emerged as a major discipline since the Second World War. As such it was heavily influenced by the positivist thinking of the time. This had two consequences. First, in establishing its credentials as a social 'science' it had itself to be 'value-free' in its search for objective descriptions and explanations. Second, positivism led quite generally to the marginalisation of ethics as non-rational and subjective. This all led to the discipline's realist tenor. In contrast the great thinkers of the past like Aquinas, Hobbes, Locke, Kant, Sidgwick and Hegel all saw their views on international relations as part of their general political and ethical theory.[6] Thinkers, both within and outside international relations, are now returning to the recognition that the normative issues in international relations have to be understood in this broader way. This complements the return to a serious interest amongst philosophers in ethics and political theory as areas of significant rational enquiry. As Brown argues, international relations cannot maintain its intellectual autonomy.[7]

A second related respect in which my approach is different from that of many thinkers within international relations concerns the issue of determinism. Many of the arguments we will consider interpret the tendency of countries to promote the interests of the state, the nation or the social group in a deterministic way, both because of the internal dynamics of group behaviour and because of their uncertain situation *vis-à-vis* other countries. That is, one reason why ethical norms are irrelevant to foreign policy is that states in their foreign policy cannot but pursue the national interest. It only makes sense to talk of the relevance of standards of right and wrong where there is a real possibility of choice between doing what is right and doing what is in one's interests. Since states are always governed by self-interest, and only do what is judged to be 'right' by some conventional standards if that happens to be in their interests, there is a sense in which moral standards are irrelevant. There is a natural tendency in international relations theory, insofar as it is a social science seeking explanation of phenomena, to suppose that what it seeks is a complete explanation of why states behave the way they do, and if an explanation is complete, it does not allow for other possible courses of action.

Tendencies however are not inevitabilities. Choices can be made, however difficult, whether this is by individuals or by representatives of collectives such as states (or businesses). If it is said that, whereas individuals are genuinely capable of choice between what is right and what is in their interests, the peculiar nature of states does not make a parallel analysis possible, then we need to argue that there *is* a parallel, and part of the underlying purpose of the book is to show how ethics can enter into such decision-making.[8] Even if we agree that foreign policy must be shaped by considerations of some kind or other, that still leaves open the possibility that moral values contribute to it, either because international actors are persuaded that they are important, or because electorates which they represent are. From the point of view of the ethical theorist, whether that 'shaping' is really 'determining' or leaves open free choice, the task of articulating ethical values remains important. Although no single theory of human nature is assumed or developed here, the cosmopolitan arguments considered and defended all rest on the premise that moral sensibilities can be extended to include (at least) all humanity, since clearly they do for many already, and the premise that moral values once genuinely accepted can motivate agents, even in the face of conflicting interests, since again there is evidence that they often do.

Although my position is in contrast to the various senses of realism above, there is also a further sense in which the 'reality' of a world ethic as a 'global social reality' does indeed depend upon what is established. This is not so much upon the norms accepted by states, as upon the norms embedded in institutions and practices which express the wider consensus of peoples throughout the world. Although I favour the development of a specific world ethic in this sense, the primary task of this book is quite different. It is the establishment of an ethical framework which is intellectually acceptable, whether or not it is established in practice. Of course if it is to be effective, it will need to become established in practice. But that is a secondary matter intellectually, though of immense importance practically.

C. COSMOPOLITAN RESPONSIBILITY AND UNIVERSAL VALUES

Earlier I distinguished two elements to the idea of a world/global ethic. This needs to be analysed further. One of the distinctive features of my enquiry will be a distinction between claims that individuals, groups and governments have obligations or responsibilities towards people, groups and other governments in the rest of the world, and the claim that values are universal, in the sense that, even if they are not currently accepted, they are applicable to all human beings, in all places and times. Cosmopolitan responsibility is about the scope or extent of duties and responsibilities. The universalism associated with a world ethic is about the character or nature of the values which are applicable in any part of the world. By 'values' here I mean such things as: key features of what human good or well-being consist of; moral rules by which people should live in their own societies; moral rights which all human beings possess; virtues; good social structures; and relationships.

The primary concern of the thinker advocating universal values is that these values are to be accepted by all human beings in regard to their ordinary social relationships.[9] It is not as such about world society or global relationships. One could imagine a situation in which various human communities were essentially isolated from one another and had minimal impact on one another, so global responsibilities towards members of other groups were more notional than actual, yet the claim could still be made that the values to be accepted in all societies are the same.

What is important about cosmopolitan responsibility is the recognition that since we live, in some sense, in one global community or society – whether or not most of us have much of a feeling for this – we do have duties to care in one way or another about what happens elsewhere in the world and to take action where appropriate. We will need to look more closely at exactly what 'citizen of the world' implies later, but it is the implication of being a 'citizen' or active member of something called the world that is significant here.

The two claims are in fact linked, though not as a matter of strict logic. Anyone who advocates some universal values, is likely to admit that, if there are universal values, then in some contexts these values will either also be expressed as global obligations – for instance rules to do with not harming others or undermining their rights – or be the basis of global obligation – for instance, if subsistence is a universal good, then in conditions of world poverty and affluence, the affluent have duties to assist the poor to achieve that good. On the other hand, anyone advocating global responsibilities is likely to hold that it is because certain values like subsistence or rules such as not harming others have universal validity in any place and time, that we have in principle, and in the modern world in practice, responsibilities of a global kind.[10]

Two further possibilities concerning the relationship are as follows. Someone could be keen on universal values but have little to say about cosmopolitan obligations, for instance because societies are seen as largely self-sufficient or because obligations are seen as dependent on established social traditions. Finally, especially in the past, often a very detailed universal ethic, based on some theological or philosophical world-view, was seen as right for everyone in the rest of the world that did not accept it, so one's cosmopolitan obligations included those of conversion and proselytising.

The distinction has immense practical importance once we recognise that the assertion of global responsibilities does not of itself entail that we have to accept a complete account of values applicable to different societies in universal terms. There may be a degree of cultural variation (and indeed intra-cultural variation within pluralist cultures) which is entirely compatible with the idea that we have obligations on a global scale, for example not to harm others or undermine their culture or forms of life, even if their form of the good or their way of life is not the same as ours. The recognition of this possibility is important to my later defence of a form of cosmopolitanism which I call 'solidarist–pluralist', that is, the defence of the idea that we have responsibilities towards the rest of the world whilst needing to respect the diverse ways in which human beings pursue the good life.

D. INITIAL STATEMENT OF THE DISTINCTION BETWEEN A GLOBAL ETHIC AS A THEORY AND A GLOBAL ETHIC AS A SOCIAL REALITY

Another distinctive feature of the account offered in this book is the distinction between a world ethic as a theory and a world ethic as a 'global social reality', a set of values and norms which are shared by a significant number of agents throughout the world and embedded in public institutions and practices. Just as there are many different world ethics as theoretical positions, so there are a number of world ethics as sets of established norms – the internationalist's 'morality of states' is one example, the moral code of the Anglican communion would be another. Two things need to be noted at this point. First, there is no one-to-one symmetry between the two. Two thinkers with different theoretical worldviews could both endorse and support the same set of moral norms as a public social reality, and conversely two thinkers whose basic theory is the same could for a variety of reasons support the establishment of different public norms. Second, each theorist will have reason to support the establishment of some set of publicly established norms, and whilst an extreme case would be the establishment of the exact set of values plus the whole worldview of the thinker, characteristically the thinker may have reason to support some common framework of publicly established principles which he knows can and will be supported by other thinkers whose theories are to some extent different.

Thus a world ethic qua theory may be a source for support for a world ethic qua agreed set of principles. So, at one level, a world ethic is about the truth or the most reasonable view, as the thinker sees it, and much of the book will be the consideration of such rival theories. In this sense, it may well be that a world ethic has a timeless reality and its principles have always been valid, even if there may have been limited opportunities for application in the past. But at another level the objective of a world ethic is one of creating an agreed framework of principles and goals in order to produce results, such as peace, development, respect for diversity and so on. In this latter sense a world ethic is precisely something which is needed now in a way it was not before.

Many thinkers will have reasons, internal to their own intellectual system, to support the existence of a shared world ethic. As I noted above, I am not saying that every thinker will accept this view. Far from it. Others may have reason to accept other agreed principles. But anyone at all committed to the kind of world ethic I have in mind will accept something like the above, and accept that there is a relationship between the common ethic and his own intellectual story such that he will find common cause with those whose 'source stories' are different. For instance, some Buddhists, some Christians and some humanists might all find common cause in principles of respect and care for the environment, though their fundamental beliefs may be different. Whilst public declarations of a 'global ethic' are not to be identified with a world ethic as a public social reality, they are important indicators and constituents of them. Thus the Declaration Toward a Global Ethic by the Parliament of the World's Religions (1993) and the Earth Charter (2000) represent important examples of the development of a world ethic (Küng & Kuschel 1993: 13–16; Earth Council 2000; Dower 2005).

The distinction between a world ethic as a theory and a world ethic as a social reality is important to my approach for three reasons. First, theories need to find embodiment in publicly agreed norms if generally effective action by people is to take place. But agreed social norms need theories through which actors can endorse and justify them. Second, to seek to establish a world in which all accepted the same theories and the same detailed norms is to seek the impossible and the attempt is dangerous too. But to seek the formation of a common core of values and global responsibilities, emanating from diverse theories and issuing in diverse local expressions, is both possible and desirable. Third, it underscores my further contention that in distinguishing different global ethics, the differences and convergences in general approach towards the kinds of actions recommended are as important as the differences and convergences in theory which people have. I identify three normative approaches which I call, since there is not a well established vocabulary for these distinctions, idealist–dogmatic, libertarian–minimalist, and solidarist–pluralist.

IV. OUTLINE OF THE REST OF THE BOOK

Part I is largely theoretical. In the next chapter I outline the main positions which I will be discussing and comparing. The outline is expository, and there is no attempt to evaluate them critically. Three main approaches to international relations are indicated – sceptical realism, internationalism, cosmopolitanism – as well as three main approaches towards ethical relations between individuals worldwide – relativism/global scepticism, communitarianism and cosmopolitanism.

In the following two chapters I then examine critically two of the three main approaches: relativism with scepticism (Chapter 2), and internationalism with communitarianism (Chapter 3). In Chapter 4 I survey various cosmopolitan theories, and in Chapter 5 I answer objections to cosmopolitanism, critically compare versions, argue for the version of cosmopolitanism I have called 'solidarist–pluralism', and relate it to communitarianism.

In Part II of the book I examine four specific areas in world affairs in order to illustrate the main theories: war and peace, aid and development, the environment, and globalisation. These are not of course all the areas that could be chosen but they are representative of the range of issues facing us in the modern world. In each of these chapters I follow a common strategy. First I set out some basic background facts, then I consider the main ethical issues involved and their relation to each of the main theoretical positions, scepticism–relativism, internationalism–communitarianism, followed by versions of cosmopolitanism, and conclude each with an examination of one or two more specific issues.

My purpose in Part II is twofold. First, to indicate how different responses to issues tend to reflect the different theoretical stands discussed in Part I. Second, to confirm through looking at issues my earlier argument for the solidarist–pluralist form of cosmopolitanism. The reader may well find these chapters intelligible without having considered the theories in Part I, but will probably find it helpful to have either read the brief survey of positions in Chapter 1 or the more detailed and critical discussions of Chapters 2–5. A glossary of key terms is provided at the end of Chapter 1 which may also be useful.

NOTES

1. The two areas are sometimes called 'normative ethics' and 'meta-ethics' respectively (though the distinction is not clear-cut and not altogether useful). See, for example, Frankena 1973 for a useful introduction to these distinctions and to ethics generally. No general definition of ethics is given here, though the idea of it as 'obedience to the unenforceable' is a useful, informal description (Kidder 1995: 61, quoting Judge Moulton).
2. Strictly other actors, such as corporations, are included, but I shall mainly focus on the two poles.
3. For the view that environmental problems are the main source of interest in 'global' ethics, see Graham 1996: 157.

4. As one IR theorist, Nicholas Rennger, put it in a conversation with me in 2004, global ethics can be seen as at the cutting edge of moral theory.
5. There are many thinkers with a vision of a new world order like, notably, Richard Falk in many works such as *A Study of Future Worlds* (Falk 1985). In many ways the quiet philosophical analysis of this book is an underlabouring to these more passionate undertakings.
6. Authors referred to elsewhere, except Sidgwick 1919: chs XV–XIII, which contains a characteristically clear and thorough account of international ethics.
7. Brown 1992: ch. 4 & p. 77. See also Frost 1996: ch. 1.
8. If free will is denied at all levels, that is another matter, not discussed. It should be noted that some determinists called compatibilists argue for the relevance of ethics for responsible choice anyway.
9. This is the emphasis of the Institute for Global Ethics, Maine, USA, which in this sense complements the emphasis of this book.
10. It is likely but not inevitable that the two will go together, because one could imagine limiting cases where the connection broke down completely. Someone could argue that there are indeed universal duties of care and non-harming in relation to certain universal goods, but insist that a crucial precondition of such duties is membership of an established society with common traditions, so although the duties and goods accepted are universal, they do not have a global dimension. Conversely someone might argue that he or members of his society had global obligations to care for others in the world, not because the objective good of those others required such moral response from them or because there were universal duties of caring and not harming applicable to all human beings, but simply because it happened to be part of the moral culture of his community that one cared for others. Whether or not these limiting cases can be sustained is another matter.

QUESTIONS FOR DISCUSSION
1. Consider the opening statements. If you disagree with any of them, is this because you have a different ethical view or you don't think ethical judgment is appropriate?
2. How far is it possible to have a world/global ethic without doing world/global ethics?
3. Does global ethics only arise because of global problems?
4. Why should someone with a global ethic as her own view be interested in a globally shared ethic?

PART I
THEORIES

CHAPTER 1

WORLD ETHICS: AN ETHICAL TAXONOMY

SUMMARY OF CONTENTS

I. First Set of Distinctions
    A. *Sceptical realism/international scepticism*
    B. *Internationalism*
    C. *Cosmopolitanism*
    D. *Assessment of the relationship between the three approaches*
II. A Second Distinction: Communitarianism and Cosmopolitanism
III. Kinds of Cosmopolitanism
IV. A Glossary of Terms

It becomes apparent very quickly from a survey of different approaches taken to ethics and international relations, that there are many different ways of dividing up the cake, some with many categories.[1] For the purpose of this exposition, I shall limit my exploration to two ways of setting up contrasts between approaches to ethics and international relations. The first is well established and is essentially grounded in international relations thinking itself, with little to say about the position or status of individuals, except indirectly. It assumes a triple division between sceptical realism, internationalism and cosmopolitanism. It is found in many textbooks and is partly associated with writers such as Martin Wight and Hedley Bull in the so called 'English School of Realists' (Wight 1991; Bull 1985),[2] and assumed by a philosophical treatment of these positions in Charles Beitz' work (Beitz 1979). The second set of distinctions comes from other writers such as Chris Brown and Janna Thompson, for whom the main opposition is between cosmopolitanism and communitarianism (Brown 1992; Thompson 1992). This contrast also addresses more directly the issue of ethical relations between individuals. These two sets of contrasts provide a useful way into the subject. This is a summary of the framework used in chapters 2–5. The latter chapters will amplify what is presented here in schematic form.

I. FIRST SET OF DISTINCTIONS

A division can be drawn between three positions, each identified by a confusingly large number of labels:

1. (sceptical) realism, Hobbesianism, Machiavellianism, nihilism, (international) scepticism, anarchism;
2. internationalism, Grotianism, 'morality of states', 'legalist paradigm', rationalism;
3. cosmopolitanism, Kantianism, universalism, revolutionism, idealism, utopianism.

A number of different contrasts are involved here. Nevertheless the following expansion represents key points which are often intended to be conveyed by the contrasts. It is useful to identify two elements to each general position: one which is descriptive, that is a factual claim about what is the case in the world; the other normative/theoretical, that is a claim about the status or content of certain values or norms which may be applicable.

A. SCEPTICAL REALISM/INTERNATIONAL SCEPTICISM

Descriptive: relations between states are generally determined by power and calculations of what is in the national interest. International relations is therefore largely a 'competitive' game, that is, one in which if one side gains or wins the other side loses. War, in Hobbes' extended but illuminating sense of being not merely actual fighting but a period of time in which there is insecurity because of the known disposition by the other side to resort to violence, is the dominant feature of international relations (Hobbes 1991: ch. 13). Such norms as develop in international relations are not really moral norms in any proper sense, but rather maxims of prudence, which are to be abandoned whenever prudence dictates. If moral language is in fact used in foreign policy pronouncements, this is generally hypocritical and yet another way of promoting foreign policy.

Normative/theoretical: many realists also assert, for a variety of reasons, that ethical norms do not apply to international relations. International relations constitutes an ethical vacuum, as moral relations simply do not exist. Striking is the famous Hobbesian argument that because of lack of a 'common power' – a world government with power to enforce and hence render sufficiently predictable the observance of norms – norms do not apply and states are in 'a state of nature' *vis-à-vis* each other, that is a state of anarchy. In this state of affairs they exercise their 'right of nature' to do whatever is conducive to their survival without moral restraint. Other arguments include the claim that governments, acting in a trustee role, always have an overriding obligation to their citizens or subjects to promote their interests.

B. INTERNATIONALISM

Descriptive: although relations between states are to a large extent dominated by considerations of national interest, there is as a matter of fact an ethical framework within which state actors operate – namely that set of norms or 'morality of states' which has come to be established in the 'society of states'. The key features of this set of norms are: duties of non-aggression and non-interference towards other sovereign states; the duty to observe the principles of the 'just war', that is, principles about when it is justified to go to war (*ius ad bellum*) and principles determining the manner of waging war (*ius in bello*); the keeping of agreements and treaties, and a diplomatic code for the treatment of ambassadors and representatives of foreign powers. States and the international system which they constitute are the dominant reality of the world. The whole point of the international system or society of states is the maintenance of the system and its order. Relations between states are a mixture of co-operation and conflict, the former demonstrated by extensive economic interdependence, in which there can be 'win–win' outcomes.

Normative/theoretical: most proponents of the internationalist position will also assert that the norms that actually operate in international relations are in fact to be accepted. That is, from the point of view of the theorist, these norms are the right norms for the relations of states. Various kinds of justification are given for the defence of the status quo. First, there are various considerations which are somewhat independent of those concerning ordinary human well-being. For instance appeals are made to convention or established practice, that is, to their being established and serving the goal of preserving the international order of states itself, or appeals are made to the inherent 'rights' of states, seen as artificial persons, somewhat analogous to the appeal to inherent rights of natural persons. Second, the norms of the international order may be defended on the grounds that, from the perspective of the defender of it, they are what is needed to promote human values in the best possible way.

C. COSMOPOLITANISM

Descriptive: despite the dominance of the inter-national order, i.e. the division of peoples into separately controlled areas of the world, there already exists in a rather undeveloped form a community or society of all human beings in the world. There are various ways in which human co-operation is of benefit, and generally perceived to be of benefit, to all human beings. Various values are already widely shared, as evidenced in the core values of each society which are the essential *sine qua non* of any human society, and in international agreements such as the Universal Declaration of Human Rights of 1948, which can be seen as having moral force as well as legal status. In addition we see shared values in religious groups (which cross national boundaries) and more recently but very significantly, international NGOs (non-governmental organisations). Obligations to help those in need (for example, international responses to disasters) and to play one's part to combat common threats to the environment are widely accepted. Many do have some sense, even if it is not well developed, of being 'world citizens' (as well as citizens of their own states or members of their own societies).

Normative/theoretical: what however is usually important to the cosmopolitan position is not an appeal to what has as a matter of fact already been accepted. It may well be recognised that global community is not well established, or is non-existent. What is important for the cosmopolitan is a theory about what ought to be the case, not about what is the case – where what is the case includes what ethical norms are as a matter of fact accepted. In this theory, we are global citizens and have duties, whether or not most people accept this now. We have duties, if our theories require this, to give aid, change our ways *vis-à-vis* the environment, work for peace, show tolerance towards other cultures, even if others do not accept this. National boundaries do not, with this approach, have any ultimate moral significance. Such theories include philosophical theories such as Kantianism, utilitarianism, natural law, Marxism and human rights theories, as well as various religious perspectives.

There are two consequences of cosmopolitan theory which are usually stressed. First, the relations between states have to be assessed, and assessed critically, in the light of the overall theory. What states do, what rules they follow, what institutions they set up, are to be judged by the theory. Do they express the values which the theory asserts as effectively as other policies, rules or institutions would do? If not, there is an argument for change – including the possibility of a change in the very nature of the international system itself towards, for instance, a world federal system or world government. However most cosmopolitans are wary of the idea of world government. Second, individual human beings need to take seriously their identity as world citizens, since in principle there is a layer of obligation which might well require of them actions which go beyond, and even in some cases, are in conflict with, what is required of them as citizens of their own states. There is therefore, either explicitly or implicitly, a challenge to the idea of absolute loyalty to one's own state.

D. ASSESSMENT OF THE RELATIONSHIP BETWEEN THE THREE APPROACHES

The three approaches, realist, internationalist, and cosmopolitan, have each been presented as having two parts – a descriptive claim and a normative/theoretical claim. Though both parts may well be put forward by a thinker about international relations, they do not have to go together. Someone could be for instance a realist in his description of the world, but still accept that states ought to act otherwise. It may also be the case that one thinker is more interested in the descriptive factual claim about how the world is, and another thinker interested in the normative/theoretical claim. This point may shed light on the following features of much 'debate' about the relevance of ethics to international relations.

Insofar as thinkers in the three positions are presenting alternative descriptive claims about the presence or efficacy of moral values in international relations, then, whilst one position could be completely right and the other two completely wrong, the probability is that they are all of them right to some degree, and wrong to some degree. Indeed that is precisely the position adopted by one writer who advocates this kind of analysis, namely Hedley Bull:

> The modern international system in fact reflects all three elements singled out, respectively, by the Hobbesian, the Kantian and the Grotian traditions: the element of war and struggle for power amongst states, the element of transnational solidarity and conflict, cutting across the divisions among states, and the element of co-operation and regulated intercourse among states. (Bull 1985: 39)

That is, it is almost certainly the case that a very large number of actions of international actors (statesmen, diplomats) are in fact governed by self-interest, even though they may say they are not, and even though our own theory may judge that they ought not to have been; that to a considerable extent the rules of international conduct are followed by international actors, when one might, in terms of one's theory, have wished them to follow more radical principles; and that to some extent there are common shared values and the acceptance of humanitarian responsibility.

What is more interesting is the relationship between the three normative/theoretical claims. For these claims are not such that each might partly be right. They are presented as claims which mutually exclude each other. Thus, if the sceptic is right that there are no ethical norms in international relations, then both the internationalist and the cosmopolitan are simply wrong in claiming that there are. If the internationalist is right that there are acceptable norms constituting a 'morality of states', which are either self-justifying or clearly the way to promote human values in an ordered way, then the realist is wrong to deny their existence, and so is the cosmopolitan who thinks there is a universal moral theory, either because he is wrong to think it is the ultimate source of validation for a 'morality of states', or because he is wrong to think that states fail to promote human values as well as they might. If the cosmopolitan is right, then both realism and internationalism are inadequate ethical theories, however well they may describe the realities of practice and the acceptance of norms in the real world.

On the other hand there can be a failure to engage, or a kind of 'missing each other in the dark',[3] where one thinker is presenting what is basically a descriptive thesis, but the other is presenting his or her thesis as a normative theory. Thus, a realist or internationalist may only be saying something that the cosmopolitan is willing (albeit with regret) to concede, namely that as a matter of fact foreign policy is largely determined by interest or rather limited norms based on the morality of states, whereas the cosmopolitan is asserting moral claims about how we ought to be ordering our global affairs. The truth or validity of this is not in the least affected by what the realist or internationalist asserts by way of descriptive observation.

If however the realist or internationalist dismisses the cosmopolitan claim by saying it is 'idealist' or 'utopian', i.e. not really applicable to the real world, this would not be missing each other in the dark. For by saying it is utopian, the thinker is saying that the values which international actors really ought to follow are different, so he is not merely making a descriptive claim about what is done or accepted, but also endorsing it, that is giving normative endorsement to it. And this is what a cosmopolitan is challenging. What he says ought to be done is meant to apply here and now. A cosmopolitan theory has to distinguish between what 'ideal theory' might require and what is practically possible in the real world, given the nation-state system itself, the international laws and institutions in place, the priorities of democratic electorates, the mutual distrust between states, and so on (Beitz 1979: pt III, sn 6). A cosmopolitan thinker who did not take into account these 'reality' constraints would indeed be 'utopian'. But it remains important that cosmopolitan thought involves claims about what ought to be done here and now, and is progressive in precisely this sense that it will put moral pressure on governments, corporate bodies (such as transnational business companies) and individuals to do more to advance the values specified in the theory than they would do in the absence of such a framework being accepted.

II. A SECOND DISTINCTION: COMMUNITARIANISM AND COSMOPOLITANISM

Several writers in recent years, such as Brown and Thompson, have set out the terms of the ethical debate in a somewhat different way. Here the contrast is between two styles of thought, one cosmopolitan and the other communitarian. The cosmopolitan position is essentially the same as that already indicated. What is significant is what it is contrasted with, namely a way of thinking about how values arise in or from established community. I am using the term 'communitarian' to cover a broad range of views, including the theory in social philosophy recently popularised under this title (Sandel 1982; MacIntyre 1981; Taylor 1989). Put informally the contrast is between two types of theory, unbounded (cosmopolitan) and bounded (communitarian).

First, there are cosmopolitan theories which identify human beings as such as the bearers of values (as pursuers of happiness, bearers of interests or rights, rational agents), and then, given that starting point, claim that in principle any such beings might, in one's relationship with them, generate duties which one has towards them. These theories may be called 'unbounded' or 'open' because the domain of obligation is in principle all humans (or beings more generally) with the relevant value-bearing characteristics. In practice, the sphere of obligation will be determined by the sphere of effective action. Such theories are utilitarianism, Kantianism, and natural law theories and the later modification and extension of these into human rights theories. The natural tendency of these theories is to advocate some kind of world ethic for individuals, as belonging to one global moral community – where community is defined in terms of the claimed moral relations, not in terms of established traditions, felt relations and shared values in practice.

Second, there are communitarian theories which limit the domain of one's duty (or at least primary duty) to those to whom one stands in some meaningful relation, the relation being meaningful if it is informed by such diverse factors as sentiment, affection, shared traditions, convention, reciprocity or contract.[4] Here the relationship rather than the independent character of the humans (or beings more generally) to whom one might relate, is central and bears the theoretical weight. These theories may be called 'bounded' or 'closed' theories of ethics. I shall use the term 'communitarian' for this approach. Theories like convention theory,[5] sentimentalism, communitarianism (as a specific social philosophy) and political theories of a contractarian form or idealist form, have a tendency either to deny the existence of global obligations or, in terms of what the theory says, regard obligations at that level as marginal and relatively unimportant. On these views world community (at least in a sense implying a moral community) is an illusion or of marginal significance, precisely because the relevant traditions and institutions are not present.

Communitarianism can be presented in a stronger form linked to ethical relativism and some form of postmodernism which deny universal value and global responsibility altogether (the general position I call 'global scepticism'). Or it can be and usually is presented in a weaker form that, whilst there may be a layer of universal values and global obligations, the facts are that the central values are those shaped by one's own social and political community. These values are generally justified on the grounds that they are socially constituted and are not dependent on any wider global theory which is there in the background.[6]

As the argument develops we will see how we will need to reach some kind of compromise between these two rather different perspectives. This can be achieved by one of two strategies, mutual acceptance or assimilation, or both. Each theory might be accepted as containing part of the ethical truth (mutual acceptance) or one theory is seen as basic but validates the values of the other as expressions of it (assimilation). I adopt the strategy of assimilation and defend a strong form of cosmopolitanism which is nevertheless sensitive to the constraints and insights which the other approach rightly identifies.

III. KINDS OF COSMOPOLITANISM

As I indicated in Chapter 1, kinds of cosmopolitanisms can be distinguished in terms of theories like Kantianism or utilitarianism or in terms of practical approaches, identified primarily in terms of the basic priorities for policy in what in fact is required of us as world citizens and correspondingly required of states. The following are not the only approaches possible, but they constitute in my opinion three important and live options in the modern world. Since the division will inform the comparisons which I will be making in Part II, a brief indication, expanded in Chapter 6, will be useful here. The differences are partly dependent upon one's basic values and partly upon one's understanding of the 'facts' about the world, its trends and real possibilities. For example different views can be taken about how much potential there is for real change without damaging or endangering what is also valuable and already achieved.

There are at least two set of polarities in terms of what cosmopolitans will actually advocate as practical priorities. One continuum has one pole with theories which give a very specific conception of the 'right moral order' which needs to be accepted by the rest of the world and is to be advanced by various forms of imposition, proselytising, even crusades.

The other pole has an emphasis on recognising and even celebrating cultural diversity, but within a framework of responsibilities of mutual support for some broadly identified universal core values shared by all societies.[7] In another continuum at one end there are theories which require radical positive action to improve the world in order to pursue global social justice by positive intervention and so on; and at the other end theories which stress the value of liberty, especially economic liberty, non-intervention and autonomy. Combining these two polarities we get three main approaches: idealist–dogmatic, libertarian–minimalist and solidarist–pluralist, which I shall refer to in later discussions, except where the context requires otherwise, as idealist, libertarian, and solidarist respectively.

1. *Idealist–dogmatic*: a cosmopolitan who has a particular ideal or vision of what values ought to inform the world (though much of the world does not share it) and works to promote this ideal. Much religious and political ideology is pursued in this way. From the point of view of those not sharing the ideal or the approach, it can be seen as based on dogmatism.
2. *Libertarian–minimalist*: a cosmopolitan who does not see himself or herself as promoting a specific ideal except liberty itself, but as advocating a world of non-intervention by states and individuals. No extensive duty of coming to the aid of others is recognised. The moral framework advocated is minimal, both for states (by implication) and for individuals. This underlies the current free market ideal of the global economy.
3. *Solidarist–pluralist*: a cosmopolitan who believes in solidarity throughout the world for promoting the essential conditions of well-being, but at the same time does not wish to promote any culturally specific ideals but rather to respect cultural diversity and a plurality of values.[8] It is essentially the approach adopted by many thinkers, especially in NGOs, who are activated by concerns about poverty, economic inequality and environmental problems.

IV. A GLOSSARY OF TERMS

Apart from the three outlines just indicated, a brief glossary of the main positions identified may be helpful for future reference.

A global/world ethic as a social reality: a set of global values accepted by a significant number of actors throughout the world and embodied in public institutions and practices.

A global/world ethic as a theory: a person's own view, based to some extent on reflection and reasoning, about what global values ought to be accepted.

Global/world ethics: the philosophical examination of the normative and theoretical issues which arise from considering relations between states and individuals on a global scale.

Communitarianism: moral values arise in established community through shared conventions and traditions.

Cosmopolitanism: the world is one moral domain in which there are some universal values and global responsibilities (within which three approaches, summarised above, are *idealist–dogmatist*, *libertarian–minimalist* and *solidarist–pluralist*).

(Ethical) relativism: moral values for individuals vary from culture to culture, are appropriate because they are thought so, and thus there are no universal values or global obligations (also referred to as *global scepticism*, and linked to postmodernist denial of a standpoint of 'universal reason').

International scepticism/sceptical realism: there are no moral norms applicable to the relations between nation-states, and foreign policy is legitimately shaped by national interests.

Internationalism: the moral norms which ought to govern the relations between states are, whatever their ultimate justification, those established and accepted by states themselves in the society of states (position also referred to as the *morality of states* approach).

NOTES

1. For instance in their recent survey book Nardin and Mapel (1992) usefully identify as many as twelve approaches, including titles such as international law, classical realism, twentieth-century realism, natural law, Kant's global rationalism, utilitarianism, and contractarian tradition. Donelan 1990 has six basic approaches: natural law, realism, fideism, rationalism, historicism: 'nation' and 'state', and historicism: 'proletariat' and 'world'.
2. This is 'realism' in a broader sense of being grounded in the realities of international practice, as contrasted with (sceptical) realism.
3. This missing each other is evidenced by my experience of teaching international relations students and philosophy students together.
4. The contract may be ideal and hypothetical but it presupposes other features such as active co-operation and perceived mutuality of interests which are real and not ideal.
5. See Harman 1977. Hume's theory of justice as artificial is also seen as a convention theory, though at another level he has a sentimentalist theory of ethics. See Hume 1888: bk III, pt III.

6. Alternatively they may be seen as necessarily the main expression of those global values. Either way, the central core of ethical value lies in membership of one's community and not in one being a member of the human race.
7. See my discussion of Küng at the end of Chapter 6.
8. Pluralism is to be distinguished sharply from relativism. See the end of Chapter 5.

QUESTIONS FOR DISCUSSION

1. How far from your knowledge of world affairs do the three positions – international scepticism, internationalism and cosmopolitanism – descriptively map what happens in the world?
2. Why do these three position as normative claims mutually exclude each other?
3. In what respects does communitarianism differ from cosmopolitanism?
4. How does solidarist-pluralism differ from idealist-dogmatism and libertarian-minimalism?

CHAPTER 2

INTERNATIONAL AND GLOBAL SCEPTICISM

I shall consider two related sceptical claims: first the claim that morality does not apply to the relations between nation-states, and second the claim that morality does not apply to the relations between individuals at a global level. I shall call the first view, following others' practice, 'international scepticism' or 'sceptical realism' and the second, somewhat stipulatively, 'global scepticism'. They are not the same views. Indeed as we shall see, it is possible to be a sceptic about the one and not the other. I shall try to show that they are both false.

Neither of these views is to be confused with general scepticism about ethics, a view that there are no moral values at all. It is assumed that we can make sense of the claim that individuals stand in ethical relations to one another within societies at least, and indeed that we can assert that such morality exists. Why might there be special reasons for denying the applicability of ethics to the relations between states or the relations between individuals at a global level?[1] I first set out the argument for international scepticism and then for global scepticism. In the second half the chapter I consider various responses to these positions, but the issues are handled in a slightly different order.

I. ARGUMENTS FOR INTERNATIONAL SCEPTICISM

A. LACK OF A COMMON POWER TO ENFORCE RULES

This is in many ways the most famous and indeed accessible argument, associated with the writings of Thomas Hobbes. If there is no coercive power to make states comply with certain norms of restraint, then states will generally pursue their interests in ways which will undermine the interests of others, and there will be no expectation of reciprocal compliance. Under such conditions, states are entitled to pursue their national interests in whatever way is effective. Under conditions of international 'anarchy', that is lack (an-) of power (arche), there are no rules.

The actual argument in Hobbes can be expanded in this way. International relations is for Hobbes a 'state of nature' and thus a state of war. War he defines as 'not Battell only [sic] ... but in a tract of time, wherein the will to contend by Battell is sufficiently known ... All other time is peace.' (Hobbes 1991: ch. 13) It is rational for human beings – indeed it is for Hobbes a law of nature – to seek peace wherever it is possible. Peace is not possible in the relations between states because of states' 'independency' from one another, and hence mutual hostility, distrust and general uncertainty about what other states will do. And where peace is not possible, each agent may exercise the right of nature to do anything that conduces to its preservation, including 'the helps of war'.

Hobbes contrasts civil society in which men do achieve peace by leaving the 'state of nature' and submitting to a sovereign 'common power' capable of enforcing rules, with international relations where the state of nature still exists, and there is no common power to hold them 'all in awe'. But he is uncompromising about what he sees as the consequence of being in a state of nature. 'Where there is no common Power, there is no Law; where there is no Law, no Injustice.' He goes on to add that there is no 'mine and thine', that is no property qua entitlement to things, because that presupposes an enforceable legal system, only 'possessions' in the sense of getting and keeping whatever you can (Hobbes 1991: ch. 13).

Hobbes was a psychological egoist; that is, he believed that all behaviour was motivated by self-interest (enlightened or otherwise). So his conception of morality underlying the above is one which assumes that the tendency towards selfish behaviour – behaviour likely to be detrimental to the interests of others unless checked – is strong and deep-rooted, and that the only reason why anyone would willingly submit to a framework of moral rules is that at least in general one will benefit from it oneself, and this would only be the case if one is confident that others around one will also generally observe the rules. Otherwise it would be irrational to accept the arrangement in the first place. Is the lack of a common power capable of enforcing moral rules then the crucial factor leading to Hobbes' denial that in international relations moral rules apply? Perhaps not. In a much later passage in *Leviathan* he acknowledges that where between particular states a level of trust has built up, it may be rational to enter into agreements and treaties precisely because one can rely on others, even though there is no power to enforce it (Hobbes 1991: ch. 22). But Hobbes' general view, and certainly the view which is called 'Hobbesian' in the literature of international relations, is one of mutual distrust, preparations for war ('battell' in Hobbes' sense) and insufficient expectation of mutual compliance to common rules.

Hobbes' argument is a special case of a more general line of argument which has the following general structure: for moral relations to exist between different people or groups, certain features must exist. These features do not exist in the relations between states. Therefore morality does not exist in the international area. Hobbes' own argument, as we have just seen, was concerned with the absence of a common power to make states obey common rules, but what really lies behind this argument is the claim that moral rules do not oblige anyone to act on them, if they have no reliable expectation that others will obey them too. To obey a rule without this assurance would be madness and contrary to one's interests. But one could similarly argue that in the international arena there simply are not the shared traditions, practices and institutions which we are accustomed to in a 'society'. This is the heart of the communitarian analysis of morality as grounded in social reality. If that reality does not exist in the international arena, then a necessary condition for the existence of moral rules is absent. So there is no morality in international relations.

B. GLOBAL SCEPTICISM

The arguments for global scepticism, that is, scepticism about there being moral relations between people throughout the world, are used to support international scepticism. The two arguments *for* global scepticism which I group under the general label 'ethical relativism' are briefly the plurality or diversity of values in different societies and the social constitution of values, and are given in a later section. What needs to be noted here is an argument *from* global scepticism to support international scepticism. Briefly, if there are no universal values or common framework of trans-boundary moral duties between individual human beings as such, there is no vantage point or 'common standpoint' from which to construct or discern an ethical basis for the behaviour of states, and each state brings its own values into its transactions with other states.

C. THE AUTONOMY OF THE NATION-STATE

Various reasons can be given (beyond the more general ones associated with global scepticism) for seeing the nation-state as an autonomous entity with its own moral logic making it impervious to any wider moral limitations.

Various Conceptions of the Nation-State

Various conceptions may be given, according to which the very nature of the social entity called the nation-state generates strong loyalty and moral relations within it, but at the same time an absence of such relationships outside. More detail is given in the next chapter when I explore what I call broadly the 'communitarian' approach.

Maxwell for instance, sensitive to ethological evidence of group behaviour in the animal kingdom, notes how groups develop strong ties of loyalty within, but hostility towards those outside the group, thus accounting for the immorality of the group in its external relationships. The modern nation-state is a particularly powerful example of this phenomenon, and 'patriotism transmutes individual selflessness into national egoism' (Maxwell 1992, quoting Niebuhr). Thus what it is right for the group to do is wrong by the standards of individuals' behaviour inside the group. In this respect the position is reminiscent of Machiavelli's position that a prince or republican leader may be justified for reasons of national interest or 'reasons of state' (*raison d'état*) to do what it would be wrong to do by ordinary moral standards: to kill, deceive, betray and so on (Machiavelli 1979: bk III, ch. XLI; 1988: ch. XV ff.). Reinhold Niebuhr, a twentieth century theologian at once attracted to the Christian virtue of love but at the same time facing the reality of international politics, concluded that inevitably humans lived in social units locked in conflict with one another (Niebuhr 1932).

Most specifically, in connection with the centrality of the nation-state, Fichte made much of the specific identity of the 'nation' as focus and locus of identity and loyalty, arguing that each nation needed to promote its well-being in competition with other nations (Fichte 2000). Nations and states are of course not the same thing, but it was assumed widely then, as it is still assumed now by many, that the only way a group of people considering themselves to be of the same 'nation' could truly be in control of their destiny was to constitute themselves as a state, that is a political unit with complete control over a territorial area, and recognised as such by other states.

Hegel's analysis of the political order points in the same general direction though in his case it is part of a large and complex philosophy, in particular a philosophy of history. But for Hegel the development of the modern rational state, within which citizens could flourish and have identity as free agents in a 'civil society', was a crucial expression of development of human potential. The meaning and identity of a person's life was constituted by the nature and existence of the political order. Each political entity as a nation-state was bound, by its very logic, to seek advance and development and therefore was in a state of competition *vis-à-vis* other states also bent on development and expansion. War is an inherent characteristic of the international system. Hegel essentially puts forward an analogue of ethical egoism for states. Just as ethical egoists say that one ought to promote one's own well-being, as this is the highest calling for action, not to be limited by anything else such as the conventional restraints of morality, so states are by their very nature bent on self-advancement, without limitation from any other 'ethic'. The picture painted in some of Hegel's writings is indeed as bleak as that painted by Hobbes.[2]

The Duty of Government

Next there is the argument commonly adduced that governments stand in a special relationship to their citizens or subjects. It is the overriding duty of government to promote the interests of their people. They act in a 'trusteeship' role. Various supporting reasons can be given for this position.

First, theories of democracy will be premised on the need for the government to carry out the wishes of the people, assuming that a satisfactory way of determining these is found. Although people may sometimes and marginally want their governments to act generously towards those outside the state, these are still the interests of citizens, and the core point is that a democratic government is committed to pursuing the national interest so determined. Second, even if a state does not have democracy, a similar argument can be mounted from 'contract theory'. People on this theory agree with one another to submit to government in return for certain goods – security, defence of liberty and property and so on. Whether the government is a party to the contract, as Locke argued in his trusteeship argument, or is itself above the contract as in Hobbes, the point remains that the role or function of government is the defence and promotion of the national interest (Locke 1960; Hobbes 1991). Third, even if we do not accept the contract analysis of the nature of political society, there are many other conceptions of the political order which stress the special relationship which a government has to its people.

The above arguments focus on the role of government, which of course is the main focus of attention when foreign policy is being considered. But perhaps the full force of this argument is not felt unless one remembers that lying behind these arguments are arguments of a more fundamental kind about the nature of social groups in general and of the nation-states in particular, which we have already considered.

Sovereignty

The role of sovereignty formalises the moral logic of the state system. The whole idea of a sovereign state is that it is not subject to any higher authority, at least on this earth. As Jean Bodin, an earlier theorist of sovereignty, put it, sovereign power is exercised 'simply and absolutely' and 'cannot be subject to the commands of another, for it is he who makes the law for the subject' (Bodin 1962: I, viii). Although he accepted as many did in his time that there was a natural law in the background, this turns out to be irrelevant so far as the relations between states is concerned, since there is no superior authority to which appeal can be made to decide an issue. This is linked to one of the arguments in Hobbes' analysis of sovereignty that the sovereign can by his decision determine the interpretation of abstract right and wrong in terms of rules and laws and settle disputes, whereas there is no such common standard in international affairs.[3]

D. THE ROLE OF ETHICAL VALUES IN INTERNATIONAL RELATIONS

Since it is clear that moral values are sometimes articulated and expressed in international relations – in what foreign ministers or diplomats say – the international sceptic needs to give an account of them consistent with or supportive of his analysis.

Morality as the Projection of Interests

The argument here is that insofar as the language of universal values is used in international relations contexts, this moral language does not refer to any genuine universal point of view, but is in fact a projection of the values of the power that uses them, and indeed may be a mask for the pursuit of interested objectives. E. H. Carr is well known for his analysis of international relations along these lines, in seeing the idealism of the dominant Western powers in the inter-war period as a projection of values which served the interests of those powers.[11] This kind of analysis is associated with but is by no means limited to Marxist understanding of international relations as imperialism. After all, just as the moral values of a society may be seen as the ideology of the ruling class within that society, so too can the universal values expressed in international relations be the ideology for the effective promotion of certain interests. A modern example of this might be the Gulf War of 1991, where the official goal on behalf of the 'world community' as President Bush called it at the time to defend the territorial integrity of Kuwait and generally liberal values was really a mask for the effective defence of Western oil interests (Carr 1939; or in Williams, Wright & Evans 1993; cf. Zolo 1997). An analogous assessment can be made about the 2003 invasion of Iraq. More generally, the ideology of 'development' as economic growth through free markets, preached as universal values for all, may seem to many in the South as a way of promoting the values important to the leading players in the global market.

Morality as Dangerous in Foreign Policy
Another line of argument well liked by realists, such as Hans Morgenthau, is that which says that insofar as foreign policy is directed to global goals it is dangerous, leading to war and conflict. The pursuit of 'moralism' or 'idealism' is inappropriate to foreign policy which ought to be inspired by the 'moral principle of national survival' (Morgenthau 1954: 10). If moral ideals are seen as particular religious or political ideologies and pursuing such moral objectives is also seen as important, then this can lead to conflict with other states which do not share these ideologies, and so the peace and order which it is in the interests of each state to preserve is undermined. Whilst we can think of rather striking examples of this in the past with wars like the crusades, and the ideological conflicts between East and West in more recent years, it is worth bearing in mind that even foreign policy directed to what may seem more modest universal goals such as the protection of human rights may also provoke conflict. At any rate, this sceptical line of argument takes seriously the point that international actors may think they are pursuing moral goals, and in a sense are doing so (because conceptions of what is right motivate what they do), but undermines the validity of that kind of motivation, as being inappropriate to foreign policy. This amounts to a form of scepticism about global morality, if the general point to be drawn from this is that any purported global goals of an ethical kind are flawed and invalid.

This argument illustrates a more general point. In terms of what people think, moral values may indeed play some part in their motivation, including moral values which they take to be universal values. But the fact that people take the values they act on to be universal does not make them so, since what people think and what is the case are often quite different. There is nothing special about this case. A person could be systematically mistaken or confused in any area of ethical thinking, for instance because, according to the theorist, he falsely believes that God exists, or that animals have moral standing.

II. GLOBAL SCEPTICISM: THE MAIN ARGUMENTS

A. RELATIVISM

Relativism is the view that moral values vary from society to society. What counts as good in one society is not the same as what counts as good in another; what are accepted as duties and to whom those duties are owed vary as well. Relativism in respect of values is strictly speaking a thesis with two parts, one empirical and the other theoretical/normative.[4] The empirical part is the claim that as a matter of fact values do vary significantly from culture to culture; that is, what is valued or held to be of value differs from place to place, and from time to time. But these facts – if they are accepted, which to some degree seems very reasonable – leave open the question of the interpretation of these facts. Whereas many thinkers more inclined to think there are some universal moral truths will say that some of the values held by people have been and are mistaken or inadequate and that there is such a thing as moral progress, the ethical relativist will interpret the variety of values as indicative that there are no universal values to be discovered, but rather that values really do vary for society to society. That is, it is not merely that what is *thought* of as right and good varies but also that what *is* right and good varies, and varies according to what is accepted in each society.

The relativist thesis is usually linked with some form of theory about the social constitution of moral values – namely that moral values arise through convention, agreement and shared traditions. It is therefore part of the relativist thesis that the duties and obligations which members of a community have are generally towards one another and not towards human beings in general. If a community did share a value concerning helping others outside the community that would be accidental anyway. The point is worth stressing because it shows that the force of the relativist position is not undermined as such by the recognition that some values (some ideas about the good or about duty) may well be the same in all or most societies. Some coincidence of value does not make a universal morality or value system. The general point is that if values arise from society – that is, particular societies – then there is no common standpoint (to use a phrase of Hume's) or universal reference point from which to assert claims about universal morality or global obligation. In the absence of such a global perspective, it is not possible to talk about a global ethic.

B. POSTMODERNISM

The relativist thesis is often presented these days in the form of postmodernism. Postmodernism is a label which can cover a bewildering range of things. In this context I shall take it to be the thesis in contrast to the modernist assumption drawn from the Enlightenment that there is something called 'universal reason' which can, if undistorted, deliver the same rationally grounded system of knowledge and value for all human beings.[5] Postmodernism 'deconstructs' this discourse and claims that there is no such thing as universal reason; there are many different systems of knowledge, worldviews, ways of life which may simply be incommensurable. The idea of a universal morality, a common system of value and global responsibilities is an illusion. It presupposes a monocentric, hierarchical and rationally ordered world, whereas the truth is that the world is polycentric with no natural or inherent order to it at all. Of course attempts to promote a system of universal values and beliefs have been made throughout history – witness in earlier centuries the conquistadors and the holy wars of the middle ages, and in the modern world the promotion of 'universal human rights' or a secular and liberal conception of 'development'. But this is really the exercise of power by one group – often European – seeking to impose its worldview and values on other parts of the world. Even though it may be the case that one day all the world will be assimilated into one value system, this would be a contingent fact about the future. It does not show that now that there is one vantage point of reason, one rational way of constructing knowledge and value. Thus postmodernism can be seen as a powerful reaction to ideas of a single global moral framework, and either, if it is optimistic, celebrates the diversity of human life, or, if pessimistic, regrets the fact that relations between states are, as the realist supposes, mediated by power, including the power to impose particular worldviews and value systems onto others.

III. CRITIQUE: ANARCHISM AND THE CONDITIONS OF MORAL OBLIGATION

Let us now turn to a critical evaluation of the sceptical arguments starting with Hobbes' famous argument from anarchism.[6] This argument depends upon a certain conception of morality and of where moral obligations come from. There are two strategies for responding to these arguments. First, to admit that the conditions are important, but to claim that the conditions are in fact met in the international area. Second, to argue that it is a mistake to suppose that these conditions are necessary for moral relations to obtain between groups. My strategy here as elsewhere in the book is to argue the latter case. But before stating this more fully, let us look at the first line of reply.

It is of course quite plausible to argue that shared traditions and practices do exist between states, and this will be one of the arguments for the 'morality of states'. Similarly it is arguable that states do come to expect mutual compliance to common rules. The sceptic may still want to argue that these agreements are not really moral agreements, merely rules followed from prudence, and abandoned when prudence dictates otherwise. If enforceability is however seen as a crucial condition for morality, then it will not be plausible to see morality in international relations even today, since the continuation of the sovereign state system seems, by definition, to deny the existence of a system of enforceability. It should be noted that even if the sceptic is right that these conditions do not obtain in the world, so moral relations do not exist, it does not follow that these conditions could not exist, at some time in the future. As Beitz notes of Hobbes' argument, the 'law of nature' requires men to seek peace where possible but use the 'helps of war' when not possible, so if states could achieve peace, then they also ought to. The difficulty for Hobbes in a world of insecure warring states was to see how to get to that point (Beitz 1979: 31–4).

But the key issue can be put in this form: does anarchism entail the absence of moral relations or peace? If there can be something called 'the anarchical society', to quote the title of Bull's well-known book, it would seem not. For if there can be a society of states, as opposed to merely a lot of states interacting with one another, then that presupposes that there are some moral rules governing the relations between the members of that society. And it is precisely Bull's contention that through custom, convention and the development of common institutions, states have come to expect for the most part settled behaviour according to agreed norms. So enforceability by a common power is not necessary to achieve the conditions of general peace which Hobbes saw as necessary for the 'articles of peace' to come into force. It is worth noting in passing that the political anarchists, such as Godwin, also believed that human beings could live peacefully in societies according to moral rules without there being coercive government to enforce any rules. Anarchy does not mean 'lack of rules', only 'lack of a ruler' (Godwin 1946). And although this idea is generally dismissed as hopelessly utopian for the relationships between individuals, it actually seems to work in the relations between states.

My main objection though is not to argue that, given the sceptic's definition of morality, the conditions for morality do after all obtain in international relations. It is rather to say that the conception of morality is itself mistaken. Morality does not depend, for its applicability, upon its being enforceable, being subject to the condition of actual mutual compliance, or being already established in traditions or institutions. All these conditions contribute towards the extent to which moral rules are in fact followed, but they do not bear on the matter of their existence or applicability. Certainly we do not generally hold that a person has a duty to tell the truth or keep a promise, only if her act falls under an enforceable law, only if others do the same all the time, or only if it is in her interests to do so.

This second line of objection, that moral rules apply to one regardless of general compliance or enforceability, may be seen as rather weak on its own unless it is added on the back of the earlier line of argument, given the following line of reasoning.[7] If we accepted Hobbes' factual analysis of international relations as a 'state of war', then surely there would be a sense in which a state is always justified in looking to its interests. If there is that degree of breakdown or absence of social co-operation, what else would any one do? We would need to say that certain moral rules are applicable in principle but are always rightly overridden by consideration of security and survival. This is a general extension of the more specific point, usually recognised, that even if it is wrong to kill, this is overridden in conditions of self-defence against life-threatening attack. So the point remains that in real terms, ethical norms would be off the scene, which is the substance of the sceptic's position. Therefore we need also to claim that Hobbes' analysis of international relations as a state of nature qua war is factually wrong as well, if we are to rebut the Hobbesian argument (see Beitz 1979: 36ff.) for criticism of the four criteria). How can we respond to this?

Clearly the lines of objection mutually support each other, but it is not clear that the second ethical one strictly requires the first. Few would doubt that in extreme situations the right of self-defence overrides moral restraints, but it hardly follows from this that in general moral rules only apply when one is completely certain about other actors' behaviour, or when some practice is actually established. My general preference for the second line of argument is not that the first is not effective (as a rebuttal of Hobbes' factual analysis), but that basic moral truths do not depend upon convention or practice.

In any case many other writers have also seen international relations as a state of nature in the sense in which there is great hostility, distrust and tendencies towards conflict, but have not drawn the same sceptical conclusions. For instance, Kant in *Perpetual Peace* accepted the negative analysis of international relations but felt that moral values applied to them (and were not to be ignored), and that there were powerful moral arguments for developing a framework of international law and institutions to make peace possible (Kant 1970b). It is one of the curious features of Hobbes' account that he sees such a clear-cut division between peace within a state and lack of it in international relations, both because he thought the latter impossible and because he thought it was less inconvenient than lack of peace in social life. But as Kant recognised, if it is rational to seek peace as the best way to secure self-preservation, it is hardly rational to secure peace within a country but allow war to continue internationally, because an individual in a country at war or in a country always liable to be at war with another country, hardly enjoys the conditions of peace, certainly as Hobbes defines it.

IV. CRITIQUE OF THE ROLE OF THE NATION-STATE

A. THE DUTY OF GOVERNMENT

The argument that governments have a special overriding duty to promote the national interest is a popular one but appears to be deeply flawed. We have to be careful to distinguish such a view as a basis for international scepticism from such a view being a consequence or corollary of international scepticism. Indeed, if for other reasons one thought that foreign policy was not governed by ethical norms, then indeed it would be clear that governments had a duty to promote the national interest (and the contrast would be with promoting sectional interests or the pursuit of power). What we are considering here is whether the duty to promote the national interest can act as a premise for the conclusion that, in practice if not in theory, governments never had a real duty to promote the interests of other states or peoples as a goal (though this might happen as a means or by-product).

The first point to be made is, following Beitz, to say that 'what people have a right to have done for them is limited by what they have a right to do themselves' (Beitz 1979: 24). That is, if some act of foreign policy, like an invasion of another country to secure control of natural resources, were such that individuals would regard it as wrong for them to do something analogous themselves, then it would be wrong for the government to do it. More generally, we do not think that the relationship between a trustee and a client justifies the trustee in doing anything to further the interest of the client. The duty of a company to its stockholders to maximise profits does not justify any measures to do so. A parent with special responsibilities to her child, is not justified in doing what is wrong, for instance stealing a toy she could not afford, in order to further the child's interests. In the latter three cases we assume that the specific duty to promote the interest of others, because of the special relationship involved, does not override the ordinary moral framework of non-deception, non-coercion, respect for property, and so on. Why should governments be any different? Locke for instance, one of the key contract thinkers in this tradition, was clear that governments were bound by the 'laws of nature' in their external relations (Locke 1960: bk 2, ch. 2, pa. 14). Perhaps however it is not the trusteeship relationship as such, but the nature of the entity which the government is acting on behalf of that makes the difference for many thinkers.

B. OTHER ARGUMENTS

The nation-state is after all, unlike most other bodies like the family or a company, a peculiarly powerful and dominant kind of social entity. Most people live their lives almost entirely within such states. The nation-state along with the society it sustains gives identity and meaning to people's lives. It is not surprising that given the will of people to flourish, develop or advance themselves within this socio-political environment, the general thrust of any such entity will be its own development. If that is so, and the rest of the world is different, separate and not part of that 'field of significance', then why should not the ethical drive of that society be to advance its interests?

This thesis, like the more general thesis of communitarianism (to be discussed in the next chapter) can be presented as a strong 'all encompassing' thesis; that is, people's identities are constituted within the nation-state and this exhausts the scope and nature of their moral agency. Even if it is so presented and is thus as 'global scepticism' seen as directly excluding a 'global ethic', it does not exclude an 'international ethic' in the form of a morality of states. States qua states still need to co-operate, so that even if individuals within states do not have any moral duty as members of anything larger than their nation-states, their governments still have to act in an international arena. It is worth noting in passing that Machiavelli, who is often seen as a key international realist, in saying that a state may have to act dishonourably in its relations to other states when national survival dictates, is not as such ruling out the applicability of moral rule in the international arena; he is merely saying that when foreign policy requires it the rules are to be ignored (Machiavelli 1988: ch. XV).

It is not however necessary to see this argument about the central role of the nation-state as an 'all encompassing' view. That the identities and loyalties of human beings are largely focused round the nation-state does not entail that they are so entirely. Apart from many levels of identity relating to smaller social groups, there may also be levels of identity relating to groups which cross boundaries as well as a sense which many people have of being members of the global community of human beings as such, perhaps inspired by religious understandings of the brotherhood of humankind, perhaps not. Membership of the human race, and, even, for some, membership of the wider community of life, may be an important level of identity. The point I am making at this stage is that, even if one takes the argument at the level of descriptive analysis, it simply is not true that the nation-state is the only, or the more important, or the widest locus of identity and loyalty. Increasingly in the modern world the processes of globalisation, particularly global travel and communications, are changing the balance.

However, the line of argument I wish to advance here does not merely depend on pointing to what is already accepted in the world. It depends upon making certain claims about human beings, their common nature and their shared condition, according to which ethically we do stand in moral relations to all fellow human beings, whether that is recognised at all, or enough, in the thinking of many people. This will be the kind of argument developed in the rest of the book.

With regard to the specific arguments drawn from the specific nature of the nation or the state, I shall reserve my more substantial discussion to the next chapter, but simply note now that whatever the value of membership of a nation or of a state, first they are not the same, and second neither entails the absence of a wider ethical framework. As Frost argues, Hegel's position can be seen as supportive of a framework of international morality in the form of a morality of states (Frost 1996).

With regard to the arguments mentioned earlier about the 'morality' of the group (namely an immorality by reference to ordinary standards of morality), we can accept this to a certain extent as a factual observation of certain tendencies in human group behaviour. But what follows from this ethically is less clear. In many ways morality can be seen generally as something which checks certain natural tendencies in our nature, and the same may well be the case *vis-à-vis* how groups interact with other groups, as well as *vis-à-vis* individuals within a social group. There may indeed be socio-biological origins to morality in which the kind of moral sensibility which initially emerged was very limited. But like other capacities which no doubt had evolutionary origins such as the capacity to count, the infusion of rationality into moral sensibility has transformed it, as it has transformed counting into higher mathematics.[8]

C. SOVEREIGNTY

Whilst a proper exploration of sovereignty would require very lengthy consideration, the following remarks may suffice to show why, on the face of it, appeal to the idea of sovereignty does not support international scepticism. If one approaches the idea of sovereignty from the inside, that is from the perspective of a people over whom a sovereign has power, sovereignty is consistent with either international scepticism or the acceptance of a wider ethical framework. It certainly does not entail the absence of wider moral values. That is, the fact that a governing power has the authority, understood as given by contract or otherwise conferred or assumed, to make laws and implement them for a given people in a given geographical area, and as subject to no higher law (other than the law of God), leaves it entirely open whether, as Hobbes supposed, such powers exist (a) in a state of amoral anarchy, or (b) enter into unenforceable agreements with other states, or (c) accept that there is a natural law governing relations between all people and groups of people, as Locke certainly held (Locke 1960: bk 2, ch. 2, pa. 14). Even if international law is seen as not really like 'hard' law at all because of its unenforceability, it is still to be understood as providing some kind of normative framework, all the more to be thought of as an ethical framework just because it is not like hard enforceable domestic law where 'law is the command of the sovereign', as the legal positivist Austin put it (Austin 1995). The point is that if sovereignty is defined in terms of not being subject to any higher 'law', then that does not affect the application of ethical predicates to foreign policy.

Characteristically though sovereignty is not defined exclusively in terms of the internal relations between governor and governed, but in terms of the relations to other states. If that is the case, then an ethical framework is actually presupposed, because sovereignty is defined as a right *vis-à-vis* other states who have a duty to respect that right, that is, to respect sovereignty and not engage in aggression, intervention or interference with it. These rights and duties are of course defined in international laws and agreements, but they still reflect a moral framework and are indeed a cornerstone of the 'morality of states' discussed in the next chapter. Whether this is an adequate account of the ethical standing of sovereignty is another matter. My point is here that it is implausible to run a sceptical line once external sovereignty is acknowledged.

One argument we noted earlier though concerns the fact that although there might be a moral law or 'law of nature' framework, it cannot be implemented because of the disputable nature of decisions and the lack of a definitive arbiter for such issues. Does this preserve the sceptical thrust of the argument? First, if indeed states had internal sovereignty but did not live in agreed 'morality of states', there would in practice be great difficulty in applying any ethical judgement to international relations (even though it would still be possible in theory and each individual thinker would still have his views on what ought to be done). But if states exist in a society of states, then there is an ethical framework, and generally it would be recognised that this extended beyond the general principles of respect for sovereignty to a number of specific rules about how to engage with other states and about the rules of war. In any case, as international law has developed, the capacity for reaching agreements over disputes increases. The fact that thinkers disagree about what ought to be done in international relations by countries in conflict is not now seen to be a reason for abandoning such discourse, any more than the fact that within societies there are very different perceptions of what ought to be done. This point anticipates part of my later criticism of relativism.

Sovereignty then does not entail the inapplicability of ethical norms to foreign policy. If it is argued that in its earlier conception it had this implication and that modern states are no longer sovereign in the way they were 300 or 400 years ago, then that merely reinforces the point that a world made up of nation-states need not be made up of sovereign states in that sense, and that one cannot rest an argument for excluding norms and values on an appeal to a definition. Whatever role the idea of sovereignty has in the real world, it is not one that can have that consequence. It is interesting to note that William Penn actually recognised as early as 1693 that if states entered into a sovereign parliament of Europe thereby transferring their autonomy, they would exercise sovereignty in respect of their own people, so he at least did not see it as an absolute concept (Penn 1993: 15). Maybe 300 years later the development of the European Community partly reflects the vision which Penn had.

V. CRITIQUE OF GLOBAL SCEPTICISM

A. AS AN ARGUMENT FOR INTERNATIONAL SCEPTICISM

First, even if relativism were to be accepted in both descriptive and normative senses, it is not clear that international ethics is ruled out. It is clearly consistent with a claim that each society is a self-contained social unit with a distinct morality within it, that between societies there are no moral relations, merely a moral vacuum. But it is no more than consistent with it, since it is also consistent with relativism to suppose that there is something called a society of states in which there has also developed, over time, a set of norms for their dealing with one another. If the thesis of relativism is that moral values arise within societies and basically are validated by their being agreed, then exactly the same can be said about what may emerge in the society of states, namely an agreed set of norms. And this is exactly what many defenders of the international 'morality of states' which has emerged since the Peace of Westphalia (1648) would say has emerged. Of course such a 'morality of states' is conservative in the sense of being based on what is already established, just as on a relativist view social moralities are. It may be self-justifying and make no reference to any deeper ethical theory of a cosmopolitan kind, since if relativism is true there is no such underlying theory in the background. We shall have reason later to reject this way of understanding and justifying the 'morality of states', but the point here is that even if relativism were true, the idea of some kind of international morality as a framework within which states operate is not ruled out, and may be seen as precisely ruled in, because such a society exists in just the same way as ordinary societies exist. Of course it is still open to the sceptical realist to argue that such a society of states is not really a society at all, and that the rules it adopts are not genuine moral rules, because for instance they are not enforceable with proper legal or social sanctions. The issue is taken up again in the next chapter. What we need to note here is that it is not self-evident that global scepticism entails international scepticism.

B. ARGUMENTS FOR GLOBAL SCEPTICISM ITSELF

The thesis of relativism has two parts to it: first a factual or descriptive claim that as a matter of fact the values of different societies are different; second a normative claim that what is valued, that is, what is counted as a value in a given society is indeed to be accepted as the appropriate values for that society. There are in fact several levels of reply to be given.[9]

Relativism as an empirical thesis: Even if the relativist is right that what is valuable or is to be valued depends on what is as a matter of fact valued, it is by no means clear that the world is as they represent it. On the one hand there may be a greater degree of consensus on key features of well-being – the value of food, shelter, health, knowledge, community – and of key duties to do with respecting life, agreements and property. As Bull remarks, the latter are the *sine qua non* of a society's existence anyway. There may also be a greater amount of acceptance of at least minimum respect for other human beings in other societies.

This is not to say that there are no real differences in cultural values in different societies. The point is that there may well be a core of values that are common, if not universal, amongst human beings, including core norms to do with acknowledging fellow human beings as having a moral status. Of course the way these values are interpreted in particular social contexts may vary from place to place. But such contextual variation is itself not sufficient reason for saying that there are no universal values.

Relativism as a normative thesis: second, the real issue which needs to be taken up is whether relativism as a normative thesis is to be accepted. Even if there are significant variations in cultural values and we accept in large measure the factual thesis of relativism, it by no means follows that we have to accept the normative claim that what is established as right or valuable in a society is right or valuable. The objections stem partly from appeals to our ethical intuitions, and partly by disagreeing with the theoretical assumptions about how moral values are established.

At the level of intuitions, one can point to the following difficulties. First, relativism is inherently conservative and makes two kinds of things impossible: internal minority dissent, internal pluralism and moral progress on the one hand, and external criticism by those outside a culture on the other. If what is valuable depends upon what is established, then where does that put the position of individuals or small groups who seek to articulate a moral view out of line with what is valuable? Progress becomes difficult to conceptualise, since there is meant to be no standard outside the norms of society itself by which one could say 'the society's norms and practices fall short of that standard'. Second, if it is recognised that in many modern societies there is a great variety or plurality of cultures, then the supposed tidy homogeneity of a society with its established values collapses. Of course as Rawls suggests, there may be areas of 'overlapping consensus' in a modern pluralist society, but of course once this is conceded the tidy move of relativism resisting the idea of common values on a global scale is weakened, since there could easily be areas of overlapping consensus at a global level consistent with more particular values in different societies within a 'pluralist' world (cf. Rawls: 1993: lect. 4).

Respecting diversity: one of the attractions of relativism and postmodernism is their supposed principle of toleration or openness towards other cultures, with the celebration of diversity and 'difference'. But there are in fact immense difficulties and tensions here. First what is this principle of tolerance or respect for diversity? As Williams remarked, this ethical principle is really a universal principle, the kind of universal principle which relativism is meant to rule out as unacceptable (Williams 1972: 'Interlude: Relativism'). I shall in fact argue that this principle is one of the key principles of an acceptable cosmopolitan ethic. The point here is that if it is recommended to any relativist from within the normative theory, then it renders the theory incoherent. If on the other hand, it is not recommended as a principle which any relativist would accept, we are into another quite opposed difficulty. If a principle of respect for other cultures just happens to be a principle which some societies have, then it is perfectly consistent with the theory that some other societies might not have such a principle of respect. If the values of any society are meant to be self-validating, then so far as the theory of relativism goes, a society could just as easily have an attitude of belligerence or hostility or superiority towards other people and regard this as part of their ethical culture. (Discourse about the 'superman' or 'super race' tends towards this way of looking at the rest of the world.) If a relativist respects other cultures, that is just an accident, not something deep within the theory, and if someone from one society justified aggression towards another society in the name of its value system, the relativist would have no right to complain. That does not accord with my intuitions at any rate. Furthermore in respect of the 'other-ness' of the Aztecs or any other non-European peoples who were seen as savages or barbarians, it is worth noting that so far from giving us reason to respect the Aztecs or other peoples, relativism is actually in danger of taking away at least the basis of restraint in the recognition that they are human like us, since if being biologically human says nothing about what is valuable in them, there is even less reason for restraint.[10] (A cosmopolitan defence of the principle of respect for diversity and for pluralism, which are part of the attraction of relativism, is given in Chapter 5.)

The use of moral language in international relations: in the course of this discussion of the weaknesses of relativism we can address the arguments mentioned earlier about the role of ethical values in international relations. What about the appeal the relativist or postmodernist makes to an intuition many of us have about the danger of imposing values on others, particularly by the powerful on the less powerful? Is not the idea of universal values a vehicle for such imposition, as Carr argued? In a similar vein, as we noted earlier, Hans Morgenthau says the promotion of ethical values in foreign policy is dangerous, and fails to pursue the higher moral goal of national survival. I take these two arguments together, not because they are the same, but because the strategy for replying to them is broadly the same. We must not throw out the baby with the bathwater. Yes, of course there are dangers in the use of universal values as an instrument of power. Yes, the pursuit of moral objectives (as for instance in Vietnam, or more generally in the cold war ideological stand-off) leads to war, great dangers, threats to peace and so on. But to reject moral goals in foreign policy on this basis is to confuse moralism with acceptable ethical principles.

In fact in both cases, there is again a kind of incoherence, because the rejection of moralism in foreign policy is premised on the value of international order and thus on some ethical principles about the importance of preserving international order, and this is a transnational value of some kind (whether understood in a 'morality of states' way or a cosmopolitan way). Similarly the criticisms of universal values discourse as a vehicle for power politics seems tacitly to concede that the world would be a better place if such power politics were not pursued or pursued in this way. If there are real alternatives, we ought to pursue them. Even

if one were a determinist on this matter – contrary to the basic premise
of this work – and doubted whether real alternatives were possible, one
would still need a perspective from which to express a view that the world
would be better place if only things were different. Arguably this is not the
relativist perspective but a supposed universal perspective, which presupposes some account of the values that would make it a better place.

Theoretical objections to relativism: turning to more theoretical
considerations, we need to confront the central contention of relativism,
that values are relative to the society in which they are accepted. Does
this seem an adequate basis for ethics? The subsequent argument of the
book will be to say that it is not, but let me mention a few points here.
At the very least it should be possible to say that the moral values of an
individual or of a social group are mistaken or inadequate, and that the
moral values which we pick up through education and socialisation might
be based on ignorance, prejudice, personal bias, or self/group interest. All
this suggests that moral values are capable of rational or critical assessment. If moral values can be modified by reflection and argument, then it
follows that what preceded such reflection might be wrong or inadequate.
If this is accepted then it is possible for a thinker to argue for a value
system, including a cosmopolitan value system, which does not correspond
to what may already be accepted. How far and in what ways rational reflection can extend or modify moral beliefs is matter of great debate. All I
want to establish here is that such rational engagement with ethical values
is coherent. But if it is coherent then reading values off from what is
established in a society simply cannot be accepted. What detailed ethical
approaches come out of this ethical reflection will emerge later.

All we should note here is that the willingness to establish basic ethical
norms on something other than what is socially accepted is consistent
with quite a wide variety of ways of developing such views. There are
many approaches, ranging from traditional objectivism, through ethical
construction by practical reason or consensus, to identifying ethical
commitment with universal prescriptivity as in a recent theory of Hare's.[11]
It may well turn out that an ethical theory does not have the character of
a culturally specific ethic, but is genuinely accessible to people of many
different cultural backgrounds.

It is of course this possibility which much postmodernist and relativist
thinking questions. Put very bluntly the question is this: is it possible for
an ethical approach to be so presented in a reasonable fashion that it is
genuinely accessible to thinkers in any culture? This is not to say that it
is now accepted by thinkers in any culture. But the same point can be
made about any ethical theory, even one that is presented as reasonable to
thinkers within any given culture. Indeed this point shows that whatever

difficulties there are in thinkers with different perspectives understanding each other, these difficulties are not as such difficulties which arise because people are living in different parts of the world. Clashes between the pro-life lobby and the pro-abortion lobby within a society may be deep and make it difficult for each side to see what the other side is saying, but this does not prevent there being at some other level some set of moral rules through which the society containing these groups continues to function. So the mere fact that there are deep differences between different cultures, for instance in the present world between liberal Western views on the position of women and that of certain traditional Islamic cultures such as Iran, does not preclude reason-based agreement on other ethical norms. It may be right to value the celebration of diversity, but in throwing out the idea of moral norms genuinely available to all reasonable thinkers, we would throw out the baby with the bathwater, and as I remarked earlier, be deprived of any real normative view about how we should treat other cultures.[12] We also throw out the whole idea of global responsibility as a moral norm to be recommended universally.

In this chapter I have examined three main lines of argument denying or questioning both international ethics and global ethics: the argument that international relations lack certain key features necessary for morality such as enforceability, guaranteed compliance or shared traditions; the argument that the state has the character it has because of its drive towards self-development and the role of government in promoting the national interest; and the argument from relativism and postmodernism that there are no universal values to be found. I have suggested that even in terms of the conception of morality presupposed in the above arguments, the picture is less clear-cut than it might seem at first, and some account of global norms and certainly an international ethic as a 'morality of states' is consistent with the views. But my main line of criticism is that the arguments rely on a false conception of what morality is and the way reason enters into the determination of a defensible moral code. The full development of the latter belongs to the later chapters.

NOTES

1. The arguments for international scepticism are drawn from a number of places, though I am mainly drawing on and combining two accounts given in recent textbooks, Beitz 1979: pt I, in which he identifies five main arguments and Maxwell 1990, in which she identifies six main arguments for scepticism, followed by six main arguments for supporting global morality (see summary on pp. 56–7). For a modern defence of sceptical realism, see Smith 1979 and for a critique see Cohen 1985.

2. Hegel 1942: III (iii) (b), pp. 212–16. However some of the things Hegel says

suggest arguments for some kind of internationalism. See ch. 3.

3. Hobbes 1991: ch. 18. Also a feature of Locke's account of international relations in contrast to the role of government of providing an 'indifferent' judge in civil society.

4. See Wong 1992 and Brandt 1967 for useful surveys. Relativism became popular in the mid-twentieth century, partly because of positivism's view of ethics as non-rational, and partly because of the impact of anthropological studies, evidenced in Benedict 1935 and Westermarck 1932. Modern defenders include Wong 1984 and Harman 1977.

5. I have in mind here the rather stronger claims of writers like Derrida, Foucault and Lyotard rather than writers such as Rorty or Habermas. The celebration of 'difference' and acceptance of an open-ended pluralism is, up to the point where it does not subvert the idea of a global moral order, to be welcomed. See Brown 1992: chs 8 and 9.

6. Beitz 1979: pt I; Cohen 1985; Thompson 1992: ch. 1; and Frost 1996: ch. 2 all contain useful discussions of scepticism.

7. See, for example, Barry 1986 for a useful discussion of the compliance problem.

8. See, for example, Nagel 1979, for an interesting exploration of this line of thought, and more generally Axelrod 1984. Part of the interesting challenge today is over the issue of the 'expanding circle', to use Singer's phrase, of the domain of ethical concern, and whether, if it happens, its expanding to include all human beings, future generations, sentient life or life more generally, is more in the nature of discovery, driven by consistency, or in the nature of creative decision.

9. For full critical discussion of relativism see, for example, Stace 1937, summarised in Borchert and Stewart 1986.

10. I am indebted to Apel 1992 for this insight.

11. Hare 1963: pt I. I mention this theory to illustrate a more general point. In his theory a moral philosopher may well argue for some form of non-cognitivism, i.e. that there are no moral truths, only commitments or preferences, but if the theory is not merely about what a person wants for himself (with nothing to say about other people or about public institutions), but it is the person's attempt to articulate what he thinks is right or valuable generally, then such a theory is hostile to relativism as a doctrine about the social constitution of ethics, and is therefore capable of being presented as a cosmopolitan theory.

12. See various papers in UNESCO 1992.

QUESTIONS FOR DISCUSSION

1. What arguments for international scepticism seem the most appealing?
2. What reasons can be given for denying that there is a global ethic?
3. Is the duty of a government to look after their nationals' interests overriding or not?
4. Given your approach to the issues raised in this chapter, what are the main features of morality as you understand it?

CHAPTER 3

INTERNATIONALISM AND COMMUNITARIANISM

In this chapter we will look at various arguments for the view that that there is a 'morality of states' and also at the type of approach which I have called communitarian according to which an important source, if not the source, of moral values which individuals have comes from the society, community, or nation-state they live in. The latter approach is significant both because it provides one form of support for 'the morality of states', and also because it provides a basis for either denying or modifying the claims of a global ethic of a cosmopolitan kind.

I. HISTORICAL ORIGINS OF INTERNATIONALISM

In 1648 the Peace of Westphalia was concluded. This brought to an end the so-called Thirty Years War which had raged on and off throughout Europe for many years. But it is usually remembered because it was this Peace Treaty that formalised what is called the international system or nation-state system (see e.g. Miller 1990: ch. 2). The central principle in the new system was that Europe should be divided up into discrete geographical areas over which secular powers should exercise absolute control and authority. This way of understanding the division of control has broadly remained until the present day (though various forces such as globalisation are now challenging it in the late twentieth century). It started out very much as a European international society of states, but has spread to the whole world, initially of course through the dominant European powers taking control of other parts of the world as parts of their 'imperium' through what we call colonialism. With the processes of decolonisation now virtually complete, the world is now conceived as made up of so many autonomous nation-states, over 190 of them, as measured by current membership of the United Nations.

It is worth stressing the implication of the above that the world has not been organised into the system of autonomous states for more than a small period of its history. How societies have been organised, who has control over what, how relations between different groups have been understood, has varied considerably in different times and different parts of the world. For a period in the so-called heyday of classical Greece, Greece was divided in many different city-states, before being absorbed as a whole into the Macedonian Empire. Rome at a later stage established an empire of the whole of the Mediterranean area and beyond to include all that the Romans counted as parts of the civilised world. After the collapse of the Roman Empire from the fourth century AD onwards, Europe broke up into many different areas of rule, some large, some small, but always continuing to be informed by the power and influence of the Roman and Orthodox churches. One of the continuing sources of conflict and tension was over the respective power and influence of the religious author-ities, under the headship of the Pope, and the separate principalities and kingdoms. Italy in Machiavelli's day (sixteenth century) was dominated by strife between different principalities, not least the Papacy itself which controlled a significant area of Italy. One of the important gains achieved in the Peace of Westphalia was the clearer division between the areas in which the Church exercised authority – spiritual matters – and areas in which secular powers exercised authority. If a system could be estab-lished in which rulers had undisputed authority to rule over their subjects in a given geographical area and in which other rulers accepted this and respected the sovereignty of others, then the chances of peace and order were greatly improved.

Although a number of other justifications for the nation-state system can be and have been given, to be discussed below, it is clear that in its origins the nation-state system was grounded in the natural law thinking of the Christian church, which in the preceding centuries, so far as Western Europe was concerned, had meant the Roman Catholic church. The natural law approach, which represents a complex tradition rather than a single doctrine, has nevertheless a central core to it which is important to the issues we need to discuss. It is, following Thomas Aquinas who is seen as the most profound and systematic exponent of this kind of theology, the 'eternal law' as that pertains to the nature of a human being but discoverable by the exercise of natural reason (Aquinas 1953: I–II, qu. 94). The first precept of practical reason is that we should 'seek the good and shun evil', and this is understood in terms of the values of three levels of human life: existence as such, our animal nature and our rational nature, leading to the moral rules not to kill, to further life and to seek life in society, knowledge of God and generally the life of reason.

On the one hand this conception is a universal conception of human well-being, and the rules of morality deriving from it apply to our relations to all human beings. Fundamentally we all belong to the *civitas maxima*, the greatest city of all human beings. So it is a cosmopolitan conception, as will be discussed in the next chapter. On the other hand, Aquinas and others recognise that because of our human frailty, weakness and proneness to sin and wrongdoing, we need to live in organised societies within which order can be maintained by coercion. That is we need to have rulers with the power to enforce moral rules, with the sanctions of punishments. Aquinas was concerned with the need to justify the use of violence and coercion where it was needed in contrast to the general use of violence. Part of his interest in arguing that rulers were justified in using force to maintain social order was to limit violence only to those who had the authority to do so. If rulers had the authority to use violence and to go to war to defend what they ruled, others did not, such as private citizens, pirates and so on. For Aquinas the authority which converted violence into legitimate rule and the exercise of law (civil law as the expression of the natural law) was essentially given by God, that is, it was a divinely instituted arrangement whereby rulers ruled particular groups of people. Other thinkers have of course given other forms of justification for rule, such as tradition, consent, democratic mandate and so on, but all seek to provide a justification for the power of the ruler or state and its use of or threat of violence either against its own citizens (if they step out of line) or against others in war, which would otherwise be sheer power and violence.

It is against this backcloth that we can understand some of the thinking which led to the international system instituted and formally reinforced at the time of the Peace of Westphalia. Although in the background there was an appeal to the universal natural law and the idea of a *civitas maxima*, the practical task was to establish principles of legitimate rule and especially the need for other states to respect the de facto division of power in the world or at least in Europe at that time.

Hugo Grotius was a key figure in the thinking of the time. He was a Dutch jurisprudentialist whose *On the Law of War and Peace* has made a large impact on the thinking behind the international system. He accepted in the main the natural law framework, but made a lot of the fact that in an uncertain and hostile world, the right to preserve oneself and promote one's interests has a centrality, which applies equally to the nation-states which had by then become the dominant reality in Europe. Unlike Hobbes, whose analysis of human nature and the human predicament was harsher still, though greatly influenced by Grotius' thinking, Grotius also affirmed the other central ethical principle that we ought not to cause unnecessary or wanton injury to others (Grotius 1925). So on these two principles, we can found a relationship between states in which on the one hand states are primarily about their own survival and advancement but are also bound to respect the like aspirations of other states. That is, this kind of morality is not a very extensive one, and has been, as we shall see in the next section, a feature of the 'morality of states' which has characterised the international tradition. But before leaving Grotius it is worth noting an observation which he made about the natural law which was that, whilst they were (of course) the commands of God (as applied to human nature), they would be valid even if there were no God to command them (see Tuck 1989: 20–3). There is an implied secularisation of the ethical basis of morality in this remark, and in many ways later thinking within the internationalist tradition not only lost the original theological anchorage but also the key cosmopolitan idea that the natural law applied to one's relations with all human beings. That is, that the ultimate justification of the moral rules governing states resides in the impacts these have on human beings as such.

II. THE MAIN ELEMENTS OF THE MORALITY OF STATES

In *The Anarchical Society* Bull identifies four values or goals of the international society. These are, in descending order of importance (Bull 1985: 15–21):

1. *The preservation of the system or society of states itself*: Like any society there is an inherent tendency towards self-maintenance. If this is a primary goal, it may well be justified from time to time, for reasons of maintaining for instance a balance of power or spheres of influence, for one country to interfere in another country's affairs or even invade it. Connected with this and with the need for the international relations to be conducted as smoothly as possible, are the complex but important rules to do with the treatment of diplomats – ambassadors, messengers, peace negotiators and so on – and the whole system of international protocol.

2. *The maintenance of the independence and external sovereignty of individual states*: This is the most prominent feature of the morality of states in practice since it concerns the key duty of other states to respect the sovereignty of states, and therefore not to attack or threaten to attack other countries, or to intervene in the internal affairs of other countries and so on. Although in certain ways of understanding the tradition, this right of sovereignty has been seen as near absolute, it does not follow that there are no occasions at all in which interference or intervention may not be justified, for instance for reasons of 'common security', which in UN terminology picks up on first goal, or for reasons to do with rectifying injustice, which links to the idea of the just war.

3. *The maintenance and pursuit of peace*: This clearly is a central goal in that it is only in conditions of peace and order that the central goals of social life can be pursued. But peace is not seen, as perhaps some idealists such as irenists or pacifists might see it, as an overriding goal, something to be aimed at above all else, since there may be circumstances, such as the need to defend oneself or one's state or the need to rectify injustice, in which peace may be deliberately and justifiably abandoned. The development of the 'just war' tradition, which very much belongs to the internationalist tradition, is an attempt to put limits on violence, by seeking to clarify just what are the limited circumstances in which the decision to go to war is justified and also by putting restrictions on who may legitimately wage war, namely nation-states themselves as 'legitimate authorities'. States reserve for themselves the monopoly in the legitimacy of the use of violence, as we noted earlier.

4. *The common goals of social life*: Bull identifies three main goals of
   society as the security of the person against violence, the honouring
   of promises and agreements, and the stability of possessions, thus
   resulting in rights and corresponding duties to respect life, promises
   and property. One might wonder whether these were the only common
   goals of social life. Perhaps, as Locke saw it, liberty is a central
   natural right along with the rights to life and property (Locke 1960).
   The value of truth and truthfulness might be given a more central
   place as a *sine qua non* for social communication, though this could
   equally be subsumed under the value of promises. Others might want
   to include more specific values, for instance of a religious kind. But
   the point remains that insofar as the international community has an
   interest in social values for the morality of states, it is interested in
   those on which there is universal agreement. In practice this does not
   mean that states have a duty or right actively to promote these values
   in other societies. Far from it, since the whole thrust of the approach
   was to protect the internal affairs of states from external interference.
   Rather, these values inform the morality of states with respect to those
   areas where interactions between states take place. The most obvious
   areas are war and commerce.

Whilst war is intrinsically destructive of life, the rules of war (*ius in bello*)
can be seen then as an attempt to limit the violence of war and its destruc-
tiveness by putting restrictions on who may be direct objects of attack
and in what ways one may legitimately fight. (From time to time efforts
have been made to ban particularly nasty types of weapons like poisoned
arrows, dumdum bullets and land mines.) Likewise if international trade
and commerce are to flourish, then there has to be accepted some general
principle of honouring agreements (even outside a framework of mechanism to enforce compliance). Similarly international law develops alongside particular agreements and treaties between states, which would not
be possible unless there was a general expectation that these agreements
would be honoured. This principle concerning the general honouring of
agreements is often still referred to under its Latin tag *pacta sunt servanda*
(pacts are to be kept).

What is striking about this international morality however is as much
what is not included as what is included. It is important to recognise
this because the dispute with cosmopolitanism arises partly because
certain things are missing. One thing that is missing is any reference to a
duty actively to promote the global common good, except insofar as the
maintenance of the society of states is itself a crucial common good, or
to a duty to promote the good of other individual states or the well-being
of individuals who may be suffering in other states.

This may be based on several lines of thought. It could be based on a scepticism about whether there is such a thing as a global common good (linked with relativism), or whether any agreement can be reached about such matters. Generally the right of states to pursue their own interests is seen as the central principle, and so long as what states do does not actively damage or undermine the interests of other states, which would be seen as a form of interference, states need not be concerned with such positive global goals, unless they have entered into specific bilateral or multilateral agreements to come to other states' aid. (I come back to the implication of this last feature in the modern world shortly.)

Beitz has characterised this general feature of the morality of states as the 'international analogue of nineteenth-century liberalism' (Beitz 1979: 66). Traditional liberalism (though reflected again in more recent years in the re-emergence of libertarian thinking) put stress on the value of liberty, economic and otherwise, on consent as the basis of transactions and on non-interference, but did not assert a general duty of positive caring for those who were less fortunate.

Another feature of the tradition is a certain approach to the status of the individual within the system. Put in legalistic fashion, individual human beings were regarded as objects, not subjects of international law. The implication of this was that in terms of the 'laws of nations' or, following Bentham, international law, states were the only legal 'persons' involved; individuals had no rights under international law, could not take legal action against states, and only affected states insofar as states took them into consideration in their dealings with one another. The development of human rights thinking, particularly in the second half of the twentieth century, does of course challenge this set of presumptions. Apart from the more technical issue to do with international law (which is changing, partly because of human rights thinking), it is in this area concerning the relationship of the individual to the state in the international context that many cosmopolitans have reason to take issue with the morality of states approach.

In summary then, we can identify the following key elements of the 'morality of states' approach:

1. States have a duty to support the system of states.
2. States have a duty to respect the sovereignty, autonomy or independence of other states.
3. States have a duty not to interfere or intervene in the internal affairs of other states.
4. States alone have the right to engage in organised violence.
5. States have a general duty to promote peace but have a right to wage war if they have a just cause.

6. States have a duty to observe restrictions in the conduct of war, if they are at war.
7. States have a duty to honour agreements.
8. States have a duty not to harm other states, but have no duty in general to promote the global common good, the good of other states or the good of individuals living in other states.
9. Individual human beings do not have rights against any states other than those they live in.

III. JUSTIFICATIONS

How is this morality of states justified? One approach, which we have already started to look at, assumes that there is a universal moral framework, one given for instance by natural law, and goes on to argue that a world divided up into discrete areas of political control where those in power act within the framework already indicated, represents the most realistic way in which those universal values can be achieved. Although this approach underlay Grotius' thinking and that of the early theorists like Vitoria and Suarez (de Vitoria 1532; Suarez 1866), many thinkers since have adopted a rather different approach to the justification of the norms in the international arena.

Thus reflection on the nature of the political community which the state represents and also on the nature of society or moral community which exists within states, might lead one to hold that the moral rules governing international relations are to be seen as something emerging out of state relations themselves. This is either because there is no wider universal moral framework, or because, if there is one, it is one about which there is so little agreement that it is not a sound basis for basing a morality of states. Various accounts may be given, such as the idea of convention, custom and tradition, parallel to a communitarian view of society itself; the idea of an inter-state contract; and the idea of states having rights within the society of states.

A. COSMOPOLITAN/UNIVERSAL FRAMEWORK

As we have seen, a natural law account can be employed, so long as certain assumptions are made that the only effective way in which violence can be contained within reasonable limits in the world is to have political rule over discrete areas of control with minimal interference from others. Whether, in the modern world, this system and these rules are most appropriate for advancing the universal goals associated with the natural law is another matter, to which I return shortly. But it is worth noting that the approach remains important. It is not restricted to natural law thinkers, but is an approach which any cosmopolitan could take, whose values and/ or reading of the world led him or her to endorse the morality of states as the best way to realise those universal values.

Kant's theory is interesting in this regard because in one sense he was a great supporter of the nation-state system. But he did not want to endorse the rules as they were and proposed various progressive articles for peace. But the point remains that Kant's cosmopolitanism still allowed him to support the existence of the nation-state as a necessary social structure, particularly in a republican form, for both containing human impulses to unsociable behaviour and giving expression to our nature as autonomous agents choosing to live under a political regime (Kant 1970; see Chapter 4 for further discussion of Kant).

A modern writer, Michael Walzer, in the course of his influential work on the ethics of war, spells out a modern variety of the morality of states which he calls the 'legalist paradigm', and provides a justification for it which is in many ways reminiscent of Kant (Walzer 1977: 51–63; 1985). Although he does not call himself a cosmopolitan, Walzer nevertheless invokes an idea of universal rights, and it is the crucial role that a political community has in protecting these rights which provides the basis for defending the legalist paradigm. In particular it is because any act of aggression attacks the political community in which people's rights to liberty are invested that the rules defending state autonomy and sovereignty must be held to firmly. More generally those thinkers who adopt a thoroughly libertarian conception in which there is no general duty of universal care but a firm duty of non-interference will also be supportive of the main lines of the morality of states approach.

B. THE CHARACTER OF THE NATION-STATE/POLITICAL COMMUNIITY

I now turn to the other approach according to which it is because of the nature of the state and/or the community within the state that the morality of states has to be understood in a rather different way, as arising from the nature of states' interactions themselves.

Contract Theories

It would not be appropriate to go into any detail about contract theories. What I need to do here is to indicate briefly the ways in which contractarian thinking can feed into the argument for a morality of states. First, the contractarian approach towards the justification of the state (and the claim that citizens have a duty of loyalty to it) does not come down clearly one way or the other on issues of international morality. Hobbes' theory for instance shows that it is entirely consistent with international scepticism. Kant's more progressive theory, which is also a form of contract theory, is grounded in a cosmopolitan framework as we have just noted, whereas other contractarians, like Locke and recently Rawls, have seen their theories as supporting a morality of states approach. Why is there this open-endedness? It is largely a function of the background theory which each thinker has, about one's account of human nature in relation to the contract story, about the possibility of universal morality (denied by Hobbes, vigorously asserted by Kant) and so on.

Rousseau is an interesting case in point. As much as any writer he has been interpreted in many ways, both in his political theory itself and in his thinking about international relations. Although some of the things he says suggest almost a Hobbesian analysis of an amoral vacuum, he did think the idea of federations was possible and that moral values applied to all human beings. But what is significant about his account is the way the social contract provides for Rousseau the very core of what gives human beings in his ideal state their moral identity. We are bound to be free, he said paradoxically, because our lower self-interested selves are made to conform to what our higher moral selves determine to be right as contributing to the general will (Rousseau 1966: bk I, ch. 7). In this sense the people are themselves sovereign and the state externally expresses the general will reflecting the interests of all in the state. As Thompson notes, this is a conception of a democratic community but it is one which by its very nature is bent on its own interests (Thompson 1992: 147). It is difficult to see how in its foreign policy it could be anything other than highly partial to the pursuit of its own interests.

This illustrates the more general feature of contractarianism, the tendency for the theory to endorse a government's giving priority to the pursuit of national interests. If after all a government is justified by its serving the interests of its people, however defined, and that is what implicitly the contract is about – 'we will submit to government in return for the following benefits …' – then it is bound to favour a moral framework in international relations which allows it to do just that as far as possible. The result is that, unless the people actually wanted policies which went beyond the national interest (for instance, serving the needs of the distant poor), the foreign policy of states would be largely directed to pursuing the national interest within the limits set by agreements with other states.

Hegel and Idealist Theories

As we have already seen, Hegel's political theory can be seen as supporting a realist understanding of international relations. But in Mervyn Frost's interpretation firm support for the morality of states is given (Frost 1996). Frost's argument has two strands relevant to our enquiry. First, having criticised standard international relations theory, he argues that we need a 'domain of discourse', an area of broadly agreed principles, which we then find a theory to account for. He claims that the current state-centred system constitutes such a domain, with agreed values to do with sovereignty, international law, modernisation and domestic values (democracy and human rights). He rejects what he calls a 'natural law' theory of the community of humankind as an alternative agreed framework, partly because it is not agreed and established. Second, what theory synthesises the currently accepted norms? Not appeals to order, utilitarianism, or rights theories, but what he calls a 'constitutive' theory based on Hegel. This he takes to be the theory that individuals are constituted by their relation to family, civil society and the state. Their status as citizens of a state requires that other states acknowledge one's state as a sovereign state in the society of states. One's status in a political community depends partly on its being recognised as such by members of other states. As Hegel says, 'every state is sovereign and autonomous against its neighbours. It is entitled to be sovereign from their point of view, namely to be recognised by them as sovereign.' (Hegel 1942: 33)

What distinguished Hegel's approach from that of contract theorists is his organicist concerns that the state is not an instrumentality serving the pre-existing ends which human beings have, but that the state is in some sense the embodiment of human fulfilment. We are what we are through our relationship to the state. This is a theme in much of the writings of the political idealists. It seems then that on these accounts even more so than on the contractarian accounts, the state will have a drive towards self-realisation; the identity of the individual citizen within the state will be wrapped up largely in his relations to the state, and not with some supposed ideal community of all human beings. Part of Hegel's vast complex system of political and social thought links him very naturally with the style of thought which has in recent years been associated with 'communitarian' thinking.

Nationhood and Political Community
One style of thought which is distinct from contractarian thinking, considerations of universal moral order, or Hegelian rationalism has been the stress of nationhood as a basis for understanding international relations. Two historical figures in this regard are the German Fichte and the Italian Mazzini (Fichte 2000; Mazzini 2004). From their point of view membership of the nation is what is most important to one's identity and loyalty. The nation is quite distinct from the state. The state is an artificial institution created, in a sense, at will, and one can choose to belong to it or not. The nation or *natio* is quite different. Janna Thompson, who

writes sympathetically about nationalism as an ethical basis for international relations, remarks: 'a nation is defined by its culture, way of life, language, history, by the conviction of the members that they form a distinct people.' (Thompson 1992: 147) Although the state and the nation are quite distinct, there is an important connection in that typically those of the same nation want to be constituted within a state recognised as such by other states, in which that state either represents their nation or at least their nation is adequately represented by that state. (Whether the United Kingdom adequately represents the Scottish nation is one of the burning issues of Scottish politics at the present time!) The tendency of nationalism then is to downgrade the significance of the global, and to be antithetical to the conception of all human beings belonging from an ethical point of view to one global society.

Communitarianism

Communitarianism as a general approach is of interest for two distinct though related reasons. First it reinforces the arguments that say that nation-states as political entities are relatively self-contained social units with an ethical dynamic or drive towards self-maintenance and advancement. The political community is definitely not a body directed to the greater good of some wider whole, such as other states, or human beings as such. (Though it might be constrained somewhat by moral rules, following these is definitely not what it is about!) Second, communitarianism as a doctrine in its own right is about the moral identity of individual human beings, according to which one's identity as a member of a particular community is far more important than membership of some notional society of all human beings. It is in its turn supported by some of the considerations already given, because contract theories, theories of the state or nation as being a primary locus of loyalty are already stories which at least in part show why our primary loyalty is not to the society of all human beings. My main discussion however of communitarianism as a general social theory, as opposed to its manifestations in the political conceptions discussed above, will be reserved until Chapter 5.

C. THE MORALITY OF STATES AS A PRODUCT OF STATE INTERACTION IN A COMMUNITY OF STATES

We are now in a position to indicate relatively briefly how the justification of the morality of states can be given, if we reject a firm grounding in a global ethics conception. If we take the message of the various theories considered seriously that the nation-state is the embodiment of community, the expression of nationhood, or the product of a contract, its primary drive will be to maintain, defend and assert itself, but co-operation with like minded-states is generally the best way forward. Though the hard-nosed realists will recognise this but read such co-operation as being based merely on prudence, most theories would see in this situation the context for the development of a genuine morality of states in which respect for one another's aspirations is built in. The justification for this will lie in one of a number of considerations.

Perhaps first and foremost one can simply point to the role of custom and convention in developing a community of states with shared values and traditions. Amongst writers who have adopted this approach are historically David Hume and in recent times Hedley Bull (Hume 1888: bk III, pt 2, ch. xi; Bull 1977). In a similar vein Nardin argues for a society of states as a practical (rather than a purposive) association, and Thompson for a 'society of communities', both picking up the point that a society may not be quite the same as a full-blown community (Nardin 1983: ch. 1; Thompson 1992: ch. 9). Nevertheless the general communitarian conception outlined above (as a contrast to cosmopolitan style thinking) both acts as the source of and the model for the morality of states. The fact that states represent separate communities seeking their own advancement leads states to co-operate, and the morality of that co-operation is itself similar to the communitarian one.

Two other forms of justification might be offered. There is an approach, associated historically with de Vattel and Wolff, but also apparent in Hegel's account of international law, which stresses the analogue with the person in a strong form: just as natural persons have rights (inherent in their nature) so too do artificial persons, and states have rights inherent in their constitution as members of a society defined precisely in terms of international law.[1] The nature of the state system simply generates these rights which are international in nature.

Finally, there is the contract approach of John Rawls which is not so much concerned with the justification of government as with principles of justice. The details of this will be given in the next chapter in connection with the use of the theory by others in support of cosmopolitanism. Suffice it to say here, Rawls himself applies his method for determining principles of justice within a society to the society of states and argues that representatives of states meeting together to decide on principles of justice to apply to international relations would choose 'the familiar principles' of the morality of states.[2]

IV. OBJECTIONS TO THE CONTENT OF THE MORALITY OF STATES

The objections to the morality of states come in two forms: objections to the normative framework, that is the content of it, put forward typically in the 'morality of states', and objections to the theoretical basis or grounding of that morality. If one objects to the normative framework, then this will either be because the value premises in the theory are themselves wrong or inadequate, or because the inference from the value premises to the normative conclusion is disputed, in the light of different readings of the 'facts' about the world and about the real possibilities of better outcomes. But even if one did not object to the normative framework, one might still want to argue for one theoretical basis over another. First let us consider the norms themselves.

A. THE NEED FOR A MORALITY OF STATES OF SOME KIND

First it must be made clear that the objection here is not to there being a 'morality of states' or international ethic (in the precise sense). So long as there is a state-system and one regards this as in some sense a co-operating society and not merely a system of interacting parts, there is bound to be, internal to its being a society of states, some set of going norms or normal rules for state interaction. Whether these rules are grounded in some wider theoretical framework or not, and whether they are seen by a thinker as 'right' or 'adequate' or not, the very fact that they are rules accepted by states, either though informal convention and agreement, or through contract or treaty, gives them some moral standing. As Locke observed, states are bound by the duty to honour contracts just like individuals. Of course if the thinker thinks that the rules governing state conduct are broadly right, then he is an internationalist in the traditional sense, but even if he thinks that the rules ought to be modified, or that more exceptions ought to be accepted (for example to the non-intervention rule), then he may still support *a* morality of states. If however he has reason to want to reject the whole framework and argue for say a world federal system, he would still accept that norms, albeit norms he cannot himself fully endorse, are needed to govern the present status quo, both because here and now there is a system of rules backed by custom and agreement, and because it does to some extent, even if inadequately, support values he endorses such as peace and order.

B. DIFFICULTIES WITH THE NORMATIVE FRAMEWORK

1. There are surely circumstances in which it is right for states, individually or collectively, to intervene in the internal affairs of other states, for instance over human rights violations. This was accepted by many

over various forms of pressure on South Africa in order to end apartheid.

2. Many problems in the world require states with the capacity to help to come to the help of others. For example global poverty does not merely require emergency assistance from time to time, but sustained and extensive action well beyond what has been assumed in the morality of states approach.

3. There are many issues especially to do with the environment which require the adoption of a common cause, well beyond what has traditionally been required. That is, for the sake of promoting or protecting a global common good, states ought to accept various forms of limitation on what they do.

4. The rights of states are not to be seen as above those of individual human beings. Individual human beings can challenge states, for instance if they fail to observe rights, and international law ought to reflect this.

5. The idea of sovereignty needs to be rejected in general and along with it the presumption that states have an overriding duty to pursue the national interest within a framework of rules.

6. The 'morality of states' presupposes a simple ethical framework on a global level, but in fact the moral situation is complicated by: the role of individuals; the way transnational companies operate globally; and tensions within the theory itself, not least the breakdown of 'nation' and 'state' within the 'nation-state' conception.

How might then an internationalist respond to these claims? First, these normative judgements might not be accepted by a defender of the traditional internationalist approach. In this case the dispute will either be at the theoretical level, which I turn to in the next section, or turn on rival empirical assessments of what is possible in the world. For instance, the negative consequences of intervention may be stressed, or the limited possibilities for useful co-operation, or the generally competitive character of inter-state relations. If however the normative judgements listed above are accepted, then there are two strategies for trying to account for them.

The first internationalist rationale for accepting them is to see them as a consequence of applying a cosmopolitan theory, according to which, whatever may have been the case at the time of the founding of the nation-state system, the application of these values requires significant changes in the rules of the 'morality of states'.

The key point about this defence is that at the heart of the internationalist position is a commitment to the international system in which nation states remain, as a matter-of-fact and normatively, the central players in world affairs. It is just that, given modern realities, new norms are appropriate. Such a position would be little different from a cautious cosmopolitan who was committed to the promotion of global values but recognised that a reformed international system was the best means to this end. The difference is one of emphasis, the cosmopolitan emphasising global values, the internationalist emphasising a certain kind of means.

The second is to resist a cosmopolitan rationale, either on the grounds that such an ethical view is to be rejected altogether – the thesis of relativism already discussed and argued against in the previous chapter – or on the grounds that, although some sense can be given to the idea of some universal values and obligations between human beings on a global scale, the rationale for the morality of states is quite independent of that. This second non-cosmopolitan rationale for justifying modifications in the 'morality of states', which is not immutable and can change over time, is to recognise change both by gradual custom and convention and through explicit treaties and agreements. Consider the historic ozone layer depletion agreement – the Montreal Protocol of 1988 – which in a sense confirmed a kind of duty of environmental restraint on states not so much accepted in the past. Such changes could be accounted for in terms of a wide variety of motives, self-interested and ethical.

As a matter of fact, some or even much of the ethical thinking going on in the background, informing the moral interests of electorates, consumers, and diplomats and government agents (as private moral thinkers) and thus influencing agreements made, might well be seen as cosmopolitan. But this from the point of view of the theorist is part of the background data explaining how states enter into new agreements and accept new norms. The theorist may still see the validation of those new norms emanating from the processes of agreement rather than from a cosmopolitan theory, if let us suppose, he himself did not accept such a world ethic.

If then an internationalist accepts the need for new norms in international relations, whether for cosmopolitan or non-cosmopolitan reasons, then he is likely to accept a more robust outward-looking role for state leaders. In this context it is worth mentioning an important new concept sometimes offered, namely the idea of 'good international citizenship' (e.g. Linklater 1992, Wheeler & Dunne 1998 and Williams 2003). Here the idea is that just as individuals can be good citizens within states, so states can be good citizen members of the society of states, and their goodness is manifested in the way their governments pursue ethical goals or an 'ethical foreign policy' like poverty alleviation, human rights protection in foreign policy and so on.

V. THEORETICAL PROBLEMS WITH INTERNATIONALISM

There are two different kinds of problem here, one to do with the role of convention, the other to do with the peculiar status of the state. Here I am dealing with those forms of internationalism which are not founded on a global/cosmopolitan ethic in the justificatory background.

A. CONVENTION AND AGREEMENT AN INADEQUATE BASIS

Agreements between states are neither necessary nor sufficient for the determination of moral values. Generally agreement and convention are hardly sufficient to determine something as right or wrong. If this were so, then anything established in a society – slavery, religious persecution – would have to be regarded as right. As I noted earlier, agreements in the sense of contracts or signing up to treaties might be seen as having some moral status of obligatoriness, but this is in virtue of the fact that we accept in any case for non-conventional reasons the value of making and keeping promises or contracts. But if we are looking at the source of the general norms of a society including an international society, it hardly seems adequate to rest the case on what is established. If we assumed this, there would be another problem too in that we would not be able to say that the norms accepted by states were incomplete, namely that states ought to include norms which they do not now include.

B. THE NATURE OF THE STATE

More specifically, there is the issue of what kind of status a state has. The internationalist who does not derive his position from a global ethic may see the state as having some intrinsic value. But is this plausible? As compared with individuals, who on most ethical theories are seen as having a fundamental status or as having intrinsic value, or as being ends in themselves, it is problematic what status a state is meant to have. States are artificial entities, and whatever good they have must from a moral point of view be ultimately cashed in terms of their value to human beings. As Bull notes:

> World order is more fundamental and primordial than international order because the ultimate units of the great society of all mankind are not states (or nations, tribes, empires, classes or parties) but individual human beings, which are permanent and indestructible in a sense in which groupings of them of this or that sort are not. (Bull 1985: 21)

Beitz notes that from a normative or prescriptive point of view, it is the interests of individual human beings that count, even if from an analytical point of view it is useful to consider states as discrete entities (Beitz 1979:

53). So that in the last ethical analysis, when the rules for states and the particular actions of states are up for evaluation, it must be with reference to the impacts on human beings. If this impact is being assessed ethically and not merely prudentially from the point of view of one country, there must be an appeal to the interests of human beings generally. This presupposes some kind of common ethical framework or global ethic, however much in the background. (How much this should be in the background is an issue which we come back to later on.)

This line of argument concerning the inappropriateness of seeing a state as an entity of intrinsic moral status invites two kinds of responses: the state as a large instrumentality and the state as the embodiment of the will of the people.

C. THE STATE AS AN INSTRUMENT OF THE PEOPLE'S WILL

On certain theories of the nature of the state, the state's interests in relation to its dealings with other states and its acceptance of rules between states, can be said to reflect adequately and properly the interests of those individuals within it. For on a contract theory the sovereign acts on behalf of the people who, according to the theory, have transferred by (implicit) contract the right to reflect, represent and define their interests. This is particularly striking in contract theories such as those of Rousseau and Kant, as we have seen. Surely a morality of states based on the policies and priorities of states so constituted would not need to be referred back to individual human well-being for validation. On the general argument here the following needs to be said.

First, not all states in the world conform to the model proposed in the political theory in question, even if one was disposed to see the contract theory as a helpful way of understanding the nature and justification of states. What gets agreed on in the international arena, both by way of general rules and by way of particular actions, is a function of the particular wills of the governments of countries, and there is no guarantee that these wills do adequately represent what their people want or authorise (according to the theory). Second, it is not clear that governments, even according to such theories, represent all the interests, including the moral interests, of their citizens. What governments do does not exhaust fully the moral interests of human beings. Therefore, what states agree on cannot represent, even in theory, all that people might want for themselves or for others. Third, the usual presumption behind contractarianism is that there are universal values and that what the contract does is to serve values – security for Hobbes, liberty and property for Locke and so on – which exist independent of the contract anyway. In this sense the state is a large instrumentality or means for achieving pre-existing goals and values.

If the morality of states failed to secure these properly or if particular decisions of governments (conforming to the morality of states) failed to secure these, then there would be grounds for criticism. It follows from this that the morality of states is not immune from criticism, by reference to the interests of individual human beings.

This universalist assumption is brought out most clearly in the case of Kant. Although this will be more fully discussed in the next chapter, it is worth noting here that although Kant supported a society of states, his own theory hardly supported the conventional 'morality of states' and his own proposals for articles of 'perpetual peace' went well beyond anything accepted in his time. His thinking was firmly cosmopolitan in character, and this is reflected in his view, much discussed in international relations thinking as the 'democratic theory' (though inaccurately since the key point for Kant was his views about republicanism), that states with republican constitutions, which are premised on the centrality of freedom and consent, would not go to war against other states similarly constituted, largely because they shared and supported the same values (Kant 1970b).

D. THE NATION-STATE AS AN ORGANIC WHOLE

The second reply to my argument that individual human beings have primacy over the state as an artificial social entity ultimately serving the interests of individuals, is to deny that the state has that secondary status. As we have seen, both Hegel and Mazzini amongst others have in different ways challenged this assumption.

Even if Hegel is right that the state is not to be seen as an instrumentality or means to values independent of it but is the embodiment or actualisation of human flourishing in its full form so that a person in a sense only fully realises himself in the context of the state, it does not seem to follow that what states do in their external relations is immune from a criticism that comes from a source other than the rules which states themselves accept. Even if Frost is right that, so far from states existing in a moral vacuum or power struggle for self-advancement, we can accept on Hegel's analysis the rights of other states because each state is what people need to fulfil themselves, it hardly follows that there is no wider framework from which criticism can be made. Indeed, in many ways Frost's own interpretations of Hegel make him into a kind of cautious cosmopolitan (though Frost distinguishes his own view from that of cosmopolitans).

If however Hegel's analysis is seen as supporting a self-sufficient morality of states, then it will not I think be because of the particular 'international relations' feature of the account, but what Hegel's organicist theory shared with many other political theories of an idealist kind like Green, Bosanquet and Bradley; namely a more deeply communitarian conception of the constitution of moral value, the deeper assumption that to a large extent, if not entirely, moral values in both scope and content arise out of particular communities, and may in any case be significantly different.

If we consider the kinds of argument we get in Mazzini and Fichte concerning the value of the nation as giving focus, identity and loyalty for the individual, we have to note that if this line of thought is right, the nation, ethnic group or for that matter other kind of social community has a status which again makes it anything other than an instrumental means. But this fact, that in some sense the nation has a primary moral status and not a derivative one and that people stand in some special relationship to it, does not by itself lead either to a denial that there is a universal frame-work of values or to an uncritical endorsement of the 'morality of states' – in fact far from it, so far as the latter is concerned.

The claim that people stand in special relationship to their nation or ethnic group is on the face of it entirely consistent with a universal value framework, like the assertion of special loyalty to one's family. Indeed in either case it could be one of the universal values promoted, acknowl-edging a special relationship to one family or nation. It is quite another thing to say that those outside the nation either have no moral standing or lesser moral standing, so far as one's actions or one's country's actions are concerned. That this is what happened in the case of nationalist movements like Nazism in Germany, is an indication of a tendency or danger, not a consequence of the theory as such.

E. NATIONHOOD AS INIMICAL TO THE MORALITY OF STATES

One of the most powerful forces which have shaped the modern world has been nationalism, where the desire for national self-expression by a people has led to creating or seeking to create a state, that is a political community with control over a geographical area which is either co-extensive with that nation or in which that national group has dominance or adequate representation in political terms. Whether nationalism has to express itself in such political terms is another matter. Mary Robinson, former President of Ireland, speaking of the extensive Irish Diaspora, expressed the view that perhaps nationhood could better be expressed and valued not through identification with the political state but through the sharing of a common heritage wherever one might be in the world (Robinson 1995). However the search for expression through political power and political community expressing it is the more usual way.

But the point has to be stressed that emphasis on the drive towards national self-determination is hardly supportive of the 'morality of states'. The fact is that the concept of the nation-state is a hybrid concept. Ever since the development of the modern international system (notice it is 'inter-*national*' we say, not 'inter-state' which would be more accurate), it has been assumed that there is broad coincidence or mapping onto each other of nation and state, either that broadly a state represents a nation or that a state may be made up of several nations (such as with the UK). But it has always been an artificial union, often requiring a lot of forcing and fudging to make it look as if it represents reality. Events, especially in Eastern Europe, since 1989 have shown all the tensions involved. Tito's attempt in Yugoslavia to 'create' a Yugoslav identity out of the various national/ethnic groups – Croats, Serbs, Slovenes and others – foundered after his death, and by the end of the 1980s had terrible consequences. Czechoslovakia split into two halves rather more peacefully. The Kurds remain split into four neighbouring countries, without proper power or political participation in any of the countries in which they are minorities.

The fact is that insofar as the desire for national self-identity leads to the seeking of political self-determination, nationalism leads to challenges to the international order which by its very nature is conservative and defensive of the existing order of states. Boutros Ghali, UN Secretary General in 1992, recognised this at the end of his influential book, *Agenda for Peace*, when he saw the secessionist tensions in recent years upsetting international security and peace and therefore needing to be resisted (even though the UN was partly founded on the principles of self-determination) (Boutros Ghali 1992: pa. 17–19). As Moynihan remarks in his perceptive survey of the powerful forces of ethnicity, ethnicity spells pandemonium on the world stage (Moynihan 1993: passim).

The point is that whatever arguments are used to support the value of the nation and the ethical importance of advancing one's nation, these come into conflict with arguments to the effect that we need to support inter-state order as we have it, and with democratic theories of how states should be governed, especially if democracies function in such a way that the interests of minority nations or ethnic groups are not properly represented.

It is difficult to dismiss the ethical significance of ethnicity and nationalism. But it is equally difficult to dismiss the importance of the rules of states qua recognised political units in the society of states. Neither, as we have seen, have ultimate or exhaustive ethical significance. But even if one had not already had reasons to require a deeper theory, this tension itself should alert one to the problem: by what principles does one reconcile conflicts or make decisions where nationalist arguments conflict with statist arguments? If both have some validity, one needs to look elsewhere for something to determine issues. As Beitz argues, what lies behind the defence of state autonomy where it is to be defended and the drive for self-determination, where that is to be justified, is in terms of a wider theory of justice (Beitz 1979: pt II).

Although it is usually the case that secessionist movements occur precisely because the dominant power in a state does not practise or enforce justice towards a minority group (so that they suffer from various forms of discrimination, economic or otherwise), it has to be acknowledged that in theory at least, if an ethnic group wanted to form a separate political community for no reason other than its desire to be separate and this will had been properly determined, it would be a form of injustice for the existing political order to prevent this from happening. But the issue of justice remains important, precisely because whatever new separate political unit may emerge from nationalistic tendencies, there will always be the issue of new minorities within geographical areas, who may either be unfairly treated, if persecuted whilst they remain, or unfairly treated in terms of being unjustly removed by forced removal or 'ethnic cleansing'.

One cannot deny then the importance of nationalist or ethnic identity. That most people have a strong sense of identity to some such group is undeniable and to be seen as entirely appropriate (within limits). However it is worth remarking how difficult a conception it is in practice. It is not as though the idea of a nation or ethnic group is a clean or tidy one, or that there is somehow *sub specie aeternitatis* or in the mind of God an exhaustive list of just what all the nations and authentic ethnic groups are, or that everyone belongs to just one or other of these groups such that there could be the world divided up, perhaps in geographically separate units, into a totally consistent exhaustive but non-overlapping set. There is too much contingency over what identities matter and what do not. No unravelling of history would ever reveal an answer: 'so now we really know just what groups we belong to and are to value'.[3]

F. CONCLUDING REMARKS

Such a 'final' answer is neither possible nor desirable. What does matter is that, whatever identities we have, we value them in ways which are consistent with respecting those of others and treating people according to general standards of justice and moral reasonableness. What the tensions between statist and nationalist conceptions reveal is the need for a moral theory which goes beyond each. This is precisely what cosmopolitanism provides. Of course what underlies the pervasive pull of the value of political community, in the various ways we have considered, is a broader communitarian conception of moral values. So long as this is accepted as the source or the main source of people's values, the government of states will be seen as justifiably promoting these values and interests above all else, and the 'morality of states' will be endorsed. If this model of moral values is undermined, then one of the chief supports for internationalism is undermined. We will return to this criticism of communitarianism at the end of Chapter 5.

NOTES

1. As de Vattel notes, 'the Law of Nations is the science of the rights which exist between Nations or States and of the obligations corresponding to those rights' (de Vattel 1811: intro).
2. Rawls' thinking developed further in Rawls 1999. See Chapter 4, II E.
3. Amartya Sen has argued eloquently for the thesis that we have multiple identities and that we can choose which identities matter. We need not be trapped in particular ethnic boxes which made certain kinds of conflict inevitable (Sen 2006).

QUESTIONS FOR DISCUSSION
1. What are the main elements of the 'morality of states'?
2. What approach to the justification of the morality of states seems more plausible to you?
3. Can the internationalist approach be understood to accommodate positive trans-national obligation e.g. to alleviate world poverty?
4. How should one handle the conflict between the appeal to nationalism and the appeal to the state?

CHAPTER 4

COSMOPOLITAN THEORIES

I. THE SETTING

The idea of being a world citizen goes back to the classical world of the Stoics.[1] Many of the Stoics like Epictetus, Pliny, Seneca and Cicero asserted in one way or another that we were 'cosmo-polites', which literally translated means 'citizen of the universe'. As MacIntyre put it: 'There is one divine universe, one rational human nature, and therefore one appropriate attitude to all men. The Stoic is a citizen of the *cosmos* not of the *polis*.' (MacIntyre 1967: 107) It is worth noting this from the outset

76

since what they were about was not primarily asserting membership of a society or political community in this world, but about a certain religious or metaphysical conception of our relationship to the universe and the divine order. Nevertheless the affirmation of our common humanity was a significant part of the conception, and what was clear was that they were distancing themselves from a view that said that one's being a citizen in the ordinary sense was a central fact of one's identity. Membership of this or that political community – a city-state, a larger state or even the Roman Empire – was merely a contingent fact of one's birth at a particular time and place. One might have been born into a quite different society – that is accidental – but one's being human is an altogether more basic and significant fact. This perception of themselves did not lead Stoics to reject allegiance to their communities or to the Roman Empire, nor did it lead to an other-worldly lack of interest in the social issues or the well-being of people.[2] Indeed one of the interesting images which they employed was that of a series of concentric rings in which there are different level of identity, meaning and loyalty – family, state, world, universe (see also Heater 2002).

Chris Brown characterises cosmopolitanism in this way:

> In the first place, cosmopolitanism has no necessary connection with the desire for world government. The Stoics lived under a 'world' government; that was precisely the problem – how to make sense of life in a context in which the coming of Empire had eliminated the previous focal points of existence. Cosmopolitanism is compatible with the rejection of politics, or with a pragmatic acceptance of existing political structures such as the states of eighteenth century Europe. What is crucial to a cosmopolitan attitude is the refusal to regard existing political structures as the source of ultimate value. (Brown 1992: 24)

A further quotation may also help to reinforce the point that existing political structures are not of ultimate value. A modern cosmopolitan, Charles Beitz reinforced the implications of asserting his thesis when he says:

> It is cosmopolitan in the sense that it is concerned with the moral relations of members of a universal community in which state boundaries have a merely derivative significance. There are no reasons of basic principle for exempting the internal affairs of states from external moral scrutiny, and it is possible that members of some states might have obligations of justice with respect to persons elsewhere. (Beitz 1979: 181–2)

II. SENSES OF CITIZENSHIP

The above discussion already reveals a crucial issue of interpretation. Just what is meant by the word 'citizen' as applied to the world? In what follows I shall somewhat schematically distinguish three different types of claim:

a claim that we are world citizens as members of a world political community, somewhat analogous to being a citizen of a nation-state; a claim that
we are world citizens as members of a global community as a social
reality in which a significant number of social bonds, background institutions, self-consciously shared values are in place; and a claim that we
are world citizens because we belong to a moral domain or sphere of all
human beings in which obligations and responsibilities between individuals anywhere exist in principle. (This is only schematic at this point:
there may be quite a wide variety of positions within the schema.)

Put very bluntly, the first claim is factually false and would only be
the case if we had a world government, or at least a world federal system
with structures and representation analogous to existing political structures. The second claim may be to some extent true but the degree of
established global community is not very great. The third claim is a moral
thesis shared by all cosmopolitans and one which, if the argument of this
book is right, it is intellectually correct or reasonable to assert. However
the point of course about the first two claims is not that they represent
what is now the case but that they may indicate what a cosmopolitan
thinker would want to be the case. Some cosmopolitans might argue that
given their fundamental claim about the moral sphere or domain, the
most effective way of realising these values is to move to some form of
world government in which we do become world citizens in something
like the current political sense. Most cosmopolitans, including myself,
would argue that we need to strengthen the existence of global moral
community if the values we believe in are to be realised effectively,
and this may involve various kinds of 'political' participation in national
and international institutions. It is however possible that someone could
accept the claim that there is one moral domain, but not see the need to
establish stronger forms of global community. The moral theories to be
discussed in the next section are all theories about the universal moral
domain in which there are common values and global responsibilities.
What the implications are for developing global moral community and
for other forms of change in the world is another matter, to be discussed
at a later stage. Before I turn to these theories, let me expand a little on
the three positions just indicated, in case what has been said has been too
schematic to be clear.

Political Conception
Clearly what initially comes to mind as the political connotations of
citizenship itself are the following features.

  1. Rights and duties defined in terms of an established political commu-

nity, both as active participants in the political community and as subjects.[3]

2. Rights to certain protections and to forms of participation.
3. Duties of obedience/loyalty and of involvement as active members.
4. Sense of identity with a strong emotional/felt character.

This idea if applied to the world may evoke several responses: it is wholly inappropriate, since no political community is in existence; it is dangerous if it is the basis for an argument for creating a world political community in which these features became the case, since people may fear world government.

On the other hand, many people, for instance through working in NGOs as part of what is called 'global civil society', do now in some sense participate in global governance. For instance proposals are made about cosmopolitan democracy that clearly involves the political dimension but not to the point of advocating world government. Furthermore in terms of the development of international human rights law, we can see human beings as members of a global legal community. The focus on political cosmopolitanism or what may be called a more broadly institutional cosmopolitanism can be on what makes someone a global citizen, but it can equally be focused on the institutional political order itself – on the nature of 'cosmopolis' (world city) not merely 'cosmopolites' (world citizen). Much interest in international relations in new forms of global governance focuses on such issues, and we will return to this in Chapter 9 (see also Dower 2003: ch. 8; cf. Pogge 1992; Scheffler 1999).

Community Conception

Let us consider a different idea which is weaker because the implications of 'political' are dropped, so that 'polites' (in 'cosmopolitan') and 'citizen' are undergoing conceptual revision:

X is a citizen = X is a member of a moral community

So if we applied this to cosmopolitanism, we would say that if someone is a global citizen, that means that he or she is a member of the moral community of all human beings in the world (note Beitz's use of 'universal community' above). This usefully links the idea of world citizen with the idea of world community but this too is ambiguous as between a stronger sense and a weaker sense.

Weak Thesis Concerning Community

The weak thesis can be stated thus:

A moral community = a moral domain/sphere

What is meant by a moral domain? All members of a moral domain have moral standing or are 'morally considerable'. To be a member of a moral domain, if one is oneself a moral agent, is to have duties in principle towards any other members of the domain, and likewise all other moral agents in the moral domain have duties towards oneself in principle. It is necessary to say 'if one is a moral agent' because not all members of a moral domain are necessarily moral agents, for instance human babies and, if one's theory supports their inclusion, non-human sentient animals. This is a rather weak claim but it is significant.

It is rather weak because there are no implications in it about the presence of institutions, about the development of emotional attachments to its values or actual commitment to the well-being of the whole in most of its members, or about the social reality of an overall unit called community. It is however significant and the cornerstone of the cosmopolitan thesis for three reasons.

1. It defines moral community (qua domain) in terms of a theory, not vice versa. The theory says: 'There is a global moral community because we have moral relationships with all human beings', rather than 'We have obligations towards other human beings because we live in a community with the following shared rules'. (The reader may note that this is one way of characterising what divides the cosmopolitan's way of approaching these issues from that of the communitarian.)
2. It allows in easily extensions to future humans, non-humans, if the theory so indicates (which we will consider in the chapter on the environment).
3. It is only if we have this basis in theory that we have an argument for wanting to create global community in a stronger sense.

This understanding of cosmopolitanism is what is often called *ethical* cosmopolitanism. It provides both an ethical basis for the assessment of what individuals ought to be, i.e. a particular form of global ethic, and it provides a basis for the critical assessment of what states and other collectives do, i.e. a particular form of international ethics. Much of the focus of this book is concerned with understanding this ethical basis and applying it to various issues.

Stronger Sense of Community
A stronger sense of community (of great significance to the communitarian thinker as well) is as follows:

A moral community is a social reality, with (perceived) interdependence, shared traditions and norms and some kind of loyalty to the whole.

This is not as strong as political community but it shares the same problem: at a global level it does not exist or only exists in rather marginal ways, and to the extent that it does exist, that is not the whole story about what ought to be the case. On the other hand it does not, on the face of it, suffer from the dangers of a global political community as a world government. Apart from the communitarian's obvious interest in this sense, we will see how the establishment of global community in this sense is one of the things a cosmopolitan may well have reason to support. The development of this is an aspect of globalization which we shall discuss further in Chapter 9 and is often discussed under the title of 'cultural cosmopolitanism'.[4] Let us now look at the reasons which might be given by cosmopolitan theorists.

III. THEORIES

There are many varieties of cosmopolitanism, both in respect of content (what values or duties are recommended), and in respect of intellectual sources (different types of religious worldview, different philosophical theories). Not all theories are necessarily radical or revolutionary, as we have already noted. Chris Brown considers three versions: Kantianism, utilitarianism, Marxism (Brown 1992: ch. 2). We can add other approaches, such as human rights, natural law and contract theory approaches, as well as explicitly religious approaches and ones that stem from environmental considerations.

What is striking about the first two approaches which Brown mentions is that they represent two main approaches to ethics generally, namely what is called non-consequentialism or deontology and consequentialism (or sometimes teleology). The key issue here is whether at bottom what is right is determined only by the consequences – actual, foreseen or reasonably foreseeable – of that action, compared with the other alternatives which could have been performed, or whether what determines one's duty are quite different considerations in addition to general consequences. For instance a deontologist might argue that keeping a promise, such as a promise to the minister of another country, is a duty and ought to be done, not because doing so will do more good that not doing so (though usually that will be the case) but because of the intrinsic character of the act, since one had accepted an obligation by one's past act, and so on. A deontologist need not be saying that there are never circumstances when it would be right to break a promise, since it might be right when there was a clash with another duty, but he would definitely rule out breaking a promise merely because more good would come from doing so. A consequentialist on the other hand might argue that since we can foresee the consequences of our omissions as well as our positive actions, we ought often give aid to others, where more good comes from this than omitting to give aid.[5]

A. CONSEQUENTIALISM/UTILITARIANISM

Utilitarianism is the best known of the consequentialist theories. In its classical form, in Bentham and Mill, it was understood in terms of the maximisation of happiness, itself understood hedonistically as pleasure. There are many variations, and later theories understand the good which was to be promoted in other ways. But at heart the theory is about the promotion of the best balance of good over bad. One of the most attractive features of utilitarianism is its global reach: 'Everybody to count for one, nobody for more than one.' (Bentham quoted in Mill 1962: ch. 5) Theoretically, the theory counts all human beings as in principle relevant, and equally so, for ethical decision making. What is crucial is whether one's action may affect the well-being of any other human beings (or more generally sentient beings), however distant in space or time. Membership of one's community or state is not the determining factor. Utility is no respecter of borders. Bentham himself was very interested in this dimension and his advocacy of international law was premised on his view that its strengthening would lead to greater human felicity.

A good example of this approach is Peter Singer's application of utilitarian reasoning to the alleviation of world poverty (see Chapter 7). Several modern writers adopt a utilitarian approach to the justification of the rules of war, and several adopt the utilitarian approach explicitly as a foundation of international ethics, for instance Elfstrom, and Hare and Joynt (Hare & Joynt 1982; Elfstrom 1990). The latter's work was an early example of the modern return to interest in normative issues in international relations, and is interesting for a strategy they adopt which is of wider significance. Having characterised the ethical point of view, in contrast to the prudential point of view, as that in which one considers everyone's interests (which strongly suggests a consequentialist approach), they then recognise that although, if we are thinking critically, we need to justify everything – actions, policies, rules, moral training – in terms of consequences, nevertheless in practice it is important that people act according to rules or the dictates of conscience without calculating consequences. This is because having well established rules and habits of conscience generally leads to the best results. So at the 'intuitive' level we appeal to rules without thinking of consequences (Hare & Joynt, 1982: ch. 1). The utilitarian is certainly entitled to argue for rules, institutions, habits of thought which he justifies on consequential grounds, but whether our judgements of what is right are to be understood in this way is precisely what a deontologist will dispute.

B. KANTIANISM

The label 'Kantian' is often used as a way of describing a general approach inspired by the writing of the eighteenth-century German philosopher Immanuel Kant. The fundamental feature of this approach is the idea of all human beings standing in an ethical relationship to one another on the basis of their being fellow rational beings or 'persons'. As rational beings we are required to act on certain principles (not based on consequences) in relation to fellow human beings.[6]

Kant saw moral duties as the demands of our 'practical reason', that is as 'categorical' demands or 'imperatives '. A categorical demand is contrasted with 'hypothetical' imperatives because whereas the latter are based on desire, namely on what reason requires us to do to get what we want, the former as a demand of duty is simply something we are rationally required to do whether we want to do it or not. He formulated this categorical imperative in several ways, including:

1. Formula of universal law (universalisability): act on that maxim which you can will to be universal law.
2. Formula of ends: so act that you always treat humanity, whether in yourself or in other persons, as an end and not merely as a means. (Kant 1949: 88 & 96)

Consider the case of a lying promise, and more generally coercive and deceitful behaviour. To act on the maxim of making a lying promise to get out of some difficulty is to act on a maxim which cannot be universalised (since communication would be unintelligible) and is therefore contrary to practical reason and wrong. Likewise to make a lying promise to someone is to fail to treat him as a rational pursuer of ends (because to respect him would be to give him a true not a false picture of the world) but rather to treat him merely as means to one's own ends. The point here is that any human being qua rational agent is the object of respect/concern, and what is universalised is behaviour by any rational being. The framework is clearly global. Kant's vision was one of a global ethical order or what he called a 'kingdom of ends'.

In *Perpetual Peace* Kant develops a threefold analysis of *recht* (right) – republican, international and cosmopolitan *recht* (Kant 1970b). He conceives of republican states as based on consent/contract and thus as the positive expression of a citizen's liberty or rational autonomy. Because of their 'unsocial sociability' men also need to live in political communities with laws enforcing areas of the moral law. These political communities will not succeed in their purpose unless states are free of the threat of external attack. Therefore perpetual peace needs to be established. For perpetual peace to occur certain articles of peace need to be accepted. Kant thus recommends a moral framework for international relations going beyond what was established on or acted on, but this was firmly premised on the acceptance at least for the foreseeable future of the nation-state system.[7] What he called cosmopolitan *recht* concerns the duty of hospitality for foreigners, that is as citizens of the world we owe certain things towards any human being. This is a surprisingly modest requirement, but perhaps understandable given the state of the world in Kant's day. What is important is the potential for more significant duties we may all have as citizens of the world, and also that for Kant the justification of international *recht* was firmly grounded in its contribution towards the well-being of all.

In the international relations literature Kant has often been associated with the label 'revolutionary', though his own actual recommendations are hardly revolutionary, nor does the Kantian approach require one to be revolutionary. (The label has stuck partly because of his support for the French Revolution.) Kant's views were certainly progressive and challenged any realist interpretations of international relations. Other writers in the Kantian tradition like Onora O'Neill see Kant's theory giving rise to a more radical critique of state practices, and as underpinning a more radical demand for social justice (O'Neill 1989: chs 7 & 8). She makes much of the principles of non-deception and non-coercion, which apply as much to the actions of corporate agents such as nation-states or companies, and also of what she calls the principle of material justice that we are required to come to the aid of those whose material need undermines the development of their rational autonomy.

C. NATURAL LAW AND THE CAPABILITIES APPROACH

The idea that there is a law concerning what is to be pursued and shunned inherent in our nature as human beings, and discoverable by the use of our natural reason, has been a very powerful theory ever since the Middle Ages (and indeed before, having its origins in the Stoic thought of Cicero), and provided a very clear basis for a universal morality and the idea of a community of all humankind. I have already given an outline of its main features in Chapter 3, since it is important to the origins of the internationalist tradition. It should be noted that it is not merely a doctrine of historical interest. It remains an attractive approach to any thinker who wants to ground morality in features of human nature, that is, in certain elements in human nature which if realised constitute human well-being. It has modern adherents such as John Finnis (Finnis 1990) and was applied systematically to international relations by Brian Midgley (Midgley 1975). It also manifests itself as one of the chief intellectual sources of the interest in human rights (via the idea of human rights as natural rights).

It is also to be noted that in many ways the natural law approach occupies a middle ground between the consequentialism of utilitarianism and the deontological approach as illustrated by Kant, since on the one hand it has a clear commitment to the furthering of well-being and on the other hand a commitment to certain duties derived from the natural law. An example of this, discussed later, is the justification of the norms of war which combined a judicious mixture of deontological thinking (like the absolute ban on direct attacking of the innocent) and the consequentialist principle of proportionality (the good pursued in war must outweigh the harm done in the course of action pursued).

A partially similar approach has become influential, especially in connection with discussions of the ethical basis of development (and will be discussed further in Chapter 7), and this is the capabilities approach. This emphasises that human beings have a range of capabilities which they need to develop and exercise and which, if realised in a full life, constitutes well being. Writers like Nussbaum want to ground this in a conception of well being derived from Aristotle's ethics, others like Sen do not, but see it as having various sources including Kantianism and Liberalism, the key point being about developing and exercising capabilities in regard to what we have reason to do and be. The appeal of this approach is that it provides a rather richer basis for understanding the good to be pursued in development in particular and in good governance generally, than is often provided by very formal accounts of the good in utilitarianism and libertarian thinking (Sen 1999; Nussbaum 2000; Crocker 1991, 1992 & 1995).

D. HUMAN RIGHTS

If all human beings have certain rights by virtue of their human nature (and rights are not all socially constituted or formed), then this universal framework provides a firm basis for cosmopolitan obligation to respect and further them. There are various theories which ground these rights (notably but not only natural law/rights theories). Note a distinction here, of wider significance to a recurring theme of the book, between human rights as (part of) a 'source' story about the nature of global ethics, and as something established by consensus (of many people throughout the world, though not necessarily all) and supported by diverse ethical theories.

A human right is a right attributed to a human being as a human being and asserted to exist on the basis of a moral theory or moral reasoning. Feinberg states: 'I shall define "human rights" to be generically moral rights of a fundamentally important kind held equally by all human beings unconditionally and unalterably.' (Feinberg 1973: 85) Thus a human right is contrasted to a legal or conventional right which exists in virtue of the laws and conventions of a given society. People have conventional rights as members of a legal community, not as human beings. Even an international declaration like the UN Universal Declaration of Human Rights (1948) neither establishes the existence of human rights nor limits what are, ethically, human rights. For instance, a right to conscientious refusal may be a human right before it is encoded in international law. (Of course the presence of a right in international law contributes towards its being part of a world ethic qua global social reality.)

A human right exists in virtue of a universal moral theory which postulates the whole world as one moral sphere or community. As Vincent says: 'it is at the level at which what is appealed to is not any kind of positive law, but what ought by some rational calculation to prevail' that the justification of human rights is looked for (Vincent 1986: 11). Amongst the approaches are theories such as the natural rights tradition, global contract theory, and a rational construction of morality theory such as Gewirth's (Gewirth 1978). A theory of human rights is therefore opposed to any form of cultural relativism which denies universally applicable values.

What kind of cosmopolitan theory we get from the assertion of human rights will depend upon a number of factors, but most notably, at the level of theory, what the rights are which are asserted, and what the nature and extent are of the correlative duties (see O'Neill 1993). Traditionally a distinction has been drawn between negative rights (liberty rights, rights of action) and positive rights (socio-economic rights, rights of recipience). Broadly negative rights are rights to be free from certain kinds of interference or harm, and positive rights are rights to receive some benefit if one has not got it. The duties corresponding to these are duties to refrain from certain kinds of action (for example, not to restrict someone's liberty, not to steal, not to attack other persons) and duties to engage in certain kinds of positive action (help or intervention) respectively.

Do all these kinds of right exist? That was a matter of great contention as part of the battleground in East–West ideological confrontation until the end of the 1980s, the West championing liberty rights and denying or downplaying socio-economic rights of recipience, and the Eastern communist bloc stressing the socio-economic rights and the collective duties of the state to provide these, but downgrading liberty rights. But there was also a more theoretical issue at stake over what conditions are necessary for the asserting of a right. Must a right be realisable to be a right? Liberty rights can be universally achieved simply by everyone refraining from actions invading these rights, whereas socio-economic rights of recipience cannot be realised for all, because of lack of resources. But if rights are not absolute (that is, they can be overridden by various other considerations including appeal to other rights), the assertion of socio-economic rights of recipience is not undermined by the impossibility of universal fulfilment. It is worth noting that even if there is a dispute about the above two kinds of rights, it is important to recognise that the right to security (not being attacked in one's person or property, and so on) is neither a liberty right nor a subsistence right, and as Luard noted, is a right universally recognised in all societies which no government of any political persuasion has any business undermining (Luard 1981: 19).

One particular kind of theory which is cosmopolitan by implication even if its adherents may not promote it as such, and which can be presented as a rights thesis, is what is called libertarianism (similar to what was called liberalism in the eighteenth and nineteenth centuries). Libertarianism is essentially the view that the right which is central is the right to liberty, especially liberty in the economic sphere. Robert Nozick is seen as a leading exponent of this approach (Nozick 1974). What is significant about it is what it excludes rather than what it includes, because the main character of an ethic is the duty not to harm others or not to undermine the range of things to which they have a right, but without a general duty of helping others or coming to their aid when they suffer from misfortune or are harmed by others. The state has no right to tax the rich to help the poor.

However for many the distinction between positive and negative rights is overdrawn. For instance, liberty rights need active defence as well as actions of restraint, and subsistence rights are rights not to have one's well-being undermined as well as to receive assistance. We should note the right to liberty and the right to socio-economic well-being in the light of the threefold correlation of duties put forward by Henry Shue in his influential study of rights. All basic human rights have three correlative duties: duties to avoid depriving, duties to protect from standard threats to deprivation, and duties to aid the deprived (Shue 1996: 52). If we see the framework in this way it is clear that both individuals and society/the state have duties in connection with virtually all human rights. The state in particular has a role in protecting people from standard threats to their rights.

But the usual point of human rights thinking is not merely to assert a range of rights and a set of correlative duties; it is to assert that those duties are in principle global in character. The duties extend in principle to all other human beings. As Shue puts it, basic rights to subsistence, security and liberty are 'everyone's minimum reasonable demands upon the rest of humanity' (Shue 1996: 19).[8] If all human beings have obligations to one another, then governments ought in their foreign as well as domestic policies, to further the realisation of human rights. If universal human rights are accepted, how far can their impact be denied or resisted by international actors? As Bull notes, 'the framework of international order is inhospitable also to the demands of human justice' (by 'human justice' he means appeal to human rights) (Bull 1985: 83). There are two respects in which this has powerful implications. First, there are direct obligations to further the realisation of human rights in other countries, for example through aid/better trade, and to play one's part in protecting a global common good such as the environment. Here the obligation arises partly because other countries actually want one to do this. Second, there are obligations to take action to prevent/discourage other countries from violating human rights within their own borders. This idea comes up against the ideas of national autonomy and UN Charter Article 2.7, and raises particular problems with regard to intervention generally, but especially by military means (for survey see Smith & van den Anker 2005).

E. CONTRACT THEORY

Several recent writers, including Beitz and Pogge have used the contractarian method, adapting Rawls' 'ideal contract' approach to argue that if we regard the whole world – as the facts require us to do – as one society, then Rawls' 'original position' method should apply, and the principles of social justice should apply to the world as a whole.[9] Beitz and Pogge (though I shall use Beitz's outline here) both want to stress the idea of international social justice and argue for a serious redistributive principle. In Part III of his book Beitz seeks to establish principles of distributive justice which apply internationally or globally. He does this by taking Rawls' famous theory of justice and applying it on a global scale. Rawls had intended his theory to apply to societies essentially within nation-state boundaries, where there are (usually) clearly schemes of social co-operation and reciprocity, and governments capable of enforcing/implementing principles of justice. What principally motivates Beitz's account is a wish to give a theoretical foundation to the intuition that rich nations ought to be doing a lot to help poor nations with development (as expressed for instance in the language of the 1974 Declaration on a New International Economic Order), which the 'morality of states' with its emphasis on national autonomy failed to recognise. As Beitz notes, there may be other ways of establishing international obligations towards the Third World, such as utilitarianism.

Two features of Rawls' theory need to be noted (Rawls 1972: sns 3, 4 & 11). First there is 'the original position' method of generating principles of justice, that is principles for 'distributing the benefits and burdens of social co-operation'. These are to be chosen under a veil of ignorance; that is, the parties do not know anything about their own wealth, abilities, conceptions of the good. Second, the principles which Rawls takes it would be chosen under these circumstances are equal liberty and, most significantly for our purposes, the 'difference principle', which states that those differences of wealth which are justified are such that everyone (including especially the poorest) are better off than they would be if there were no differences allowed. It will quickly be apparent that if this method were applied to the world as a whole, that is the parties to the ideal contract or 'original position' were all human beings, there would be a 'global difference principle' which would have immensely radical consequences for the redistribution of wealth in favour of the very poor, through large aid programmes and trade reform at the very least.

Beitz argues for such an interpretation, by examining why Rawls himself does not take this step. This is basically because Rawls, like many other thinkers, thinks of nation-states as largely self-sufficient entities and, partly for this reason, does not think of the world as a whole as being a 'society' in the relevant sense. On the other hand nation-states are capable of some interaction (which may be damaging) so Rawls does conceive of a separate 'ideal contract' of states which yields, as we saw in the previous chapter, much the same limited set of rules of non-interference as the 'morality of states' view. In Rawls' later work *The Law of Peoples* we get a somewhat richer account. Rawls argued for a wider range of eight principles, especially to do with human rights, that would be agreed between liberal and decent hierarchical societies, but his position remained an internationalist one rather than becoming a cosmopolitan one (Rawls 1999).

Beitz's cosmopolitan argument however proceeds on a twofold basis. First he argues that even if states were largely self-sufficient entities (which they are not), the great differences in natural resources would lead state representatives in the original position to accept some distributive principles. Second, he argues that the degree of interdependence, especially economic interdependence, in the world as a whole is such as to make the world as a whole a 'scheme of social co-operation' in which principles of justice are fully applicable.

He recognises however that there are impediments to realising such global principles of justice (particularly the global difference principle), and that one has to recognise the difference between 'ideal theory' and its application in the real world. But the duty to 'further justice' requires significant action now such as more aid. One kind of impediment is the fact that neither adequate international political institutions nor an adequate international sense of community currently exist. This difference between ideal theory and what ought to be done in the real world is of course something to be faced by any cosmopolitan theory.

F. MARXISM

Although as Brown notes, Marxism provides us with a kind of cosmopolitanism based on the collective interests of the working class which as a class transcends national borders, the way in which Marxists provide us with a cosmopolitan global ethic is not straightforward. This is partly because there is a real issue within Marxist thought about how important or relevant morality generally is in the analysis. On the one hand there is certainly a conception of the working class, the proletariat, as belonging to one society throughout the world. 'The worker has no country'. The conception of the communist utopia is one in which the state 'withers away' because through the development of greater material abundance and of moral maturity, the antagonisms both within and between states and therefore the need for their existence will have disappeared. The movement of history is towards such a realisation of, in effect, a cosmopolitan world order. The conflicts in the world as it is are in large measure the products of conflicts between the ruling classes, not the conflicts between the ordinary people within them whose interests largely coincide. In this sense there is a cosmopolitan vision, and behind it a view about the conditions of human flourishing and about the need for action to be taken, insofar as human endeavour can play an active role in advancing, by revolution, those conditions.[10]

On the other hand, morality is generally seen as part of the ideology which the ruling class uses to maintain its power and oppression, by for instance representing its interests as though they were the interests of all, and both utilitarian ideals and human rights come in for criticism. In a parallel way global ideals and ideas of universal values are seen as expression of the interests of the dominant powers on the world stage, as we noted earlier in connection with Carr. Similarly Marxist analysis of North–South relations stresses the systematic nature of the exploitation by developed countries of developing countries, whether it was the more naked imperialism of the colonial era or the more subtle forms of neo-colonialism in the modern world (e.g. Frank 1975).

G. RELIGIOUS THEORIES

It is worth noting here that many theories emanating from religious belief will also assume a cosmopolitan dimension. But there will be a wide range of such theories, advocating very different normative positions, even within each major religious tradition. On the one hand there is the deeply pessimistic position of Reinhold Niebuhr who saw state action as necessarily immoral by the private standards of love (Niebuhr 1932), or the defence of economic liberty amongst right wing evangelical Christians in the USA, and on the other hand there is the commitment to major social change, in liberation theology or ideals of social justice. Religious convictions may lead to challenges to state authority, one example being pacifist conscientious objection, though there are many other kinds of challenge.

The natural law theory already noted has its origins in a theological conception, though its validity may still stand without religious presuppositions. The converse of this is that many religious thinkers will in effect employ arguments like the ones outlined above which they can share with secular thinkers. Certainly there is a natural tendency for a theological understanding of the world to take a global view. After all if God as creator created all human beings with a common nature, it is natural (though not inevitable) to suppose that we stand in some kind of ethical relationship to humanity in general and that there is in some sense a 'brotherhood of humankind'. On the other hand the division between true believer and infidel, if taken seriously, may lead in practice to differential treatment of, and attitudes towards, different groups of people.

H. ENVIRONMENTAL THEORIES

Finally in this restricted survey of cosmopolitan theories, I need to note that the advocacy of environmental ethics tends to be either implicitly or explicitly cosmopolitan in character. Many environmental problems are global in scope and require for their solution co-operation between many countries and citizens acting in appropriate ways. Environmental ethics comes in two forms: human-centred and nature-centred. Briefly, an ethical theory based on long term human interests is at heart one that takes seriously the consequences (usually unintended) of human activity, and therefore the effects on others, irrespective of whether they live here or elsewhere, now or in the future. It will either be a theory such as Kantianism, utilitarianism or human rights theories, suitably applied or extended, or be one very like them in terms of its commitment to human well-being generally. If, on the other hand, one adopts a biocentric perspective according to which either non-human living things or whole ecosystems or both have a value, one is likely again to accept an ethical theory which puts emphasis upon the effects of activity on any beings or things affected by it, and not to accept a moral theory which tries to limit the domain of responsibility to the geographical area of one's community.

I. COSMOPOLITAN ETHICS AND GLOBAL JUSTICE

In recent years there has not only been a strong increase in interest in global/cosmopolitan/international ethics, but a specific interest in *global justice* (e.g. Jones 1999; Pogge 2001 &2003; Drydyk & Penz 1997; van den Anker 2002). Several things need to be noted. First, the theory/set of beliefs constituting a global ethic need not be a theory/set of beliefs about global justice. Assuming, as a more robust cosmopolitan form of a global ethic does, that a global ethic is about trans-national or trans-boundary obligations and responsibilities, it may or may not be claimed that these obligations are obligations of justice. Three considerations motivate the wish to see global obligations as obligations a global justice. First, a claim is made that the obligations are substantial or significant, rather than minimal or merely 'charity' (seen as either a lesser duty or beyond duty and so 'supererogatory'). Second, a claim is made that global obligations need to be based on institutional arrangements which specify quite clearly which bodies have which duties to deliver justice (and some like Nagel had denied the propriety of global justice precisely because of the current lack of appropriate institution arrangements) (Nagel 2005). Third, and linked to this, it is often claimed that our obligations are based on the human rights of others which are either violated by the global economic system (Pogge 2003) or fail to be realised because of it.

If we look at the various theories we have been considering, several can be seen to be theories of global justice. Marxism is quite explicit about the injustice of capitalistic exploitation, and Beitz' theory in applying Rawls' theory of justice is explicit in applying it globally. On the other hand, other theories such as utilitarianism, Kantianism or environmental ethics could all be presented as theories of justice, but equally they need not be. Singer for instance presents a powerful utilitarian argument for alleviating world poverty (see Chapter 7), which does not directly refer to justice. On the other hand the utilitarian may be the first to argue for rules and institutions of distributive justice as powerful instrumentalities for achieving maximum human well-being. Although calling a theory a theory of global justice may be motivated by the view that duty is significant and/or needing institutional expression, it certainly does not follow that a global ethic not expressed in global justice terms is necessarily the opposite, as the case of Singer illustrates.

IV. STRENGTHS AND WEAKNESSES OF PARTICULAR COSMOPOLITAN THEORIES

It would of course be an impossible task in a book of this nature to give a proper critical assessment of all these theories. Since each represents a major ethical position, an adequate assessment would require a much fuller exposition of the theories and their background assumptions. My purpose here is to indicate what I see as some of the main strengths and weaknesses of each position and to suggest the elements of a position which in some sense combines features of several theories. Whilst part of the interest in the theoretical debate is whether the major theories exclude each other or can be to some extent mutually accommodated, it seems important to recognise two things. As compared with denials of global ethics it is important to recognise what all these theories have in common; and as important as the theories themselves are the general prescriptions and priorities which the theorists advance. Over the latter theorists may find they have common cause with some but not all other theorists whose theories may be somewhat different. Sometimes different theories may support the same practical priorities, and sometimes the same basic theory may lead to different priorities, if two thinkers understand the empirical facts about the world very differently. Still each person who has a view about ethics and world affairs will have some theory or other, even if it is in the background and something he or she hardly thinks of. It is therefore worth looking at these theories and comparing them, whilst recognising that reasonable people may simply differ on what theories to accept. My strategy in what follows is not so much to assess the deep theories – there simply is not the space to do that here – as to test the theories against certain intuitions which I at least have and hope other thinkers may share. If you do not share these intuitions then clearly you may wish to assess the theories in different ways. I look at a sub-set of these theories, not all of them, but sufficient to map out the kind of approach which I commend.

A. ASSESSMENT OF UTILITARIANISM

One of the strengths of utilitarianism is precisely its explicit global reach. It says all human beings are to count as having the same moral weight, and that in coming to a decision we have to take into account the effects on anyone, however far away they are, psychologically or geographically. Another, related to this, is the recognition that I am responsible in my actions not merely for what I aim at or intend as a goal but also for those other effects which are reasonably foreseeable that lie beyond the aimed at goal: in a sense 'I intend all that I foresee'.[11] Likewise since my refraining from doing things (omissions) can also be deliberate and their consequences can be foreseen, we are responsible for what we allow to happen as well as for what we actively bring about (the thesis of negative responsibility) (e.g. Harris 1980). Apart from its global reach it also gives us good reason to include people who are distant in time, that is future generations, since what is important is the question whether we can affect the well-being of others by our actions. Our responsibility extends as far as the capacity for effective action.

On the other hand, utilitarianism suffers from serious problems. First, and most notably, it leads us to do what may simply be wrong, for instance, to execute a man not proved to be guilty to prevent a riot that would cause more deaths. Suppose the dropping of the bombs on Hiroshima and Nagasaki were justified, as many argued, on the grounds that the war in the Far East was shortened with overall reduction in loss of life, would that show it to be right, if one thought that directly targeting civilian centres in that way was intrinsically wrong? Second, utilitarianism fails to take proper account of special relationships, like the special duties and rights we have in relation to our spouses, parents, children or friends, or at another level to our community or nation. I do not act for the sake of these people because more good comes from doing this than acting for the good of others generally. Third, utilitarianism does not do justice to what Fishkin calls 'the robust zone of moral indifference', the fact that we are not expected in all our actions to promote the greatest good since there is a significant space in our lives in which what we do is for our own good, according to inclination or to what furthers our own projects (Fishkin 1985: 2–6; cf. Dower 1983: ch. 2). Another kind of problem often identified in utilitarianism is its having an altogether too thin or open-ended account of human well-being, defining it in terms of pleasure, preference satisfaction and so on (see also Chapter 7).

B. ASSESSMENT OF KANTIANISM

Kant's theory, though opposed to utilitarianism in most respects, does share its strength in providing us with a thoroughly global conception of ethics. We belong to a kingdom of ends, that is, a kingdom or community of all rational beings. Its deontological insistence on the rightness in principle of certain kinds of action is a healthy warning against the temptation in foreign policy to follow the advice of Machiavelli and to engage in acts of deception or coercion when reasons of state require them. Coercion and deception cannot be universalised, so they are always wrong. Kant's ethical position is also as forthright as any in showing that what ought to be the case is quite different from what is the case or from what people think ought to be the case, a distinction at the heart of the whole approach adopted in this work.

On the other hand it seems to suffer from two defects, both of which happen to be illustrated by issues to do with the environment. First, in identifying what gives human beings a moral standing as ends in themselves or rational ends, Kant sets the rest of nature on the other side of a fence as mere 'things' with only instrumental value for being with ends. Apart from whether nature as a whole should be seen in this way, this raises serious problems about the attitude we have towards sentient animals, assuming that they are not rational in the relevant sense. This problem reflects back on the case of humans too because arguably one important level of our 'good' is our bodily flourishing and avoidance of physical suffering, a level we share with animals at the pre-rational level. Can Kant's approach adequately account for this? The other weakness in Kant's theory is that in putting such emphasis upon the will or intention as the bearer of the moral worth of action, there is a danger that not enough attention is paid to the consequences, whether actually foreseen or not, of actions. This dimension is striking when we look for instance at the cumulative effects of human activity on the environment for example in climate change.

C. ASSESSMENT OF THE NATURAL LAW APPROACH

The natural law approach has the strength of giving an account of human nature and basing morality on furthering what is good so understood. Like the Aristotelian approach it wishes to give a fuller account of what human well-being consists of, rejecting an account in terms of pleasure as misguided and an account in terms of the exercise of rationality as also one-sided. In many ways these theories combine elements picked out by utilitarianism and Kantianism to advantage. Again the idea of the natural law determining duties derived for the precept of practical reason is a useful corrective to any conception of moral rules being relative or dependent upon what societies happen to agree on. It provides a clear standard of assessment.

On the other hand in terms of its historical origins and what is still associated with it by its adherents and critics alike, it is perhaps unduly wedded to a rather specific view of well-being and more particularly, specific moral rules which are said to be derived from the general principle of seeking the good and shunning evil. Insofar as it is associated with a particular religious background, especially that of Catholic theology, there is a danger, which I think exists in many religions, though many adherents including Catholics to a religiously inspired global ethic would not share this perspective, that in terms of the conception of the moral and religious order which the moral law enjoins us to create, a certain attitude may be adopted towards those people and societies who do not share that conception. This is an attitude of intolerance, opposition and a drive towards conversion, missionary activity and generally proselytising practices, and thus of dividing the world into true believers and infidels.

This is also as I see it one of the problems with the Marxist approach, since, whatever its merits in recognising that a genuine moral framework globally is one in which human potential is realised everywhere and in recognising the dangers of false ideals masking the pursuit of power, its prescriptions for conflict and antagonism hardly seem justified, especially as the belief in the inevitability of progress towards the future utopia has not been vindicated by events to date.

The modern development of Aristotelianism in the capabilities approach however does not suffer from this kind of problem. Its exponents are generally keen to demonstrate that the approach is consistent with a variety of interpretations partly dependent on cultural context. Where the approach may be a little weak and needing support from other theories is some indeterminacy in regard to the nature and scope of the obligations to support the realisation of capabilities, particularly at the global level.

D. ASSESSMENT OF HUMAN RIGHTS THEORIES

The strength of human rights theories lies in the way the elements of human well-being picked out by what rights are said to exist, are identified in having a kind of primacy. J. L. Mackie once argued that, if one contrasted a right-based theory with a goal-based theory and a duty-based theory, the case for the first emerged by seeing the inadequacy of the other two. A duty-based theory without reference to the good which the duty was meant to promote was sterile, whilst a goal-based theory simply saw good as something to be maximised. A rights-based theory at least emphasised that it was individual humans that mattered (Mackie 1984: 169).

On the other hand human rights theories, diverse as they are, are incomplete and require supplementing by further theory, both to do with the good, spelling out what are the elements of human well-being to which we have rights, and to do with duty, spelling out who has what duties. Although I outlined Shue's analysis with favour, the thesis that there are three types of correlative duty and that their scope is global is not something that can be automatically read off from the idea of a right. As I have said before, saying a value is universal, that is, it is to be accepted everywhere even if it is not already accepted, does not entail cosmopolitan responsibility to promote it. So Shue's claim that human rights are the minimum demand of everyone on everyone discussed earlier is, whilst plausible, not strictly entailed by the idea of human rights. The other danger which any of these theories faces but is accentuated by a human rights theory (if it is not handled carefully) is the danger of over-specificity, that is the danger of a set of values which have largely arisen from a particular cultural context such as the European Enlightenment then being presented as appropriate for the rest of the world.

There is one kind of thesis which I have introduced in the context of human rights (though it could be seen as more separate) and this is the libertarian position. It is a rights thesis in the sense that it homes in on one kind of right, namely liberty rights, and makes this the central plank of the theory. It is a genuinely global theory (though its adherents might not proclaim it as such), but it is one which will not support the idea of a positive responsibility, for instance to go to the aid of others. It underlies much of the commitment to the relatively unregulated global economy/ market, and as such is seriously flawed (see Chapter 7 IV E).

E. ASSESSMENT OF GLOBAL SOCIAL CONTRACT THEORIES

Beitz's attempt to construct a theory of global social justice is instructive and important because it rightly sees the point that if we can talk of social justice at a domestic level for a society within a nation-state, we should be able to talk of social justice at the global level too. What this theory does is to bring out the importance of a conception of a justly ordered society in which the distribution of goods is such that the basic needs of all are met. Applied to the world this is a powerful conception. If we took it seriously we might for instance see foreign aid as a kind of global income tax, as Paul Streeten has observed, reflecting the thought of an earlier cosmopolitan Barbara Ward (Streeten 1999).

But there are difficulties too. First, there are difficulties with the contractarian method in general for establishing principles of justice. It is not clear that we need to invoke the idea of hypothetical contract in order to argue for a society in which goods are so distributed that everyone's needs are met – other theories can generate this conclusion. But second and more particularly, Beitz's argument relies too heavily on an empirical assumption being met, namely that the world is interdependent economically, that it is a society in the relevant sense parallel to domestic society. This makes the theory of justice applied globally too dependent upon a disputed factual analysis.[12] But he is right that a full conception of justice requires us to think of a society as a whole as just, not merely individuals in their private transactions. But this society or community can be thought of in the first instance as notional, the product of the theory not vice versa, and thus to be worked towards as a social reality, as the theory requires.

F. CONCLUDING REMARKS

The above assessment has necessarily been selective and at the level of assessing strengths and weaknesses against intuitions, but may at least have alerted the reader to some of the issues which arise in trying to decide which kind of cosmopolitan ethic is to be accepted. Any theory may have much more to be said for it, such that one might wish to adjust one's intuitions in the light of the theory.[13] In the next chapter I outline the kind of cosmopolitan ethic which I believe to be reasonable and which, I submit, theorists of various persuasions would be willing to endorse.

NOTES

1. Actually the idea first surfaced amongst the less influential Cynics.
2. The issue is discussed by Nussbaum and her critics in *The Boston Review*, October 1994. For a fuller discussion see Heater 2002.
3. Note Rousseau's distinction between citizen as law-maker and subject as subject to laws in Rousseau 1966: bk I, ch. 6.
4. See Dower 2003 and Dower & Williams 2002 for different approaches to global citizenship. A useful survey of types of cosmopolitanism is given in the Stanford University Encyclopedia 2006 by Brown & Kleingeld. For cosmopolitanism as a way of seeing the world see Appiah 2006.
5. For useful discussions of the two approaches, see Frankena 1973 and Smart and Williams 1973.
6. For fuller accounts of Kant's complex theory, see, for example, Brown 1992: ch. 2, Thompson 1992: ch. 2, and Donaldson 1992.
7. In the later essay (Kant 1970a), Kant sees a natural evolution towards a cosmopolitan world order but it lies a long way off.
8. The implications of this for international relations are further explored by Luban 1985.
9. This is an example of how a global ethic could be constructed rather than simply discovered as an objective truth, but it is a rational construction, not something based on what is already accepted. See Beitz 1989 & Pogge 1989. The discussion is further developed in Rawls 1993 & 1999; Pogge 1995.
10. On the ethical side of Marxism, see, for example, Peffer 1990.
11. This observation is attributed to Bentham but I do not know the reference.
12. In the later edition of his book, Beitz no longer relies on the condition of economic interdependence (Beitz 1999: afterword).
13. See Rawls 1972: sn. 9 for discussion of the 'reflective equilibrium' method of mutually adjusting theory and intuitions. My own theoretical position, not developed here, would be a mongrel one which combined elements from several theories.

QUESTIONS FOR DISCUSSION

1. In what senses, if any, do you think of yourself as a global citizen?
2. What are the main features of the cosmopolitan approach?
3. What are the main differences between the Kantian approach and the utilitarian approach to global ethics?
4. In what form, if any, would you defend a conception of global justice?

CHAPTER 5

COSMOPOLITANISM AND COMMUNITY

I. OBJECTIONS FROM NON-COSMOPOLITAN PERSPECTIVES

In the last chapter we compared a number of cosmopolitan theories with one another. The kind of cosmopolitanism which I argue for will be stated shortly. First we need to consider some of the objections to the whole idea of universal values and global responsibilities. Many of the objections to cosmopolitanism from other quarters have already emerged in the earlier chapters, for instance in the arguments for international scepticism. But a quick summary of the kinds of difficulties will be useful here.

A. OBJECTIONS

The Tendency Towards Hegemony and World Government

The argument here is that the inner logic of the cosmopolitan theory would lead, if followed, towards world government, but before that the development of international institutions which would concentrate power in the hands of powerful nations, or perhaps at the present time just one – the USA. This has been the theme of a recent book by Zolo, entitled *Cosmopolis* (Zolo 1997). It is significant that the title says 'cosmopolis' rather than 'cosmopolitan', which is putting emphasis upon the idea of a world 'polis' or political institution rather than on the idea of being a 'world citizen'. World government and indeed hegemony by a super-power are dangerous for various reasons but also lead to the following difficulty.[1]

The Projection of Universal Values and the Tendency Towards the Homogenisation of Cultures

The danger is that those in positions of power project the values important to them as if they were universal values equally applicable to all peoples, whereas in fact values vary from culture to culture. What is in fact occurring, as writers such as Sachs and others argue, is that the development of the global economy is undermining local cultures in ways which are disastrous for human flourishing (Sachs 1992). We can call this the thesis of cultural pluralism, which is often associated with what the relativist claims (though as we shall see this is not necessary).

Inappropriateness of Idealism

A somewhat different argument is that the tendency of cosmopolitanism is to introduce ideals into decision making and thus insofar as politicians or others are influenced by them, they may be led to do things which are inappropriate in the real world. Thus so-called Wilsonian idealism is often criticised (by Carr and others) as leading to a disastrous peace settlement after the First World War. Woodrow Wilson's idealistic principles led to punitive action against Germany and the setting up of the unrealistic League of Nations, both of which arguably contributed to the return to war twenty years on. Analogously Anscombe criticises pacifism on the grounds that by setting too high a standard, it sets all forms of violence on the wrong side of the moral fence and this in fact encourages the abandonment of ethical constraints in warfare (Anscombe 1970: 48).

The Prosecution of Holy War/Ideological Conflicts

Another related danger of cosmopolitanism is that in the name of partic-ular religious or political ideals or ideologies which are seen by their adherents as universally applicable in a world which does not share those ideas, engagement with other countries in the world in order to 'convert' them leads to conflicts of a military kind, and thus in the past to holy wars like the crusades, and more recently ideological conflicts between East and West, often through so called 'proxy' wars in the Third World. There are dangers that conflicts between Western liberalism and Islamic theocratic ideals may lead increasingly to such conflicts in the future, as we are now witnessing in the polarisation implicit in the 'war against terror'.

The Undermining of Loyalty to the State as Citizens

Another line of argument will be that insofar as ordinary citizens are concerned, the spread and strengthening of cosmopolitan ideals will lead to a weakening of respect for and loyalty to the state. Apart from pacifism, which has always been seen as in some sense subversive of the state because of a refusal to defend it in ways required (and because it provides a view of the world in which the state's legitimacy, premised on the right of military defence, is challenged), other forms of cosmopolitanism may lead to challenges to state authority. Someone who smuggled in refugees or gave sanctuary to them may do so inspired by a global ethic which certainly challenges state authority. If we are world citizens, can we still be state citizens, at least in the sense we have always assumed?

B. REPLIES

First, none of the theories as set out earlier strictly entails any of these consequences. As theories about a universal ethical domain, they leave open in many ways the issue of how these are to be translated into policies in the real world. Certain theories are more likely to have some of these consequences. Marxism is more likely to endorse conflict, as are certain more proselytising forms of religious faith. Libertarianism is likely in view of its robust defence of individual liberty as a universal value to lead to economic processes in the world which do indeed undermine local cultures. Any of the theories may lead a thinker, given her more detailed interpretation and development of the theory and her view of what changes in the world will most effectively realise these values, to advocate things which will lead to these consequences. A vigorous champion of human rights may well advocate intervention leading to conflict and may well promote ideals which lead to unintended unfortunate results.

One response of the cosmopolitan may be of course a robust defence of these consequences as acceptable. Yes, world government is something to be aimed at; modernisation does require the transformation of traditional cultures; idealism may sometimes lead to bad consequences but sometimes bad consequences are the cost of acting on principle[3]; sometimes wars have to be fought in order to promote values not yet accepted elsewhere (because these values are after all right); and transformations in our attitude towards the state are exactly what we need.

The strategy adopted here however is that of accepting that the objections pick out some real dangers, but to argue for a version of cosmopolitanism which avoid these dangers. Not all cosmopolitan theories or normative positions are equally acceptable. Indeed the challenge in world ethics is as much to engage with alternative cosmopolitan theories and positions on norms to be advocated as to argue against those who would deny a global ethic altogether. The kind of cosmopolitan ethic which I give next would I think not generally have the dangers we are considering (though it does involve a re-evaluation of the nature of citizenship, which I return to shortly).

II. TYPES OF COSMOPOLITAN APPROACH

A. OUTLINE OF A NORMATIVE APPROACH

Briefly the kind of cosmopolitan ethic I commend is as follows. An analysis of human nature shows that there are a number of main elements of human well-being or flourishing: nutrition, health, shelter, security, family, community, liberty/autonomy, recreation, exercise of (other) rational capacities.[4] Because of their tendencies towards selfishness human beings need to live in society, which is an intrinsic good as well. To live in a society certain basic rules are needed: non-deception, non-coercion, respect for life, liberty and property, benevolence. But this recognition of the need for society requires us, on rational reflection, to accept all of humanity as part of society, as susceptible to the good and bad impacts of our actions, including omissions, for which we are responsible. It also requires us to extend concern to non-human life as well. But our responsibility towards others is coupled with a recognition that the ways people interpret the basic goods and the basic rules may be somewhat varied, and it is not our business to impose our conception of the good and the right on others. Responsibility requires us, in accepting a value such as truth or justice, not only to act justly or truthfully but also to promote these values. This responsibility is extensive but not exhaustive, since the right to pursue our own lives and to have particular attachments and relationships is also to be sustained.

What is important to the kind of world ethic qua set of agreed principles which I am trying to develop and which both expresses the above values and would be supported by a range of theoretical approaches, is this. First, it is sufficiently broad to allow for diverse manifestations of value in different contexts and to allow for diverse intellectual sources of support. Second, its main elements of global responsibility will be: commitment to maintain (and promote) the conditions of well-being, peace, justice and environmental care, that is commitment to not harming others and helping them in respect to the primary elements of human well-being; along with commitment to respect for diversity, both in relation to life-style and culture and with regard to beliefs including beliefs about moral values.

The distinctive nature of the approach which I call 'solidarist–pluralist' will become clearer when features of it will also emerge in the various discussions of issues in Part II, but also if we contrast it to two other approaches. All these approaches are cosmopolitan in both the respects indicated earlier. First, a set of values is postulated as values to be accepted everywhere. Second, there is some notion of active responsi-bility to further these values and to oppose those who frustrate them, either through wilful wrongdoing or through commitment to inappro-priate moral values, though there may be different views taken about the appropriate means to adopt. Indeed one of the hallmarks of any global ethic which is presented as cosmopolitan is precisely the emphasis upon positive responsibility to further what is valuable. Put formally, if x is a basic value (truth, liberty, peace, reverence for nature), then ethically we are not merely committed to expressing these values in our own behav-iour (acting x-ly) but also to promoting x in appropriate ways.[5]

It must be stressed that there are no sharp divisions: the different elements of each position could be combined in different ways. In any case perceptions will vary. A libertarian who vigorously promoted individual liberty by opposing other illiberal cultures would merge into a form of idealist-dogmatism (and would be perceived by others as such), but if he stressed the liberty of others in other cultures to choose a non-individu-alist way of life, his position would merge into pluralism. Likewise in the pursuit of social justice and human rights someone who saw himself as a solidarist–pluralist may be seen as a dogmatist by others. What follows is a kind of framework for interpreting approaches; it does not provide a simple or agreed analysis.

B. IDEALIST–DOGMATIC

First, there is what I shall call, somewhat stipulatively, an idealist–dogmatic cosmopolitanism which asserts a fairly specific and definite set of moral norms or ideals, which it sees as emanating from the specific worldview, religious or metaphysical, which it also asserts. What is important to this kind of view is not only the set of values which is recognised as not gener-ally accepted elsewhere in the world, but also the worldview from which the values emanate, which it also sees as important that other people and societies, with other worldviews, ought to accept. Such was the basis of much religious crusading and proselytising in the past. It is currently a feature of fundamentalist Christianity, as well as of militant Islam (though we must note that this is not as such a general characterisation of Islam or Christianity in the modern world). It is also a feature of some modern worldviews of a non-traditional religious kind. A militant humanism or atheism which saw the suppression of religion as important to its goals would be one such, but so too would a radical ecological outlook which saw it as more important that other people give up their anthropocentric views than that they give up environmentally destructive lifestyles, whatever their reason for doing so. Whilst the passionate pursuit of an ideal may well be done through negotiation and dialogue, there is a greater tendency within this approach than within the others to let the end justify the means in terms of the use of coercion and manipulation.[6]

With regard to the type of world ethic which is a proselytising world ethic, where the goal is projecting one's own specific values (seen as universal) and thus converting the rest of the world to it, two issues can be raised. Practically, one has to argue that this approach, especially if it comes up against alternative proselytising approaches, simply results in antagonism at various levels, wasted energy and at worst destructive conflict and states of affairs which undermine other universally accepted goods which the different worldviews would include as desirable. Theoretically, the issue is also raised as to whether it is even desirable that the worldviews of all peoples should be the same or that people should behave in the same ways. So long as a common framework is observed that enables people to lead fulfilled lives, the variety of ways of living should be no problem, and similarly though with a qualification, the variety of worldviews is no problem.

The qualification is this: worldviews, whether religious or otherwise, have a 'truth' component, as indeed, on many views of ethics, ethical beliefs and theories have themselves. Am I saying then that it does not matter whether different individuals or groups hold different beliefs about what is true and hence that some hold false views? I am not arguing this nor am I saying that disagreement about truth matters in other areas but not in respect to what is important in ethics, because that prejudges the issue as to whether there are ethical truths which matter, as opposed to certain patterns of satisfactory behaviour. But there is an issue concerning the relative importance of the correctness of intellectual formulations, in religion or ethics, as compared with certain patterns of articulated practice. If we accept the importance of the latter, we may be in a position to see the issue of intellectual disagreement in a context that shows that the need to make everyone else believe what I believe does not have such great importance.

C. LIBERTARIAN–MINIMALIST

Second, there is what may be called the libertarian forms of cosmopolitanism. This on the face of it is at the other extreme in that it precisely does not advocate a specific set of values, but rather stresses the value of freedom or choice, coupled with a rejection of intervention, aid or generally the positive promotion of goods. There is no general duty of doing this, as opposed to the duty not to harm others, though action to establish freedoms and oppose illiberal practices may be seen as right, and in terms of the ethics of the means, there will be a general preference for the way of consent. However organised attempts to come to the aid of others generally represent a form of interference which is contrary to the principle of liberty. The trouble with extensive aid is that it requires bureaucratic structures which are invasive of liberty, privacy and so on. Such a view tends to be supportive of the society of states and the more limited 'morality of states' and of course to be supportive of the global economy and the principles of the global free market.

Theoretically allowing people to do their own thing, to pursue their own conception of the good, allows not only for personal diversity but also cultural diversity, since the way a group lives should be up to them as well. However, although it is opposed to the dogmatic forms of cosmopolitanism, there is a danger that it assumes its own forms of dogmatism, insofar as its stress on the free choice of individual agents is not neutral between different value conceptions in different parts of the world but is a specific value of a liberal Northern culture and therefore insofar as it is presented to or projected onto the rest of the world, it becomes a value to be promoted elsewhere where it is not already accepted. The current dominance of the Western market model of economic development as the key to the good life can be seen as a combination of a minimalist approach in some aspects with an attempt to proselytise for a dominant image of the good life on the other.

Both the acceptance of the global free market and the acceptance of the morality of states can be seen as expressions of this libertarian approach. As such this approach may be supported by a number of different theories, and thus constitutes an important form of consensus or agreed global ethic. There is however another kind of agreed global ethic and that is the one which I have characterised as 'solidarist–pluralist', to which we now return.[7]

D. SOLIDARIST–PLURALIST

Third, there is the cosmopolitanism in the middle, which can be called solidarist–pluralist, and takes its starting point to be the observation that if ethics is about enabling people to flourish and to flourish as far as possible consistent with other people doing so, we need to be clear what the basic conditions of flourishing are (cf. the idea of responsible pluralism, e.g. in Drydyk 2003). The basic values of peace, reliable access to elements of well-being (food, shelter and so on), a healthy and resource-full environment to live in, stable community and relationships, autonomy (in the sense of a level of self-direction which enables a person to have dignity) need to be affirmed. Of course a libertarian or an idealist cosmopolitan may by and large agree with this list. But whereas the idealist thinker will see this as only the starting point for a wider set of objectives to be pursued (the acceptance of specific values and beliefs), and the libertarian will in stressing liberty as the value sustained by the other goods, downplay the level of obligation needed to make it possible for all to enjoy these values, the solidarist–pluralist cosmopolitan will deny the importance of promoting these other values and beliefs but assert the importance of obligations at the global level to bring these values into existence. That is, he or she will combine the twin values of plurality or diversity and global solidarity or global responsibility; solidarity because we need a firm basis of positive obligation to promote these goods, and plurality because in not being as concerned about whether other people's beliefs and values are the same as his or her own, he or she is saying in effect: 'differences of values and beliefs between individuals and cultures do not matter as much as the promotion of common and indeed commonly agreed values'. He or she will almost certainly have his or her own more complex set of values plus supporting theory, but the promoting of these is not seen as of overriding importance or indeed relevance. Up to a certain point diversity of belief and practice is something to celebrate anyway.

There are two abiding motivations for the kind of approach I have advocated. First, we need desperately an ethic of global responsibility (reflected in changed state priorities) for dealing with the evils in the world – poverty, environmental degradation, lack of peace and so on. Second, we need a humble recognition, at least for those of us coming from Northern cultures, that in discharging this global responsibility we should not be in the business of promoting or projecting values – ideas of the good life and ways of living in society – which are actually culturally specific to our own cultures. There is a great need to respect the great cultural diversity in the world, to allow for significant variations in the ways people pursue development and so on. One of the great dangers, to be explored later, is precisely that in the name of development we are projecting a specifically Eurocentric model of development on the rest of the world, which for a variety of reasons may not be appropriate.[8]

What matters then to the cosmopolitan position I am advocating is the building of a consensus of agreed values, not the finding of or the creation of agreed fundamental beliefs. This does not mean that she is not opposed to other beliefs. She is certainly not seeking the lowest common denominator. She is opposed to dogmatic cosmopolitanism as much as to denials of cosmopolitanism altogether, as she will be opposed to libertarian versions which deny extensive global obligations and endorse models of development that actually make things worse for the poor. But she is seeking alliances of convergence for practical principles and policies, in order to build a world ethic as a social reality of genuinely shared values. In many ways the position I am developing is similar to that put forward by Arne Naess, since he recognises that what is important in the environmental movement is agreement in practice to oppose the dominant economic paradigm, not agreement on the 'ecosophies' themselves which are diverse.[9] Whilst the position does not rule out the use of force *in extremis*, its strong preference will be for the way of peace, dialogue and negotiation.

E. THE ISSUE OF PLURALISM

More needs to be said about pluralism in order to distinguish it from the relativism which I criticised earlier. The three main differences are that the assertion of pluralism is linked first to the assertion of global responsibility; second there is still assumed to be a common value framework but one which allows variable interpretations; and third, there are limits to what is seen as acceptable. The following remarks will bring out the differences.[10]

First, however we characterise universal human goods, this needs to be done with a sufficient degree of flexibility and sensitivity to significant variations in interpretation. These variations according to cultural or personal factors may be, for instance, in the values associated with liberty or autonomy, with stable relationships, and with community and participation in it. The duty of others to respect these ways of living depends on the general value of things like liberty and relationships, even though there may be variations in how these things are interpreted both between and within societies.

Second, the fact that some moral rules or principles are seen as universal does not entail that all such rules have to be seen as universal. Some rules and customs within a society may simply have local significance and validity. One of the reasons for this is that part of the moral force of rules (the cosmopolitan cannot accept 'all') derives from what is established and customary and thus, because agreed upon, has the moral force which agreements as such, as a universal value, carry. That is, promising, contracting, agreement or consent are not merely acts, states or processes which create obligations in otherwise neutral individual acts but can also create obligations which inhere in new social structures and rules of behaviour.

Third, whatever the variations in non-universal culturally specific norms and in expressing universal values, it remains true that certain goods and rules have a universal validity, because they are preconditions for the more specific forms of life and the moral culture which depend on them. Access to subsistence and adequate means to a range of actions which make up a meaningful life, generally good health, a healthy environment, freedom from arbitrary attack (basic security), along with the basic ground-rules of not lying, killing, attacking, breaking promises, can all be seen as universal features of any society, and therefore give rise to obligations, in principle if not in practice, in others in other societies not to undermine those preconditions.

The acceptance of diversity of values is not meant to be an 'anything goes' approach, amounting to a *de facto* relativism of values. If one is to avoid being shipwrecked on the Scylla of the traditional objective of proselytising or missionising promotion of values, there is of course the danger of hitting the other rock, the Charybdis of relativism. The need to steer a middle course between these two extremes is part of the challenge for anyone advocating a sensitive but radical world ethic. My view is not meant to be, and I hope is not perceived to be, an admission of relativism. This is for two reasons. Global obligations are a central part of the story, and they are what are denied by relativists. More to the point, the argument is not that all values – all ways of thinking of the good or of moral rules – are equally valid and are simply to be accepted because they are dominant in a given culture.

Some values are to be seen as universal, even if needing to be characterised in fairly non-specific terms, and it may well be the case that what is dominant or practised in a society simply is not acceptable from this universal point of view. This may be both because certain elementary rules are simply ignored or distorted in established practice, as when there are violations of the kinds of human rights which concern Amnesty International, or because what is established may well be a reflection of a certain power structure which simply does not reflect the perceptions and values of other groups in society. These may be majorities, like blacks in apartheid South Africa, or minorities such as persecuted religious sects or ethnic groups, or just half of a population, in the case of women in a male-dominated society.[11] Discrimination, persecution, exploitation and slavery are all extreme examples of the more general phenomenon of voices not heard which should be heard.

No one, least of all me, is pretending that deciding what is legitimate cultural variation and what is not is an easy business. It is not. Many controversies will exist over these issues. But the framework has to be acknowledged in which these dilemmas arise. It would be a false escape either to retreat into an old-fashioned 'we know what is right and good and the rest of the world had better change' or to retreat into a relativist 'whatever is thought good or right is good or right', which apart from anything else undermines the whole idea of global responsibility anyway.

III. COSMOPOLITANISM AND COMMUNITARIANISM

A. COMMUNITARIANISM

We have referred to communitarianism in many places and it has featured significantly in the discussion of internationalism. There the main emphasis was on the idea of political community and its bearing on the arguments for internationalism. Here I turn to the underlying general idea of morality arising from socially constituted community and the implications it has for the relations which individuals have to others in the rest of the world (see Sandel 1982; Taylor 1989). The idea is a more general one partly because there may be many kinds of community, small or large, linked to a geographical area or made of up members geographically spread out, none of which are communities corresponding to political units. The same issues concerning the relationships between members of such communities and those outside them arise.

As with the theories discussed in Chapter 2, I expand the communitarian position already given there into two parts: first a descriptive claim, then a theoretical/normative claim.

Descriptive: ethical relations as a matter of fact exist in terms of how they are perceived to be and are embedded in social practices and traditions. Conceptions of well-being and identity are not given in the abstract but grounded in concrete cultural particularities of time and place. The relations which people have with the community or society as a whole, to the 'nation' or the 'state' are of central significance in their lives. It is in the context of shared values and social sanctions that most people are adequately motivated to act in accordance with the agreed norms.

Theoretical/normative: what is important however to the communitarian approach is usually the theoretical understanding that goes with the above analysis, namely that these facts about the social constitution of ethical norms provide us with the key to their justification. Ethical norms are justified precisely by being embedded in custom, convention and tradition. The values of people's identities are indeed constituted by the social context of their lives. The society, the nation or the state do provide the context in which the nature and scope of ethical norms and values are to be located. One of the key elements in this style of thought is the recognition of the importance of the contingent in the formation of people's identities and moral values. That is, what is important is the particular time and place one lives in, the particular traditions one is part of, the national group one happens to be born into and so on. These are 'non-rational' elements, because in a sense they are arbitrary and not something equally relevant to any rational agent.

On the face of it, the general thrust of communitarianism seems to be in conflict with the general thrust of cosmopolitanism and to give support for a global scepticism and for either internationalism or international scepticism. The communitarian is saying that moral values arise out of actual community and shared traditions, whereas the cosmopolitan goes back to a basic theory which his own reasoning supports and says in effect, 'given my reading of human nature, the human situation, what reason requires, and so on, these are the values which apply to human relationships generally'. However the conflict is not direct nor, as we shall see, necessary. Although communitarian thinking can support and be linked with ethical relativism, it need not be. Whereas relativism precisely denies what the cosmopolitan theory asserts, communitarianism has a different primary agenda, and allows for various possible accounts of values in the world as a whole. What follows is a somewhat schematic consideration of different logical possibilities, and how one might respond to each.

B. WHY IS THERE A CONFLICT?

In fact the opposition between communitarianism and cosmopolitanism can be seen potentially in several different respects. First, they may be in conflict over the source of moral values, as I have just indicated. Second, they may be in conflict over the nature of moral values. If the cosmopolitan says that there are moral values which are universal and obligations which are global in scope, the communitarian may say that because there is no relevant global community, such values and obligations do not exist. Or as a variation, there may be a conflict over the strength or importance of global norms: the communitarian says they are weak because that is the extent to which they are accepted in a weaker global community, whereas the cosmopolitan claims that they apply in principle and with a strength in practical terms that is not generally acknowledged.

Clearly the conflict will be most conspicuous if the first two bases of conflict are combined. That is, there is a disagreement both about the source or validation of moral norms and about whether they exist at all at the global level. The arguments against communitarianism in this case will be the arguments against relativism which we have already given in Chapter 3. Briefly, it conflicts with deep intuitions that we do stand in some kind of ethical relations to all human beings simply in virtue of our common human-ness, it undermines the idea of progress measured by any common yardstick, renders unintelligible internal minority dissent, and makes external assessment of social practices problematic.

The disagreement would not be as intense if for one reason or another the communitarian did acknowledge the existence of global values in some form. This might arise in a number of different ways. First, if he thought that some kind of global moral community already exists, as evidenced by levels of agreement about core values and duties of mutual aid. Second, if he recognised that many global organisations are made up of individuals who share global ideals, that is moral values internal to the organisations in question and thus part of their globally shared traditions and agreed norms. Third, if people generally within one's own community shared concerns for the outside world, cosmopolitan values could become part of the traditions of that society.

Let us suppose that sometime in the future there emerged a world in which all these features above were well established – well established global community, many people endorsing global values through the organisations they belong to, and a strong sense of commitment to other human beings internal to most communities throughout the world. If this happened, the strength of commitment to global responsibility would not be weaker than what a cosmopolitan advocates. Indeed, such an outcome would be exactly what a cosmopolitan wanted. For reasons to be developed below, the best hope for any cosmopolitan theorist to get what his theory recommended actually done is to create the characteristics of community just indicated. So the eventual convergence of what the communitarian stresses as necessary to morality and what the cosmopolitan recognises as the necessary means to what she advocates would be recognised.

However, even in these cases where it is recognised that the world as it is now has actual levels of moral concern for the rest of the world, and that in the future such concerns might be well established (to the heart's content of a cosmopolitan), there would still be a fundamental area of disagreement, namely about the nature of the source of those values. The existence or strength of cosmopolitan values do not depend upon what is already established in a global community. Nor are cosmopolitan values contingent upon what a community happens to care about. If people in a country happened to care about distant poverty but what made that valuable was the fact that the values are shared and accepted, then if that community ceased to care or never had cared, it would no longer be or would not have been a value. Such contingency is contrary to the cosmopolitan position. Third, the moral conventions within a country may be no more right, in the last analysis, than the morality of states, and the fact that they are in either case accepted does not cut off the question: are the norms acceptable or adequate? Convention, custom and tradition are neither necessary nor sufficient for valid moral claims to be made. What is customary even at the global level may be wrong and something that ought to be done may not be accepted as a duty. On its own then communitarianism would seem to be seriously inadequate.

C. CAN WE COMBINE THEM?

Do we have to take communitarianism on its own though? Perhaps there is some way in which we can combine the strengths and insights of communitarianism's thinking with some form of cosmopolitan theory. After all many of the values in a society, to do with conceptions of well-being and social norms, do seem to vary, as we noted in the section on pluralism, and their being valuable in the way they are can be accounted for by the fact that they are shaped and accepted in the traditions of that society. The fact that they are contingent does not necessarily make them ethically questionable. Communitarianism also provides useful insights about the conditions necessary for the general observance of moral norms.

There are three ways in which one can respond to the disagreement between the two positions. The first is to accept the conflict as fundamental, and argue for one against the other. The second is to adopt a strategy of mutual accommodation, and argue that both theories have part of the truth about the nature and source of ethical values. The third strategy is one of assimilation, that is of taking one approach as fundamentally correct but interpreting various features of the other approach as derivative from the basic theory (and mistaken by its advocates as being fundamental).

Both the latter two strategies seem promising. Although the kinds of ethical theory – Kantianism, utilitarianism, natural law – associated with cosmopolitanism tend to be presented as *the* bases of morality, thus excluding any other type of theory as well as each other, there is no reason why morality could not be seen as deriving from a variety of sources. Certainly, communitarianism can readily be seen as open to the possibility of there being a layer of obligation we have towards fellow human beings in virtue of our human-ness, alongside the values which arise from established society. This is one reason why communitarianism cannot be identified with relativism. Part of the attraction of pluralism is that there may be a variety of ways in which moral values arise.

But it is one form of the third strategy which I adopt here, that is to argue that cosmopolitanism is basic and that many of the things which the communitarian stresses can be seen as applications or expressions of universal values. But we need to recognise that it is possible to adopt a 'communitarian cosmopolitanism' too, arguing from the development of community at the global level. Thus a communitarian might argue that ideas of universal values and global responsibilities arise naturally out of the traditions of societies and increasingly in the modern world out of the shared values of the 'society of societies' (Thompson 1992).[12]

Why do I prefer my form of cosmopolitan thinking? First, since agreement and consent are universal values (they are not valuable merely because people have agreed to value them), many practices and ways of life peculiar to local domains are indeed valuable. Second, the existence of a political order and participation in it are indeed important both because such arrangements are necessary means to the fulfilment of universal values but also because, as Aristotle stressed, such participation is an intrinsic and important good (Aristotle 1988: esp. bks 1 & 2). Third, apart from the political order, living in communities is both valuable in its own right and a vital source of motivation for moral agency. Thus a cosmopolitan might say that the values internal to living in a particular community are to be derived from a fundamental theory as expressions of it.

My reasons for preferring this strategy are twofold. First, it is theoretically sound. Whatever the practical importance of values established in community, we will not seek to create them, unless we have moral reason to do so, prior to and independent of their creation. Second, unless we have a fundamental ethical basis, we will not be able to argue for significantly progressive cosmopolitan obligations. Without this we will not counterbalance the tendency in practice for communitarian arguments to resist active expressions of global citizenship.

In the mid-90s there was an interesting and important exchange between Martha Nussbaum and her critics in a special edition of *The Boston Review*, in which she defended cosmopolitanism and the need for a cosmopolitan education (Nussbaum 1994; see also Cohen 1996). It is very striking that in this debate very few of the respondents actually reject a framework of a global ethical kind in which it is acknowledged that there are duties towards the world's poor, to protect our common environment and defend human rights. But most of the writers nevertheless reject Nussbaum's call for 'cosmopolitan education' which would take seriously the *teaching* of the idea that we are citizens of the world. Their reasons for rejecting this are various but many were ringing the communitarian bell that identities have to be primarily national. In another context Alasdair MacIntyre, whilst he is not hostile to some framework of common values in the background (after all he is deeply influenced by the natural law approach) nevertheless rejects strongly the idea of world citizenship on the grounds that makes us rootless citizens of nowhere lacking any real identity in a particular culture (quoted in Almond 1990: 102).

What the responses to Nussbaum's article showed was not only great resistance to cosmopolitan education in the American context but also, more positively, the point that the issue is not simply between good cosmopolitan education and bad national citizenship education. Both cosmopolitanism and patriotism can have their pathologies as well as wholesome forms. If the cosmopolitan education was informed by a less than satisfactory set of values like a form of fundamentalism, as discussed earlier, that would not be better than an education which taught a pride in national identity and loyalty but with a 'live and let live' approach to other cultures and countries. If an education in citizenship stressed, as officially the American way of life or constitution reflects, the ethical values of liberty, democracy and respect for rights and these are seen as universal values, then in principle such a citizenship could inform enlightened foreign policy. But if that education was based on the idea of the superiority of one's own nation or country and the legitimacy of putting one's own country's interest before all others, then that would be unsatisfactory because it was inconsistent with reasonable cosmopolitan values. There is therefore a false tension between the two kinds of citizenship, and cosmopolitanism needs to acknowledge the importance of ordinary citizenship and indeed the values of established community (see also Tamir 1993 & Tan 2004 on the complex relationship between cosmopolitanism and nationalism).

Although I have indicated my reasons for preferring a cosmopolitan theory theoretical basis and seeing communitarian values as both expressions of this and means towards its fuller realisation, it remains important to stress the two senses of global/world ethic discussed earlier. If a global ethic is an ethic widely shared across the world, then in effect we have a community of shared values and if that shared-ness is not merely coincidental but the product of negotiation, consultation and transnational dialogue, then even more evident is the emergence of global community. As Parekh notes, an emerging global ethic should be one we can both assent to and consent to (Parekh 2005: 27). I have already stressed the importance of assent – which each one of us can give, given our (different) comprehensive intellectual/spiritual standpoints. But part of the rapprochement between communitarianism and cosmopolitanism is precisely the recognition that an ethic needs consent too and the wider the better, consistent with fidelity to our own starting points, and that this consent is also part of what gives the shared values their validity.

D. GLOBAL CITIZENSHIP

We can now return to the idea of global citizenship and consider what the appropriate form of implementation is. Does global citizenship really exist in the world today? If so, is it in competition with or complementary to the citizenship we have as members of particular nation-states? Invoking the distinctions I drew at the beginning of Chapter 4 we can state the position as follows. The idea of global citizenship as something strictly analogous to ordinary citizenship simply has no application in the world as it is. The idea of global citizenship as the assertion that we have duties in principle towards all fellow human beings is of course both intelligible and, if the arguments of this book are sound, valid. It does not however depend at all on whether or to what extent global institutions exist to give it expression. What we need to recognise is that there is something between the two interpretations which is important to advocate and for which the nature of international institutions is important and critical.

To be a global citizen in this sense is first to accept the moral thesis above that one has duties in principle towards anyone in the world; second, to believe that there are a range of ways in which individuals can act so as to make a difference towards what happens in the world; third, to engage to some extent in patterns of action which one believes to be an exercise of one's global responsibility, patterns of action which one would not have engaged in but for this belief. What any individual does may of course vary considerably from private acts of, say, recycling glass, not using one's car when one could have done, or giving donations to a third world charity, to active engagement in NGOs campaigning for change on global issues, engaging in the education of others, or taking part in political parties in order to influence their foreign policy priorities.

For such activities to be engaged in (and the idea of global citizenship not to remain an unactualised ideal), there needs of course to be a backcloth of institutions through which one's actions can take effect. Without a charity like Oxfam, donations to help the poor in distant lands could not readily take place. Without environmental organisations, neither action in solidarity with others (who are doing the same) nor appropriate political influence would be possible. Without democratic institutions within countries the capacity of ordinary citizens to influence foreign policy decisions, through voting, lobbying or whatever, would be lost.

A good example of global citizenship engagement was the Jubilee 2000 campaign – a campaign that is ongoing – to get the debt of the poorest countries cancelled (Jubilee Campaign 2006), along with commitment by many to 'fair trade' and 'ethical consuming'. Another recent example of the exercise of global citizenship, and of the importance of the influence of international NGOs is the World Court Project which I shall focus on because it is less well known. On 8 July 1996 the World Court in the Hague delivered an advisory opinion on the legality, in international law, of not only using but also possessing and thus threatening the use of nuclear weapons. It ruled that the threat or use of nuclear weapons would generally be contrary to the rules of international law applicable in armed conflict and also clearly stated that there was an obligation for nuclear disarmament negotiations to be pursued and concluded. This was the culmination of a number of years' work by many activists in a citizens' movement called the 'World Court Project'. The Project organised the collection of a large number of 'declarations of public conscience' by ordinary citizens throughout the world, which the 'de Martens' clause of the World Court constitution requires it to take heed of. This led eventually a motion in the UN General Assembly in 1994 which asked for an advisory opinion.[13]

There are a number of interesting issues raised by this case. First, is it helpful or relevant? Experts have dismissed it as irrelevant to the real challenges of checking nuclear proliferation. Certainly it has to be acknowledged that as an advisory opinion, this judgement, like other 'soft' parts of international law is not enforceable. On the other hand, it may well contribute towards the building up of a pressure for the reduction of nuclear arsenals. It is important to remember that the whole process would not have taken place at all but for the development of groundswell of public opinion, as expressed in the declarations of public conscience. It is difficult to see how this now activated level of public awareness can simply be dismissed as having no effect.

Second, this was an exercise of world citizen power or global civil society. That a body like the World Court can be responsive to such influences is of course, from a cosmopolitan point of view, much to be welcomed. The fact that a lot of people think the threat and use of nuclear weapons is wrong or the fact that a judgement tends to confirm a position in international law, do not, either of them, actually establish that the possession or use of nuclear weapons is wrong. People, even judges, are fallible. Nevertheless for any thinker who for reasons other than the fact that it is already accepted by others or embodied in a public and authoritative advisory opinion, believes reliance on nuclear weapons to be wrong, such influential processes in global civil society are encouraging signs for the future.

But global citizenship, if it is to be an effective idea, does not merely involve a range of activities which the committed person engages in for the sake of some global good. It must also involve, to some extent, a change of attitude towards his own society and political order. Recognition of a meaningful membership of a global community of humankind may not lead one to questioning one's general loyalty to the state or to question the special place membership of one's own community or society has, any more than recognising the value of the wider society undermines family loyalties, but it must involve some reordering of priorities. At the very least, if one gives generously to Oxfam, it is reasonable counterfactually to suppose that had one not been ethically concerned about distant poverty, one would have given more to some domestic charity. If one had not campaigned for the saving of whales, one would have campaigned for something else closer to home. At a deeper level, one may in terms of one's concerns, be led to break the law in acts of civil disobedience. It is not merely that commitment to some moral or religious ideal can lead one to defy the state – this can always be the case, whether the ethic is global or not – it is rather that the claims of community and state may have quite generally less of a pull, if one really does think of oneself as having an identity as a citizen of the world and one sees a significant part of one's responsibility as a moral agent being exercised at this level rather than at a more local level. The development of international institutions, aided of course by the recent massive explosion of global communications, all contribute towards these trends, so that global citizenship becomes more a practical reality, as the institutions which embody its ideals are themselves developed (see Carter 2001; Hutchings & Dannreuther 1999; Parekh 2002).

One example which illustrates what the implications might be of this revised perspective is that of refugees. The flood of refugees has grown dramatically in the last few years and now stands, according to official and therefore conservative estimates, at over 20 million people (UNHCR 2006). The refugee crisis is one of the major issues facing the world today. Many countries, especially the wealthy countries, have very strict and unhelpful procedures for admitting political refugees and countries generally do not accept 'economic' refugees at all. Many cosmopolitans would argue that the rights of individuals to escape persecution or extreme poverty should lead to a relaxation of the tight frontier controls which are maintained. To be sure, such relaxation will have effects on existing citizens, who may prefer not to undergo possible reduction in economic well-being or not to have others who are not part of their community entering the country, and these preferences may well be seen as democratic justifications for not doing so. But it is not clear why these considerations should take precedence over meeting the basic needs of others. In many ways our attitude towards refugees is a litmus test of how far we accept a cosmopolitan way of thinking and how far we retain a traditional communitarian approach and support for internationalism.

Nevertheless the importance of community for cosmopolitanism in the sense that the communitarians stress can be underlined if we recall the distinction between a world ethic as theory and as social reality. In this sense it is a truism, but an important if neglected one, that a cosmopolitan ethic, like any other ethical code, is more likely to be realised, the more people accept it. Therefore the development of a public ethical culture which embodies the values in question is clearly crucial to the more effective realisation of the values involved (see e.g. Boulding 1990). For instance, if one's theory says that the rich ought to be generous towards reducing extreme poverty, then the more people who believe this, the more individuals will be motivated ethically to do, the more such behaviour will be strengthened by the perception of like behaviour and the more governments are likely to reflect such electoral preferences in aid programmes. So whilst a cosmopolitan may actually be more interested in the normative/theoretical part of his claim, it is clearly important that this ethic becomes more fully represented in the 'global social reality'.

So the argument must be to create the appropriate kinds of social structure to embed the idea of global citizenship, so that it is not either membership of a global political order or merely membership of a moral domain. What those structures are is the challenge. 'We are global citizens with tribal souls', as Piet Hein once remarked (quoted in Barnaby 1988: 192). The challenge is: how can we acquire our global souls? Bradley, the English political idealist, once suggested that a morality has both body and soul, the body being the social institutions and public practices and the soul being the individual moral wills which breathe life into that body (Bradley 1878: 177–81). If a global ethic is to exist in the fullest sense then it will need both body, the public social embodiment in shared norms and institutions, and soul, the beliefs of a sufficient number of moral agents who believe that ethics is global in character. Cosmopolitan theories provide us with the soul of that morality. Communitarian thinking provides us with the insight as to what must also exist for that morality to be embodied. We cannot do without either.

NOTES

1. Toulmin's earlier book *Cosmopolis* also criticises the tendencies of modernity.
2. See also Chapter 9 for discussion of world government.
3. Note the deontological theme, illustrated by the Latin tag '*fiat iustitia ruat coelum*', i.e. 'let justice be and the heavens fall'.
4. But note that not all have to be satisfied in any one life for that life to go well.
5. A 'global' ethic could assert certain universal values but make light of or deny any duty to promote these values worldwide, but it would hardly be

called 'cosmopolitan'. See Introduction, Section IV.

6. See Ceadel 1987: ch. 4 for discussion of 'crusading' approach. He distinguishes five approaches – militarism, crusading, defencism, pacific-ism and pacifism – which whilst not the same as my distinction are sensitive to the same kinds of issues of ends and means.

7. My criticism of the conventional 'morality of states' has already been given in Chapter 4. My criticisms of the libertarian basis of the global economy are given in Chapter 7.

8. For a balanced survey of different cultural values see Laszlo 1993.

9. Naess 1989: ch. 2. Hans Küng argues similarly for peace values (Küng 1990). See Chapter 6.

10. For a useful discussion of pluralism, see Kekes 1993. He also sees pluralism as a middle way between traditional objectivism and relativism. The general upshot is similar, but the theory somewhat different.

11. One of the biggest gaps in this work is a lack of discussion of feminism's contribution to thinking about international relations. Some though not all feminist themes are I believe reflected in my approach and may have influenced it indirectly – questioning hierarchical models, celebrating difference, and valuing caring and the way of peace and negotiation. These values are all supported by feminism, as indeed postmodernism and ecological visions, but I do not see them as essentially depending on such theories. See Peterson 1992 and Robinson 1999.

12. Nagel discusses these issues of strategy in several papers in Nagel 1979. His distinction between agent-centred ethics and outcome-centred ethics, both of which he argues have some validity, is similar to but not the same as the distinction between communitarianism and cosmopolitanism respectively.

13. For an account of the background to this, see Mothersson 1992 and World Court 1996.

QUESTIONS FOR DISCUSSION

1. Are any of the objections to cosmopolitanism effective?

2. In what respects is solidarist-pluralism different from the other two main cosmopolitan ethics discussed?

3. Is cosmopolitanism incomplete without some insights from communitarianism?

4. Was the World Court Project a paradigm case of global citizenship action?

PART II
APPLICATIONS

CHAPTER 6

PEACE AND WAR

I. SOME BACKGROUND FACTS

War has been a significant feature of the life-conditions of people throughout history. War and preparations for war affect the economic and cultural conditions of people. War and the threat of war have shaped the boundaries and existence of states, and determined the status of people as free citizens, subjects without political rights or even slaves (Bull 1985: 179). Generally speaking however human beings have wanted to live in conditions of peace, preferably a kind of peace in which the threat of war was absent, but at least peace as a period of existence in which there was no need to engage in fighting other groups of human beings, with the consequent loss of life, injury, loss of land and damage to property, all seen as damaging vital human 'goods'. This crudely is the problem war poses: we do not want it, but we tend to resort to it.

123

The tendency towards war is of course a particular manifestation of a more general tendency to resort to violence, the tendency of individuals and groupings of individuals to resort to attacking people and their property, either for private gain or to advance some goal which the group has adopted. What inclines us to call certain forms of violence 'war' is the fact that it is 'organised violence carried out by political units against each other' (Bull 1985: 178). Whether or not there is any deep ethical significance in distinguishing between these different types of violence, it should be noted that ever since the development of the modern nation-state system, it has been a key feature of its rationale that nations-states are the units, and no others are, who can legitimately use organised violence in pursuit of their ends. That is, there is a claimed monopoly in the legitimate use of force enjoyed by nation-states. There are various challenges to this assumption, especially in the modern world, stemming from civil wars, wars of secession, and conflicts between states and terrorist groups or what Kaldor calls 'new wars' (Kaldor 2001).

Whether or not one thinks that the party fighting a currently established government, namely, the other side in a civil war, the seceding area or the terrorist group, could be doing so legitimately, two facts remain significant. First, such struggles, insofar as they tend to be thought of as war, are still broadly political struggles because the party not in government has political objectives, such as the overthrowing of government, the creation of a new separate state. In this sense Clausewitz, the famous nineteenth-century Prussian philosopher and military strategist was near the mark when he characterised war as 'the continuation of politics by other means' (Clausewitz 1832: ch. 1, pa. 24). Second, most of the wars in the second half of this century have not been wars between states, but various forms of internal strife, as in Korea and Vietnam, and more recently, former Yugoslavia (particularly Bosnia) and Ethiopia.

Indeed it is one of the most striking features of the second half of the twentieth-century that there have been countless wars – well over 150 major conflicts – ever since the end of the so-called Second World War (1939–45). It is true that there has been no large-scale war involving Europe as a whole or North America since then, which has given a superficial plausibility to the claim that the 'cold war', based on nuclear deterrence, between the NATO countries of the West and the Warsaw Pact countries of central Europe led by the former Soviet Union, 'kept the peace' for more than forty years. Whether nuclear deterrence did play the crucial role claimed for it of preventing war in Europe is a debatable matter. What is rather clearer is that it did not prevent a large number of conflicts in the rest of the world. Perhaps the possession of nuclear weapons actually made it more difficult for the superpowers to get directly involved in regulating conflicts elsewhere, and some would argue that some of the wars in the South were actually 'proxy wars', that is wars fuelled by super-power rivalry.

The United Nations was set up at the end of the Second World War. Its primary purpose was to provide a realistic framework for maintaining international security.[1] Although it has not succeeded in this primary aim, it nevertheless provides a framework of rules and procedures, which, if they were followed by states, would achieve a large measure of genuine peace in the world. Its Charter underscores an important (though disputed) assumption that aggression is wrong, that states are not, save in exceptional circumstances, to go to war at all, and that military action should always be authorised by the UN Security Council in the interests of 'common security'.

II. APPROACHES TO THE ETHICS OF WAR

We can identify three main approaches: realist, middle position ('just war') and pacifism. Whilst the realist position is, not surprisingly, linked to the sceptical realist approaches discussed earlier, and pacifism is (at least in its normal formulation) a form of cosmopolitanism, it would be a mistake to think of the middle position as aligning with the internationalist position as such, which I will explain when I have described the middle position.

A. REALISM (REALPOLITIK)

Turning to the specific ethical issues in war, we should note that realist arguments come from two features (e.g. Wasserstrom 1970a). The lack of moral restraint could be claimed in regard to the reasons for going to war or to the way war is to be fought or both. Clearly the sceptical position discussed in Chapter 2 precisely claims that the decision whether to go to war or not depends on considerations of the national interest. It is thus natural to think of the realist position in international relations theory going hand in hand with realism about war. This would certainly be the case for any realist who denies there is a global morality since, in denying this, he is also claiming that morality does not apply to the way war is fought either, though as I remarked earlier there may be reasons of prudence to abide by some rules. But, as we noted in Chapter 2, a realist position in international relations is consistent with accepting a very modest global ethic applying to face to face relationships between people in different countries which could of course include the face-to-face relationships of soldiers fighting each other. So a realist about foreign policy might accept some moral restraint in regard to the way war is fought by appealing to some principle of humanity.

On the other hand there is a realist view about how wars are fought which is not necessarily based on a general realist position in international relations, but on a view about how war itself undermines morality. There may be a perception that whatever moral rules govern the relations of states in peacetime become suspended in wartime. If for instance obligation is seen as extending as far as there is conventional agreement, community or reciprocity in actions, then if war breaks convention, community or reciprocity, obligation would cease too. Such a position does not depend on sceptical realism. It might accept that foreign policy ought to be guided by moral norms, for instance in deciding whether to go to war or not. But once war has started, as the American general Sherman remarked in the American civil war, 'war is hell'.

Whilst extreme views of these kinds may rarely be held as such, the process of the totalisation of war, the use of weapons of mass destruction, and accepting the possibility of legitimacy in what non-state violent actors might do by way of arbitrary violence makes this approach never far from the thinking of many people.

B. MIDDLE POSITION/JUST WAR TRADITION

On this view, in one form or another held by most thinkers, some waging of war is morally legitimate, whilst some is not. As Grotius put it, there must be a middle way between those who think in warfare everything is permitted and those who think nothing is permitted (Grotius 1925: proleg. pa. 29). This position is usually associated with (though many modern supporters of it would not wish so to identify their position) the 'just war' tradition within catholic moral theology. A large body of international law and norms like the Geneva and Hague conventions has grown up over many years establishing both the rules of war on how war is to be fought, and the circumstances in which it would be legitimate for states to declare war, and these are developments of the just war tradition.

This tradition combines a complex mixture of consequentialist and non-consequentialist elements. It is in any case a tradition or approach, not a single position.[2] Two branches of the just war tradition are usually accepted:

1. *Ius ad bellum*: the rightness/justice (*ius*) of waging war or going to war;
2. *Ius in bello*: the rightness of the manner in which one conducts the war (whom you attack; what weapons are used, and so on).

The following elements of *ius ad bellum* are usually identified:

1. The war must be declared by a legitimate authority: this is usually taken to be an established government of a nation-state.
2. The war must be waged for a 'just cause', such as the right of self-defence in warding off an aggressor or rectifying an injustice.
3. The war must be pursued with a right intention: that is, what one is aiming at is morally acceptable (which may or may not be the same as the just cause).
4. Waging war must be the last resort: all other remedies must have been tried.
5. There must be a reasonable prospect of success in achieving the goal, since otherwise it is a futile gesture involving unnecessary suffering.
6. The principle of proportionality must be observed: that is, the amount of good to be achieved must outweigh the harm that is done in waging the war.
7. The war can be fought according to *ius in bello* principles: that is, the war can be fought by using ways which are not ruled out as immoral in themselves.

Considerable differences in practice will emerge depending on the interpretation of the various clauses. In particular, (1) and (2) can give rise to serious disagreements: for instance, is the established government of a nation-state the only legitimate authority, as Anscombe claims? (Anscombe 1970: 42–6) If not, what other groups are legitimate, like governments in exile such as the African National Congress before 1994, or other groups with political or other causes? Is defence against aggression the only just cause, and conversely is aggression the arch international sin, as the UN Charter Article 2.4 assumes? Or can just causes include violent intervention for the sake of stopping injustices or serious human rights violations? Can a pre-emptive strike be seen as a just cause? Furthermore (5), (6) and (7) raise questions about permissibility in the waging of nuclear war (see below).

What are the issues raised by *ius in bello*? This relates to the manner in which war is waged.[3] The principles of the reasonable prospect of success and proportionality also operate here (with regard to particular operations). Perhaps the most significant element (philosophically) is the limitation on who may be a direct object of attack. It has generally been held that only combatants may be aimed at, and that it is wrong to aim to kill civilians or indeed soldiers once they have surrendered, become disarmed or become prisoners.

This was traditionally based on the principle that it is wrong (absolutely) to kill the innocent. Since the innocent, whether in the sense of 'innocens' ('not harming'), or in the sense of 'morally blameless', are often killed in war, this principle also depends on the doctrine of double effect. This is that we can make a morally significant distinction between what we aim at in our actions ('first effect') – what our goal is and our chosen means to it – and what may or will come about as a result of what we aim at ('second effect') but is not itself aimed at. Saturation bombing of cities in the Second World War clearly violated the traditional doctrine, and the policy was a matter of grave moral misgiving for many at the time, as killing civilians in order to demoralise the enemy was an instrument of policy not a side-effect (Walzer 1974).

Before looking at more modern variants of this middle position, we should note two things. First, in the just war tradition, whilst the principles of *ius in bello* and *ius ad bellum* can and arguably should be combined, there is, for some thinkers, a certain tension between them. If one stresses the justice of the cause of one side (and thus the injustice of the other side) one may be less concerned about the morality of the means to victory. Whereas if one does not believe that there can be objective or at least internationally agreed principles of justice to settle which side has a just cause, one will be, as the internationalists like de Vattel earlier and Oppenheim more recently were, primarily concerned with the limitations of violence via agreed rules of war (see Bull 1966).

Second, there is an issue as to whether the checklist of conditions is meant to be a set of conditions, all of which need to be satisfied for a war to be satisfactory, or whether it is one in which if a sufficient number of them are satisfied, then a war may be justified. This issue is illustrated by the Gulf War of 1991. It was very apparent at the time that the decision to engage in military action in January 1991 to oust Iraq from Kuwait was being publicly justified in just war terms. Clearly Iraq had flouted international law in invading Kuwait, so there was a palpable just cause to rectify an injustice; there was legitimate authority, especially as the action had been endorsed by the UN Security Council; and there was a reasonable prospect of success. On the other hand, others argued that it was not the last resort; that further attempts at negotiation could have been made; and that behind the just cause lay an unacceptable intention to protect American/Western oil interests in the Middle East and to demonstrate American hegemony in the 'new world order' (see e.g. Zolo 1997). If the latter analysis was correct and if all the conditions on the checklist needed to be satisfied, the action was not justified.[4]

There are in fact various ways of marking the ethical difference between combatants and non-combatants.

Various forms of deontology/absolutism: by this I mean forms of argument which try to draw a principled distinction between two categories of person, such that it would be wrong inherently to attack people in one category, but permissible or even obligatory to attack people in the other category. Apart from the traditional account above, several attempts have been made to get round difficulties with defining innocence and combatancy and with the doctrine of double effect. These include Fullinwider's account of the right of self-defence which cannot include civilians who are not attacking one, even if in all sorts of indirect ways they are supporting the other side; and Nagel's account of the special relationship of hostility between those who recognise one another as agents fighting each other.[5]

Consequentialism: the alternative is to find some basis for the distinction either in considerations of general utility, or in considerations of prudence and mutual interests. The utilitarian justification is that the general good is promoted if there is strict adherence to certain rules: rules concerning not attacking civilians, disarmed soldiers, not using particularly nasty weapons like anti-personnel mines, and so on. Richard Brandt and Richard Hare have argued this case (Hare 1974; Brandt 1974). Three things are worth noting about utilitarian justification. First, it is the interests of all those affected which have to be taken into account – enemy soldiers, enemy civilians as well as soldiers and civilians in one's own country – and we should add, in principle people in other countries, future generations, and so on if these are affected. (See discussion later of nuclear weapons.) Second, utilitarian thinking cannot rule out situations in which exceptions to these rules would be justified. Third, it can be argued, as indeed Hare himself argues in another paper, that utilitarian thinking, properly thought through, actually rules out going to war in almost all cases and would, if generally adopted, lead to peace (see Section VI).

If the reasons for limiting the way war is fought are based on prudence and mutual interests, then at best the rules of war are based on conventional agreement, since there would be no motive for limiting one's behaviour unless the other side did so, and this would not happen unless there was some kind of understanding or agreement. So it is simply convention for mutual benefit that limits warfare. Would such a way of understanding limitations on warfare constitute moral restraint rather than merely prudence or enlightened self-interest? This touches on more general issues in ethics as to whether the kind of account of morality given by convention-theorists such as Hume, really counts as a proper morality? (Hume 1888: bk III, pt III) The issue partly turns on whether once the conventions are up and running, the obligation to observe them overrides the pursuit of interests when they clash. If, in the case of the rules of war, the view is that they do override considerations of interest, or do so if the general interests of all are served, as a utilitarian might argue, then it can count as an ethical constraint based on convention. If the view is taken (Mavrodes 1985), that once the other side has abandoned a restraint, one no longer has any obligation to stick to it, then one might see this as verging on the non-moral. Indeed it is very similar to the line taken by realists, that there are really no moral restraints, though prudence may dictate certain limitations, so long as the other side does the same. An example of the issue here was the commencement of saturation bombing in the Second World War, since this policy did break the traditional ban on directly targeting civilian populations.

It will now I hope be apparent that there are many bases for grounding the claim that there are moral restraints in warfare, both in regard to decisions about going to war and in decisions about how to fight a war.

C. PACIFISM

I identify pacifism as the position that all waging of war or resorting to violence is morally wrong. As such it is a universalised prescription, since the judgement 'it is wrong to kill any human being' is applied to all people. In this form it has radical, not to say subversive, implications for international relations, since it challenges directly the legitimacy of the international order, as the rights of sovereignty include the right to use force. There are two forms in which this universal prescription can be justified. First, in absolutist terms, the claim is that it is simply inherently wrong to kill any human being, innocent or otherwise. It is like the traditional just war position banning the intentional killing of the innocent, since both are absolutist principles; it is unlike it in extending the ban to all human beings (and many pacifists extend this to other higher animals). Often there is a religious understanding informing the position. Second, there is a form of pacifism sometimes called 'contingent pacifism', contingent because it is dependent upon the empirical fact (or claim) that the way of non-violence always in the long run serves human well-being better than the way of violence, since violence begets violence, and so on. Henry Ballou, a famous nineteenth-century pacifist, strikingly remarked on how much suffering violence has caused (quoted in Wasserstrom 1970a: 91–2). On the whole pacifists combine the two lines of thought.[6] If one was an absolute pacifist who did not believe that overall human well-being would be served by it, one would be in a very pessimistic position.

It is worth remarking that pacifism need not be presented in this light. A pacifist might see his pacifism as a personal commitment or calling, without thereby universalising his position (Ihara 1978). Although some might argue that this position is incoherent, on the grounds that it cannot be wrong for him to fight if it is not wrong for others to fight, it seems to be possible to formulate a coherent position in which certain people can make commitments to ways of life which are not realistically possible for all, but point in the direction of what may be possible in the future, and thus have a role and importance in so doing. This view is less striking in its implications for international relations, since it does not rule out some uses of force by others. Even if such a pacifist does not universalise his position, he does not think that what is right for others depends simply on what they think is right. He will condemn hawkish militaristic attitudes and behaviour, and generally advocate 'the way of peace'.

Two standard difficulties with universal pacifism are often raised. The claim that it is incoherent has been advanced by Narveson, who argues that pacifism is based on the right not to be attacked, but the condition necessary to realise that right is that one defend it by all necessary means which includes the use of force (Narveson 1970). On the face of it the pacifist can reply that his is a duty-based theory rather than a rights-based theory, that is, we simply have a duty not to kill others. Even if however he accepted the premise that we had a right not be attacked, it does not follow from this right, any more than from any other right, that one has the right to absolutely anything in order to defend what one has a right to. No doubt most people do think that the right to life includes the right to defend oneself with, if necessary, killing force when attacked, but it does not follows as a mater of logic that such a right is contained in the right to life.

Second, the claim that it has counterintuitive implications has been advanced by Glover in a generally useful survey of ethics of war issues (Glover 1977: ch. 19). First it depends upon an extreme and unacceptable division between acts and omissions. If it is wrong for me to kill someone, it is surely wrong for me to let someone die whom I could prevent from dying. The pacifist has either to claim that he is only responsible for what he does rather than what he lets happen, or he cannot maintain the absoluteness of his position, since there may be circumstances in which he ought to kill in order that more may be saved.[7] It is not clear how telling an objection this is, since the essential spirit of the position could be preserved if one simply said that one should always do what least undermined human life. Second, Glover argues that there is an unacceptable trade-off between the value of life as such versus that of liberty, justice and so on. Is not the preservation or regaining of liberty worth sometimes fighting for, even if in the process some lives are lost? This exposes the weakness of the 'non-violence pays in the long run' argument, because, even if that is true, it may be that here and now people's rights are violated, rights which could have been protected if a fight had been put up. However, if someone is killed, his or her right to liberty and other values has gone, so there is also a here and now loss in respect of the same things. Further doubts are raised about the simplicity of these trade-off situations, especially if one accepts that actions (killing) do generally carry more negative moral weight than omissions (letting others take away liberty) and so on.

Whether or not pacifism can be defended as a universal prescription, it can be argued that its value in the modern world lies elsewhere. Pacifism nowadays seems more concerned with a certain perception of the dynamics of human nature, by examining the ways of peace, the roots of personal and social violence and the remediable causes of war and conflict, and provides a powerful motivation for pursuing the way of peace which may be called pacificism. Pacificism may of course be pursued by many who do not call themselves pacifists as well (see Ceadel 1987: ch. 6). As a contribution to the ethics of international relations it has to be developed into more than a statement about the wrongness of the actions of individuals, since there have to be answers here and now for what nation-states should do. So a whole theory of peace – how to promote, make and keep it – is required.

III. THE THREE APPROACHES TO INTERNATIONAL RELATIONS

I now turn to the three main approaches to the ethics of international relations and the related views on the position of individuals. In many ways the positions are most clearly defined in this area, because it is in the area of war and peace that the issues which shaped thinking about international relations were prominent.[5]

A. SCEPTICAL REALISM

On the Hobbesian analysis, discussed earlier, war is the primary reality, and peace is seen as an interlude between wars. Since there are no moral norms regulating the external behaviour of states, what they do in relation to other states is to be determined by calculations of national interest. If declaring war or threatening to do so will advance national interests, then that should be done. Such rules as exist in international relations (and reflected in international law) are essentially rules of prudence, to be abandoned when it suits the state to do so. On this view there are no moral restraints in war and in principle 'anything goes', though in practice there may be some restraint for prudential reasons. The maintenance of military forces is an essential part of foreign policy. If a country has the capacity to develop nuclear weapons, then there is nothing wrong is so doing, and if it can thereby exercise a hegemony or dominance in international affairs, then it should do so.

As noted in the previous section, if the realist denies a global ethic altogether, then, in the absence of any wider sphere of ethical allegiance, the individual has duties of allegiance to his or her state, and if someone is called on to fight in an army for his country, then he should do so, and observe or flout conventions of war as he is commanded in his country's interests. That is, although as a human being he may feel some very basic compunction about causing unnecessary suffering to other human beings (whether or not they live in his society), the main reason for any limitations of what he does or whom he fights, has to do with the advantages his country gets from such restraint. If that advantage no longer exists, military necessity dictates what should be done.

B. INTERNATIONALIST/COMMUNITARIAN PERSPECTIVE

In this approach the pursuit of peace is seen as a key goal of the international society of states, and this is partly to preserve itself as an international order. The rules of war limit violence in the world, and the conditions under which war is legitimate, like having a just cause, put limits on going to war. Violence is limited in two ways, both because states themselves are to abide by the rules agreed, and because no other bodies have the moral right to use violence at all. In the modern world, where some countries have nuclear weapons, deterrence is seen as a crucial ingredient in the picture, because the balance of power and the mutually assured destruction involved are vital means towards maintaining such peace as is realistically possible. Thus on this view deterrence is not merely based on prudence but an ethical argument that the most effective way of preserving the peace must be pursued. More generally the rules of war are grounded in convention, both general agreements hallowed by custom and tradition and specific agreements like the Geneva and Hague conventions. But in saying that they are conventions, they are still seen as genuinely ethical conventions, which require states to comply with them even if it is not in their interests to do so. Clearly from an internationalist point of view, the society of states is grounded in the right to sovereignty and the legitimacy of states using military force both to defend themselves and to defend the society of states itself when challenged by acts which threatened international security. The UN, insofar as it is based on statist assumptions, assumes the legitimacy of actions to preserve the sovereignty of member states and common security. The rules of war are seen as validated because they have come to be agreed and accepted, formally or informally, by members of the society of states. The general position here is fairly clear, whatever account one gives of the basis for the morality of states.

The internationalist position generally goes hand in hand with a communitarian conception of the nature and scope of the obligations of individuals, or at least a form of global ethic that falls short of full cosmopolitanism, in which one has duties based on common humanity, in face-to-face relationships. If they were, then the internationalist defence of the 'morality of states' status quo would not stand. Thus on this view, individuals have duties of allegiance within the framework of the rules of war as agreed. Individuals would be bound by the rules of war, because these are agreed, but unlike the realist position above, they would act wrongly in breaking these rules, and their government or superiors in a chain of command would be wrong to order them to do so, even if it was in the interests of their country, or the other side had failed to observe them. Furthermore, as subjects or citizens they would not be in a position to criticise their government's decision to go to war on grounds of global injustice, only on the grounds that their state was clearly in breach of the agreed international norms governing war, or it was acting imprudently or contrary to the values of his society.

C. COSMOPOLITANISM

According to the cosmopolitan there is a common moral framework through which to assess issues to do with war and peace. The pursuit of war and peace is to be determined by the deeper question concerning the well-being of humankind generally. Rules of warfare are humanitarian in the deepest sense of being grounded directly in fundamental moral laws of human transactions, not merely on conventions. The individual as a world citizen is not just answerable to his own state and may have reason to criticise his country's decisions concerning war and peace and take a stance against the state, arguing for instance that its action was wrong even if it was in its interests. Pacifism is a striking example of this kind of position but there are many others.

The cosmopolitan approach, broadly stated, does not lead to any particular agreed positions on the rules of war, deterrence, intervention or terrorism. Unlike scepticism, which denies the relevance of ethics and the internationalist position which takes its lead from the established conventions, cosmopolitanism brings an independent moral yardstick to the matter in hand. But what that yardstick is depends upon the particular theory, and there are, as we have seen earlier, quite a variety of positions, differing either in the basic values asserted or in the applications of these values to the real world, given the thinker's reading of these realities, or both. Below I consider the three kinds of cosmopolitan thinking identified earlier. The first two do not in practice lead to practical views all that different from the views already considered, but the third one is more genuinely different and challenging. However it should be noted that cosmopolitans generally accept the rules of war approach, though their reasoning may be different from that of an internationalist. Even the pacifist cosmopolitan might accept that the rules of war are preferable to no rules at all.

Cosmopolitans other than pacifists will also support generally the middle position, but depending on their values and reading of what is realistic in the world, will give different emphases and interpretations, on what a just cause would be, on what rules really are for the good of all, and so on. The point is that the rules and norms accepted by states are, in principle, subject to criticism. The concern for the rules of war relates directly to the relationships between human beings involved in war, rather than being mediated by what happens to be agreed amongst states. In a parallel way, some cosmopolitans, not necessarily pacifists, might argue that there ought to be a right to conscientious refusal to engage in military service – an issue much argued over in the Human Rights Commission in Geneva for many years – even though most states do not recognise this, nor are there (yet) international agreements about this.

What is characteristic though of many cosmopolitans, particularly those whom I have called 'solidarist–pluralist' is a certain conception of the world in which the impulse towards peace is dominant, and there is a tendency to say that though organised violence may sometimes be justified, in practice such occasions are rare. This is linked to a certain way of looking at peace itself, which I return to later in the chapter.

Idealist: if one's cosmopolitanism is based on a religious or political ideal which it is important to promote amongst those who do not share it, the pursuit of it will lead to conflict, including war. Consider in the past the holy wars or the conquistadors in South America, or more recently East–West conflicts in the cold war era. So on this view, peace is not the overriding goal of international relations, but the framework within which generally the ideal can be best promoted, but sometimes is not. Hence such cosmopolitanism is seen as 'revolutionary'. Such a thinker will have a clear idea about the justice of one's cause (and the wrongness of the other side) which may justify going to war or risking it and which may also lead to less interest in the importance of the rules of war than many internationalists have, because 'the end justifies the means'.

Another link which this form of cosmopolitanism has, perhaps surprisingly at first sight, is with terrorism, if the latter is driven by ideals and disregard for rules. If one combines the assertion that people are citizens of the world, and therefore their loyalty to a particular political order is not ultimate but conditional, with what is distinctive of this particular form of cosmopolitanism, the commitment to a moral, religious or political ideal and the need to promote it amongst those who do not accept it by whatever means, then quite generally individuals may feel called upon to act in unlawful and even unpeaceful ways for the sake of their goals. Taken to extremes this may provide the basis for someone to be committed to terrorism. As Fullinwider remarks, terrorism motivated by a call to change the political order is not inspired by a lack of moral commitment but rather a refusal, following Locke's analysis, to hand over 'the executive right of nature' to the civil authorities, as the rest of us in effect do, and to adopt any means including the indiscriminate killing of the innocent (Fullinwider 1988). (See also discussion of terrorism in section V.)

Libertarian: this position basically supports the 'live and let live' philosophy which underlies the morality of states approach. The rules governing the waging of war are grounded in a deeper theory than convention or what is necessary to preserve the society of states. That is, given the twin values of order and liberty, these should apply to states as well as to individuals, because the order and liberty of states conduces to these values for individuals. So the rules governing war are to be strictly adhered to since peace and order are central values. Even if there may be objectively 'right or wrong', generally speaking there cannot be agreement about this, so accommodation is generally to be preferred. Only very exceptionally would intervention be justified.

Solidarist: the middle position, which I have argued for, is held in tension between the importance of peace, accommodation and non-prose-lytising on the one hand, and the importance of actively pursuing the goals of human flourishing, basic human rights, environmental care, and so on.

What is distinctive of this position is the importance of both means and ends. First, the means generally to be preferred are the ways of peace, accommodation, dialogue and negotiation, both because this process, whether between individuals or between states, is intrinsically to be preferred, and because many of the differences of values in different societies are to be accepted, so the attempt to try and convert others to one's values and thus risking conflict and even war, is not justified. Second, what is important to this view is an active commitment to pursuing those values which are generally shared in all societies but which, for one reason or another, like lack of resources and knowledge, disasters, or human injustice and mismanagement, are not realised.

In claiming that this active commitment is feasible and combinable with the way of peace as the general rule, the position offers a genuine alternative both to a passive acceptance of the way the world is for the sake of peace and order, but also to an aggressive and unpeaceful promotion of particular ideals. The position does not as such rule out the resort to war, as humanitarian intervention for the sake of human rights might be justified, but it would be very much a last resort. On the other hand a pacifist could accept this position, apart from simply ruling out war as an immoral means, whilst being vigorously committed to change in other ways. He is not as such a 'passivist', though a pacifist who adopted the 'minimalist' position above might be.

Characteristic of the cosmopolitan position will be a generally radical appraisal of the international situation. Peace needs to be defined in a richer way in order to incorporate other values such as justice (see Section VI). The role of responsible world citizenship to promote these goals will need to be stressed. Certainly there will be no overriding loyalty to the state, or resting content with *de facto* social identities and commitments. There will also be a distinct challenge to much conventional wisdom on defence, especially nuclear weapons.

I will now illustrate some of the tensions indicated above with some of the more detailed issues which arise in connection with war and peace.

IV. NUCLEAR WAR AND DETERRENCE

Although since the end of the cold war (1989) the threat of a nuclear war between the two superpowers, the USA and the then USSR, has gone, the dangers and problems remain. The nuclear powers still have large stockpiles of these weapons of mass destruction, and although Russia is no longer regarded as the enemy, its uneasy relations with the expanding NATO needs to be noted with caution. In any case, with the increasing power of China, and proliferation of nuclear weapons to more countries, the general problems remain. It is still worth analysing the ethical aspects of the long-standing nuclear deterrence scenario, partly for the light it sheds on the way we think of international relations. One of the central issues of philosophical interest arises for those who believe that the actual use of nuclear weapons, either offensively or in response/retaliation to nuclear attack, would be wrong, is whether it is nevertheless morally acceptable (or even obligatory) to rely on a policy of nuclear deterrence, that is threatening to use them under certain conditions.

A. USE OF NUCLEAR WEAPONS

It would generally be accepted, even by a hard-nosed realist, that, with the possible exception of the limited use of battlefield weapons (where it is assumed, no doubt naively, that such use would not escalate to full-scale use), the use of nuclear weapons, whether as counter-value weapons against cities or as counter-force weapons against enemy weapons centres, would have devastating consequences from blast, fire, radiation and nuclear winter effects on millions of people who may include: civilians in countries involved; people in countries not parties to the dispute; future generations; and the biosphere as a whole.

What follows from these facts from an ethical point of view? A realist might claim that what happens to countries other than his own is not his concern. On the other hand even he would need to take seriously the argument that it would be imprudent or even simply irrational for a country to launch a nuclear attack or to retaliate if already attacked, considering the effects on its own population, present and also future. But for most thinkers who adopted the middle position discussed earlier, it would be very difficult to justify actually using such weapons on moral grounds. In traditional terms the principle of proportionality would be completely violated, as well as, in the case of the bombing of civilian centres, offending the traditional ban on killing the innocent (see Kenny 1985; Lackey 1974). Generally consequentialist thinking would also lead one to suppose that no overall good for all affected everywhere could be achieved, either from the point of view of a potential attacker or a retaliator.

Arguments against the permissibility of using nuclear weapons could come either from an internationalist perspective or from a cosmopolitan perspective. In terms of the rules of war agreed internationally, the use of nuclear weapons is ruled out, if not by the implications of humanitarian law and of restrictions on other 'weapons of mass destruction', then arguably by the 1996 judgement of the World Court.[8] Interestingly the internationalist can make much of the point since the rights of other nations would be undermined by the collateral damage almost certainly caused for them. Any cosmopolitan argument will at least stress the unacceptability of causing extensive harm for no comparable gain, especially to third parties, that is, to people in countries outside the conflict and into the future.

B. DETERRENCE

This depends upon one's having a nuclear weapons system capable of causing unacceptably high damage to the side that might attack. There are two elements essential to this system's actually deterring:

1. A retaliatory strike can be delivered: namely the other side cannot either wipe out one's entire weapons system in its first strike or adequately defend itself from incoming missiles with ABMs (anti-ballistic missiles) or 'star wars' technology. This was why ABMs were banned by treaty because they could undermine deterrence, and why the development of the star wars programme (Strategic Defence Initiative) in the 1980s, which did not come to fruition at that time,

partly because of inordinate expense, proved immensely dangerous for international relations in a period of cold war tension.

2. There is a reasonably high probability, as perceived by the other side, that the weapons will actually be used if there is an attack. This requires a perception that there is a weapons system which is operational and capable of being activated and at least a willingness on the part of those responsible to activate it. For this perception in the other side to exist, there would have to be either a firm intention to use it if attacked (the most likely situation), or a willingness to use it (with no intention not to use it) or an extraordinary feat of sustained bluffing.

The defence system is therefore meant to work on the basis of MAD (mutually assured destruction). Interesting questions arise over (2). What makes it the case that it is probable that the weapons would be used in response to attack? If it is taken that it would be either irrational or immoral or both actually to use them, what is the likelihood that they will be used? The other side would have to believe that one will (or might well) do what is immoral and/or irrational. That is not impossible since people do both. Deterrence 'works' precisely because each side fears that the other might very well do what is wrong/irrational.

It can be argued on both deontological and utilitarian grounds that deterrence is ethically unacceptable. One of the ethical questions arises over the structure of the threat itself. Can it be right (or rational) to threaten to do what it would be immoral (irrational) actually to do? That is, if doing x (under certain conditions) is wrong, is intending to do x (under the same conditions) wrong? Does then the conditional intention carry the moral attributes which the action intended carries?

A deontologist (someone who believes that certain kinds of action are in themselves right or wrong) is likely to assert that it does. After all, as Kant argues, it is the will involved in an action which carries the moral value, and the same will is already involved in the prior intention or plan to do it. Does the deontologist then have to conclude that the threat to use nuclear weapons is inherently immoral because of this connection between intention and action? Many, especially catholic thinkers invoking the just war theory, have so concluded and become in effect what is called 'nuclear pacifists' (Stein 1961).

There is however a way of looking at the situation which may allow even a deontologist to accept nuclear weapons. Does the fact that the conditional intention is subordinate to a higher intention, namely to prevent the condition occurring in which the conditional intention would be carried out, make a moral difference? This of course requires that the conditional intention be publicly declared and embodied, as it were, in a publicly functioning system. This is precisely what is the case with nuclear deterrence. Hockaday for instance argues that the *prima facie* wrongness of intending to do what it would be actually wrong to do may be outweighed by other duties to preserve peace or other values (Hockaday 1992). However, this move, whilst possible, seems unacceptable, if one notes that such peace is inherently unstable with the risk of massive destruction and that the other values are not necessarily worth that risk.[9]

A consequentialist on the other hand is more interested in the actual or reasonably foreseeable consequences of acts, and so although there is obviously an important connection between intention and responsibility, the consequences of the act are to some extent separable from the consequences of having an intention or plan at an earlier time. Thus a consequentialist can recognise that intentions, particularly publicly embodied ones (stated and prepared for) such as the nuclear weapons stance, have their own sets of consequences and may therefore be evaluated differently from the acts intended. Although the consequentialist is able to evaluate the deterrence stance independently from the use of nuclear weapons, it does not follow that he will then justify nuclear deterrence. It will depend on a calculation of the likely consequences of different strategies. Thus a quite different way of handling the ethics of deterrence is to do a utilitarian calculation comparing deterrence with unilateral disarmament. Lackey argues reasonably that a good utilitarian would opt for unilateral disarmament, and that on the whole even prudential reasoning, for instance merely looking at American interests, goes the same way. His article works on complex empirical estimates of probabilities, which can of course be disputed.[10] The different positions discussed – deontological and consequentialist – are of course different approaches to global ethics or cosmopolitan thinking. Cosmopolitanism itself does not provide any particular answer. Realists are likely only to be interested in the prudential arguments just mentioned. An advocate of the morality of states approach is likely to agree with the cosmopolitan analysis of the issues if she thinks the morality of states is grounded in a global ethic. But if she thinks it is based on convention, then the question becomes: what conventions are to be accepted – the right of states to defend themselves in principle with such unacceptable threats or the right of states not to be so threatened?

V. TERRORISM AND THE SECURITY AGENDA

Terrorism has been a significant feature of international relations for a very long time (Wilkinson 1986). What it has gained is a certain prominence since the '9/11' 2001. The response to the attack on the twin towers and the Pentagon was first the bombing of Afghanistan which toppled the

Taliban regime that was linked to the terrorist network called al-Qaida. Since then it has been an American-led 'war on terror' and the pursuit of a certain 'security agenda'. Although rather curiously one of the 'justifications' given for the invasion of Iraq in 2003 was the supposed link between terrorism and Saddam Hussein's regime, generally this war is not a war in a conventional sense. Whilst there have been some skirmishes where terrorist cells have been located, hundreds of people had been detained without trial in Guantanamo Bay, and intelligence operations have intensified to locate terrorist cells before they strike again, there is no war as such. What there is is the demonisation of an enemy. Whilst there is indeed something quite terrible about the means taken by terrorists, and whilst historically terrorists have come from many different religious backgrounds or none, the general consequence in the current global context has been that, given that the terrorists are Muslims, there has been a polarisation between the secular West and Islam – even though the vast majority of Muslims are deeply disturbed by terrorism too.

The topic is vast and I shall restrict myself to two related points, the first about terrorism and the second about security. If one asks what is wrong with terrorism, the two most plausible factors may be the means taken – arbitrary violence against ordinary citizens – and their proximate goals – the inducing of terror in populations. As such, terrorism can be engaged in by states ('state terrorism') and, although it is not usually called this, saturation bombing against civilians in a conventional war between states in order to induce terror fits the model as well. I say 'proximate goals' in order to distinguish this from the ultimate or at least higher-level goals. These may include the liberation of a country (e.g. from apartheid or military occupation); advancing the cause of animals or the natural world (eco-terrorism); fighting Western materialist values or hegemony; fighting against the Western presence in the Arabic states such as Saudi Arabia; or responding to gross inequality in the world. Freedom fighting is not an alternative to terrorism: freedom is one of the things a terrorist may fight for by causing terror (Graham 1996).

If the last three goals – fighting materialism, fighting Western hegemony, protesting against global inequality – are amongst the goals of current Islamic terrorists – and these are the goals which are commonly mentioned – we have to ask two questions about these goals. Is it the goals we object to or merely the ways they are pursued? Even if we do not accept the goals, would it be prudent nevertheless to adjust what we do in order to address the root causes of terrorism?

The idea that we can stop terrorism simply by trying to stop people from doing what they are motivated to do is arguably unrealistic. Maybe it is necessary, but it is certainly not sufficient. If we want to reduce the likelihood of people becoming terrorists, we do need I think to question Western dominance, tackle gross inequality and extreme poverty which give terrorists a certain credibility for many, and generally build better inter-faith/inter-cultural relations. As things are, we continue to assert Western dominance, fail to tackle gross global inequality and actually make things worse in global relations.

If then the war on terror is arguably counter-productive, that is one reason to change it. But even if it were effective, it would rest on a one-sided understanding of security which, I argue, is unacceptable. It is widely recognised that security is not merely about freedom from attack on an individual or a state, it is about being secure in one's environment, health, or economic situation as well. These are all dimensions of what is called human security (UNDP 1994; see also Atack 2005 Chapter 8). Furthermore, if we recognise that from a cosmopolitan perspective, the security interests of most people in adequate conditions of health, economic well being and environmental safety are far more important than the narrow security interest underlying the current security agenda, then very different priorities in foreign policy would be taken. What this reveals is that the response to terrorism by Western countries is still dominated by internationalist if not realist premises (see Dower 2002a; see also Honderich 2003).

VI. PEACE

So far in this chapter I have been looking at the general positions which can be taken over war and peace and at the various justifications for going to war. But before we conclude this chapter we need to look more carefully at the idea of peace and ask the question: are we collectively doing the right things, and all the right things, to promote peace? I take it for reasons which will become apparent that peace is a positive value and war is a negative value. It is worth noting however that this is not an uncontentious claim. Certainly there have been warrior tribes in the past where fighting with other groups was a positive part of life. In any country with armed forces, the life of military persons may well be seen as good, all the more so when in action. A country may get a positive sense of its own worth if it engaged in successful military action.

Nevertheless there is a sense in which peace is necessarily the preferred state in most normal situations. Just as Plato remarked that even in a gang of thieves there must be honour, basic rules and trust amongst themselves internally, whatever they do to others, so a basically peaceful framework in a social group is a prerequisite to people being able to function and achieve well-being within that group. We have seen earlier how Hobbes saw peace as something the law of nature requires us to seek where possible, for without it life would be solitary, nasty, brutish and short. Augustine, noted that we wage war in order to get peace, but we do not seek peace in order to wage war (Augustine 1947: bk XIX, ch. 12). However, he also noted that, because the kind of peace generally achieved in the 'earthly city' was, unlike the eternal peace in the 'city of God', dependent on one group dominating another, the tendency for war and conflict to break out again was endemic (Augustine 1947: bk XI, ch. 4).

This last point leads to a crucial problem about the idea of peace: peace may not be a truly satisfactory condition to be in, if one group, for instance, maybe the loser in a conflict, is oppressed or unjustly treated. It is common to distinguish between two conceptions of peace, the positive and the negative. The negative conception is that of peace being the absence of war. The positive conception, as for instance advanced by Macquarrie and Curle, involves a set of relations characterised by harmony, wholeness and lack of fracture (Macquarrie 1993), or positively peaceful relationships and a sense of justice involved (Curle 1981).

Whilst both conceptions are available to any thinker, pessimistic or optimistic about the human condition, realist or cosmopolitan, the question arises as to which conception is of practical importance. The sober realist who is not very optimistic about the human condition, may feel that the negative conception, thin as it is, is what is important to try to achieve. Ideas of peace in the richer sense are at best utopian abstractions, at worst dangerous because they may tempt people to sacrifice such peace as we have now for the sake of an illusory peace with justice in the future. The more optimistic thinker may feel that the richer conception is important because in many cases it is realisable, or at least something we can move towards, and that to settle for peace as merely the absence of war or overt conflict is to ignore the perspective of those who may not benefit from such peace as much as they ought, and in any case is to settle for something somewhat unstable and unsustainable into the future.

In fact it may be more helpful to distinguish not merely two conceptions but a range of positions. At the one end there is the idea of peace as a relationship between different people or groups of people over a period of time in which there is an absence of war or overt conflict. Such a period of time may be characterised by fear of possible attacks, military threats, preparations for future conflicts, as with rearmament in Europe in the 1930s. Compared with a period of war, it has many advantages which are real and important, because of basic social order, people not being killed, property not being destroyed and so on.

Then we have a conception of peace in a stronger sense as a period of time in which there is neither war nor the threat of war, perceived or actual. This was actually Hobbes' conception. It would have many advantages over the thinner conception of peace for international relations if it could be achieved, which Hobbes doubted. One advantage is arguably that if there is no threat of war or conflict there is no need to prepare for war or handling conflict, so more time, energy and resources can go into pursuing other positive goods in society (the 'peace' dividend).

However it might be argued that the way to achieve no real threats from enemies is precisely to have sufficiently strong defences. Here is one of the key litmus tests on the optimist/pessimist divide. If the only way to get security is through having bigger military forces than your neighbour, then we have a necessarily win–lose scenario with all the inherent instability that entails. If on the other hand levels of military security can be achieved which create a positive feedback loop of generally scaled-down defences, we have a potential win–win scenario.

Even if we had a peace in which there was no explicit threat or corresponding preoccupation with military preparations, such a peace might not still be entirely satisfactory, because there might still be injustices or at least perceived injustices, either within societies or between societies. As Curle stresses, such a peace which is consistent with injustice is hardly satisfactory, so we need a conception of peace which incorporates the absence of injustice, the violation of rights or other morally unsatisfactory elements, such as the absence of democratic participation. So long as there are those who are in this position, there may well come a time when if their situation changes or they become more empowered, conflict will emerge. So a peace which lacks justice is problematic, both because it may be currently unsatisfactory in sacrificing other moral values, and because it is unstable.[11]

Finally, as an extension of the last point, a peace which is truly sustainable into the future will be one in which so far as can be avoided the 'seeds of future conflict' are not sown in present polices or practices. This may seem unduly idealistic, but it is in principle a dimension to what a wholehearted commitment to peace involves. Interestingly the eighteenth-century Quaker John Woolman warned that in the desire for possessions the seeds of conflict may be sown, and in the modern world the competition for economic goods, given the stark contrast between North and South, may very well be a case in point.

The value of peace can be reinforced if we link it to security. These are often treated as the same concept but in fact they are distinct concepts with somewhat different logical structures. Peace is a relationship between different people, security is a relationship a person has towards certain things which he values. Generally if people are secure in the things they value, they are more likely to want to be peaceful towards others.

Amongst the various kinds of security we want are physical security, freedom from arbitrary attack on one's person or property, being part of a society which is itself free from attack, economic security, environmental security, health security and so on. Generally the condition of peace is to be preferred as a way of securing the range of goods for now and in the future that people want (Dower 1995; Atack 2005: ch. 8).

What the above discussion suggests is that the promotion of peace is a multifaceted process. Much of the promotion of peace has to do precisely with stopping or preventing overt conflict, but much of it is not. To suppose that the promotion of peace was no more than the stopping or preventing of war, would be rather like supposing that the promotion of health was merely the avoidance of or treatment of illness and injury (Jenkins 1993).

I have talked above about the promotion of peace. Do we have a duty to promote it? It is important, as we noted in Chapter 6, to distinguish between acting peacefully and promoting peace, and to advocate the idea of responsibility for promoting values. Given the immense positive advantages of peace, and duly noting the need to see it in the context of other important values, it seems self-evident that there is some kind of duty to promote peace, at least for anyone committed to some form of cosmopolitanism. Hare argues for instance that if we pay sufficient attention to everyone's interests and avoid the errors of nationalism (putting more value on the interests of one's own nationals) and fanaticism (putting more weight on ideals rather than interests), then there would generally be no case for going to war.[12]

If we take seriously the idea of living in one global society, then the commitment to play one's part in creating the conditions of peace and other values seems to follow naturally. Most people accept that within a society one has some kind of role in helping to maintain peace, so it needs to be shown that if we want international peace, there is parallel duty to work for it. At any level peace does not just happen, it is something which involves active commitment. The recognition of this especially at the global level would make a significant contribution towards creating a more peaceful world. This is one contribution that the development of cosmopolitan thinking can make.

But not all forms of cosmopolitanism will do this equally. As we noted earlier some forms of cosmopolitanism are more conducive to the spread of peace than others. Those that are committed to promoting a particular ideal (religious, political) are less likely to create the conditions of peace than those which are more accommodating of difference. Hans Küng has argued the thesis that there will be 'no peace in the world without peace among the religions; no peace among the religions without dialogue among the religions' (Küng 1992: cover & passim). His argument is that we need to accept an attitude of tolerance and welcome diverse forms of religious faith, whilst being committed to our own faith communities, since peace and other basic human values are common values to all cultures. We need to acknowledge our shared 'global ethic' and not worry too much about the diverse sources and theologies from which they derive. Peace therefore is not just something we all want. It is something which we all have reason to work for. This and other common values are far more important to share than other things we do not share but which we may be tempted to promote at the risk of conflict.

NOTES

1. For fuller discussion of the UN, see Chapter 10.
2. For accounts of the just war conditions see, for example, Smith 1961, or Graham 1996: ch. 3.
3. If there is no legitimate manner in which a particular war can be waged, that would of course rule out the rightness of initiating it also. Perhaps a war reliant on the use of nuclear weapons would be a case in point.
4. Furthermore, it might be argued that the long-distance bombing of Baghdad and the mass destruction of the retreating soldiers on the 'road to Basra' were serious violations of *ius in bello* principles.
5. Nagel 1970. This is a wide-ranging article of interest because of its attack on consequentialism and its general distinction between outcome-centred ethics and agent-centred ethics.
6. See Holmes 1990, for useful survey of positions, including those of Gandhi, Tolstoy and King. See also Quaker Peace Testimony, presented to Charles II in 1660, in Britain Yearly Meeting 1995: para 24.04. These stances are seen as both principled and effective.
7. Cf. Bernard Williams' famous example of Pedro, Jim and the Indians, where Pedro offers Jim a choice between killing one Indian with nineteen going free and watching Pedro's men kill twenty. See Smart and Williams 1973: pp. 98–100.
8. See discussion of the World Court Project in Chapter 6. The key part of the opinion reads: 'The threat or use of nuclear weapons would generally be contrary to the rules of international law applicable in armed conflict … In view of the current state of international law … the court cannot conclude definitely whether the threat or use of nuclear weapons would be lawful or unlawful in an extreme circumstance of self-defence, when the very survival of a state would be at stake.' The advisory opinion is sufficiently unclear on a key point to allow both the World Court Project supporter to claim a substantial victory and at the same time to allow the nuclear powers to argue that it does not affect their nuclear policy at all. The latter interpretation is I believe hardly tenable. It can hardly be argued that the very survival of the UK, or

indeed any other nuclear power, depends on the threat of nuclear weapons. Certainly without nuclear weapons a country's standing in the international scene might change, and not necessarily for the weaker, but that has little to do with the survival of a state. If this point is correct, the unclarity of whether it is lawful or unlawful to have nuclear weapons in such circumstances is irrelevant, since these circumstances do not apply, and therefore the general ruling in the opinion applies, namely the holding of nuclear weapons is contrary to international law.

9. Those troubled by the 'conditional intention' problem have considered such moves as: the threat could be based on bluff, or on the possibility (danger) of response but with no intention either way. Both moves are ethically problematic since either deception is involved, or there is still a present 'willingness that the system may operate'.

10. Lackey 1974 and Kavka 1974. One issue raised here is how to compare alternative policies when there is uncertainty about the outcomes of each.

11. As Penn noted, 'Peace is maintained by justice, which is a fruit of government ...' (Penn 1993: 8).

12. Hare 1972. He sees this as the consequence of utilitarianism but the point has more general validity.

QUESTIONS FOR DISCUSSION

1. Is the distinction between going to war and fighting a war in a certain way of ethical relevance to the realist?

2. If a cosmopolitan supports the rules of war, does he do so for the same reasons as an internationalist?

3. Are the objections of either Narveson or Glover fatal to pacifism?

4. If we are interested in promoting peace, what kind of peace should we be most interested in?

CHAPTER 7

AID, TRADE AND DEVELOPMENT

I. SOME BACKGROUND FACTS

One of the most important dimensions of the present world situation is the great disparity between the wealth and economic prosperity of different nations. Not only is there an immense gap, it has been getting larger in the last fifty years, and has been happening over a period in which the international community has actually set itself the task of reducing the gap between the rich industrialised countries in the 'North', as it is called with little geographical exactitude, and the poorer countries in the 'South'. There has also been in absolute terms an increase in the number of people, mainly but not wholly in the South, who are 'absolutely' poor – living below a level of human decency, in terms of malnutrition, hunger, disease and inadequate shelter. In the 1970s the figure of 800 million was often mentioned, but now estimates tend to be in the region of one billion, a fifth of the world population.

This poverty and inequality exists alongside an ever expanding global economy. More and more people are drawn into a vast global market in which goods made or produced in one part of the world are through a chain of transactions used or consumed in other parts of the world. Increasingly, through investments by other countries or companies based elsewhere, people are employed by organisations which are primarily based in other countries. The so-called multinationals and transnational companies like Nestlé or Ford play a very large part in this process. Their operations are so large that they dwarf the economies of some very poor countries.

Increasingly loans have been made, by governments or private banks or by the international institutions like the International Monetary Fund or World Bank, to governments, particularly of poorer countries, to stimulate economic development, to facilitate developed countries' exports or to bail countries out because of serious debt problems which were incurred earlier. One of the most pervasive features of the global scene in the last thirty years has been the crippling effect of the 'debt crisis'. Overall it is estimated that the amount that governments are paying in debt servicing is more than what such countries overall receive in official aid. This debt servicing combined with austerity measures cutting public services and food subsidies, often imposed by the IMF as conditionalities for financial support, has contributed to greater poverty in many countries.

On the other hand ever since the Second World War the international community has seen itself as committed to helping poorer countries, referred to by Truman in a famous inaugural speech in 1949 as the 'underdeveloped regions of the world', to achieve development and catch up with the (relatively) developed North (Sachs 1992: 2). Many public documents assent to the need for countries to co-operate in this, not only for richer countries to provide development assistance, but also to organise international trade and investment so as to provide development in poor countries. In 1970 the rich countries committed themselves in the UN to providing 0.7 per cent of GNP in official assistance to poorer countries, a figure that has generally not been reached ever since. Later in that decade there was in the UN a declaration on a New International Economic Order (NIEO), which included a call for a radical redistribution of resources from North to South. Although the idea was endorsed in 1980 in an influential report called *The Brandt Report* or *North South – A Strategy for Survival*, which tried to persuade rich countries to support development by stressing the 'mutuality of interests' argument, the ideas in the NIEO were largely swept aside by the harsh economic climate of the 1980s with the return to a more robust philosophy of the unregulated free market (WCD 1980).

Despite these trends the middle of the 1980s saw two significant documents, one the *Declaration on the Right to Development* (UN 1986) and the other the *Brundtland Report* called *Our Common Future* (WCED 1987). The former is not well known, but it is significant because it attempts to spell out a framework of global obligations in which, for instance, richer countries have an obligation to help poorer countries realise their right to development. Whether this will result eventually in legally binding covenants laying down such obligations is another matter, especially since the rich countries were not really in favour of the declaration anyway. The latter, *Our Common Future*, was by contrast an immensely well publicised document spelling out a range of measures intended to integrate environmental and development concerns into a coherent strategy for sustainable development. The report recommended an international conference five years later in 1992 and this took place in Rio, the so-called Earth Summit. Since then there had been a number of further conferences, and significantly the declaration of the millennium development goals or MDGs (UN 2000), which indicated eight general goals for combating poverty and various aspect of it.

There is no doubt that if one surveys these factors and notes what countries do and say, moral language plays a significant part in it. The question we need now to ask is: what interpretation should we put on what is done and said about international aid, economic co-operation and development? As in other chapters I propose first to look at what each of the three traditions has to say on the issues, before focusing on one or two more specific issues.

II. REALIST/RELATIVIST APPROACH

It may be thought that in this area the realist position which denies a global ethical framework is not a real position. This however is not so. Aid and co-operation are both things which can be engaged in for a variety of motives, and all the realist has to do is claim, plausibly enough at least for many cases, that the motive for aid and co-operation is national self-interest, and furthermore dismiss the moral language used by government officials in international documents as either a smokescreen and vehicle for the more effective promotion of interests, or based on an illusion. It must be noted that the sceptic as well as the cosmopolitan is perfectly entitled to say of the internationalist values which may actually be accepted and acted on by a group of actors, that the belief in these values is based on a false set of assumptions. In the realist case these would be false assumptions about the possibility of global morality; in the cosmopolitan's case about what the nature of the values is.

Aid is to be seen as an expression of the interests of the donor country and/or the views of the electorate. If sufficient of the electorate want aid to be given to help the poor or think the country ought to do so, then this is part of the 'moral interest' to be pursued by the government, but the duty to give aid is a function of what the electorate want and/or thinks ought to be done. There is no external yardstick according to which a government ought to do this for the sake of the poor elsewhere.

Similarly, when we turn to trade, loans and investment, the picture is the same. These things are engaged in by governments because they contribute to the national economic interest. A parallel analysis can be given of the operation of private companies across borders. It is well recognised that multinational companies like any other businesses are driven by the profit-motive, and it is often held that this is morally acceptable. These interests and the values internal to the operation of such companies are of course transnational in character, but that does not make them global in the relevant sense denied by the realist. On the realist analysis countries clearly co-operate with one another through international institutions and at international gatherings, but this is only evidence of prudential commitment not moral commitment, and if circumstances change such that the national interest is better served in some other way, such support would cease.

On this view not only is development seen as part of the national interest, it is also as such usually construed as economic growth, partly because there is a natural tendency for those in power to want greater power within their own country, and partly because that is what most people want. The right to development will, if that language is allowed at all, be given a different interpretation from that assumed in the *Declaration on the Right to Development* (UN 1986) where the idea of the right to development is meant to entail a correlative duty on the part of other states to support it. A realist will prefer to interpret it as a right without correlative obligation, parallel to the Hobbesian idea of the 'right of nature' as a right to all things but without any duties of restraint either by others or towards others. If one country's development comes into competition with another, then on this view the first country would have no reason to restrict its pursuit of development, even if the development needs of the other country are greater.

If, parallel to the realist view of international relations, a relativist view is also held about the nature and scope of an individual's obligations, then he will have no reason to accept or advocate as a universal ethical position duties towards distant peoples, either to give aid, to support development or modify international trading arrangements. Development is whatever people within the cultural ambience of their own society determine 'progress' to be, and that conception cannot, in terms of the theory, be universalised. It is true that many of those who advocate relativism, or some form of a postmodernist view of a polycentric world, see it as a consequence of the approach that one can support diversity of cultures and hence diversity of development paths and models. This attitude concerning development is in many ways to be welcomed, but as I indicated earlier, such tolerance for diversity by no means follows from relativism, and is better accounted for in a form of cosmopolitanism that combines such tolerance with a firm moral commitment to international aid and co-operation.

III. INTERNATIONALIST/COMMUNITARIAN APPROACH

In many ways the position of the internationalist will be fairly similar to that of the realist, in respect to the policies which are actually pursued, though the rationale for doing so will be different. That is, if states have a right to pursue the national interest, then the pursuit of their development is part of that, and is only restricted by whatever is regarded as undermining the similar rights to development of other countries. Aid is both an aspect of that policy of pursuing the national interest, and also the expression of moral commitment. It can be the latter in two quite different ways. First, if the electorate wants the government to give aid for moral reasons, that is for the sake of the poor country or its poor, then as an expression of that mandate it should do so. Second, if a country enters into an agreement with another country or signs up to an international covenant, then it is morally bound to act accordingly, in terms of the requirements of the 'morality of states'. These obligations are functions of what electorates want and what international agreements are made, not direct reflections of moral arguments endorsed by the thinker in question (Dower 1993).

Multinational companies, driven by the profit motive, are entitled to pursue their economic activities within the confines of what countries allow them to do, either within the confines of domestic laws, which of course vary considerably in content and effective enforceability in different countries, or within the confines of such international law as is applicable to their regulation. On the one hand most rich countries accept this because these companies are actually national companies, repatriating profit and contributing to the development to their own base-country and are only called 'multinational' in a misleading way because their operations are transnational. On the other hand they are accepted in poorer countries, largely because their operations are seen as contributing to development there too, at least as understood by governments. However this is often not as much as poorer countries would like, and is seen as the lesser of two evils compared with no operations at all, given the poorer countries' weaker economic power and their relative inability to enforce effective legislation.

To be sure the right to development is acknowledged as giving rise to international obligations (as based on agreements amongst states), but the extent of those obligations is not great, certainly not as great as what many cosmopolitans will advocate. Certainly every country would retain a right to its own development, even if it was in conflict with that of others, not least because electorates would expect no less. This links in with the point that on the internationalist approach, development is generally assumed to be economic growth, usually qualified nowadays as 'sustainable' economic growth, both because that is what electorates want, and it is the duty of governments to deliver this, and because that is how the society of states themselves have agreed to understand development. These understandings are part of what many cosmopolitans will challenge (though of course other cosmopolitans may accept these, but simply argue for more committed promotion of such development for all countries).

The communitarian conception of morality, which I suggested earlier tends to go along with the internationalist approach, will not provide a robust set of arguments for individuals to make donations themselves to help the distant poor or to support aid, to adjust to a life-style which witnesses to a more equal world or to advocate reform in the international economy, or to challenge development paradigms on the grounds that they are not appropriate to the global situation. The content and scope of a persons's main obligations are shaped by the community he or she lives in. This is not to say that individuals may not have some moral feelings, some impulses of charity and generosity, in relation to distant poverty and be moved to act accordingly, or to say that a community may not have as part of its own collective moral culture a concern for good relations with other communities, and concern for the suffering of others (or concern for the environment). But in either case the extent of this concern for well-being beyond the community is a contingent fact about the particular developments and traditions of that community or the particular sensibilities of individuals. It is not something which the theory says ought to be accepted.

IV. COSMOPOLITAN APPROACHES

A. GENERAL PERSPECTIVE

Although cosmopolitans will adopt a number of different approaches to these issues, what is important is that the range of issues to do with aid, trade, investment and development are all assessed in terms of a basic theory of value, and are indeed assessed together so that basic consistency of policy is achieved. This can be illustrated as follows. If we accept, as most cosmopolitan thinkers except libertarians do, that there is an ethical argument for aid (and it is not merely seen as an instrument of foreign policy), then two issues arise.

First, we need to avoid inconsistency between aid and other practices. If there is an argument for reducing extreme poverty, the same argument in principle ought to inform the international policies for trade and investment and the development priorities within countries themselves (I return to this issue in section IV E). Second, what is in any case the object of aid? Is it the reduction of extreme poverty or the stimulating of the poor country's economy? Whilst the internationalist may say that inequalities between countries are themselves the key problem (partly because the representatives of states have decided on this), the cosmopolitan is likely to stress that it is the well-being of people that counts ultimately. If a form of aid to a poorer country resulted in no significant improvements for the very poor or even led to their situation getting worse, then it would be unclear why a poorer country should receive aid.[1] However we should note that a cosmopolitan like any other thinker could take the view that aid does not work – after all this is an empirical issue not tied to any particular ethical theory. There is a cluster of arguments to the general effect that aid either does not generally, or cannot, work and so there is no duty to do what is impossible. Such arguments are either to do with the general nature of aid, with the argument that it necessarily creates dependency, or to do with the long-run ecological consequences of aid, particularly emergency food aid.[2]

These arguments are based on empirical claims, and the replies to them have to be of the same kind. That free markets and enterprise contribute to general well-being may be granted, but to accept that measures to regulate markets and to use redistributive mechanisms to advance the economic well-being of others can never be effective, flies in the face of much evidence. The specific argument that aid does not or cannot work looks like a duty-excusing move and is quite untenable. That much aid does not work is to be granted. That all aid does not work or cannot work is simply defeatist. Riddell's survey of aid shows clearly that much aid is effective. In any case, if some aid does not work, the response needs to be 'Let's make it better!', not 'Don't do it!', and will be if one takes the moral argument seriously (Riddell 1987).

B. LIBERTARIAN APPROACH

The libertarian position also seeks consistency in its position on aid, trade and so on. If there is no general duty to give aid (outside positive agreements to give it), this is consistent with the model of the free market. On this view the basic values are those of liberty/autonomy, coupled with duties of not harming others or violating their rights to liberty. The value of liberty, especially economic liberty, may be justified in its own terms, and if a consequence of this is that the weaker suffer, that is a regrettable but not morally culpable consequence. States in their economic relations are justified in their dealings with others if they pursue their interests within the framework of law, without coercion or deception, and thus with the consent of other parties. Likewise businesses pursue their transactions within the framework of the market, and so long as they do this within the 'ethics of the market', they do so legitimately. Thus the libertarian takes a different view from that favoured by realists, that businesses are entitled to maximise profits (at home or abroad) in whatever ways they can get away with, or the view that they should maximise profits within the framework of legal regulation, national or international. The basic moral framework underlying economic freedom, requires non-coercion and non-deception, whether enforced or not.[3]

Generally, the libertarian position is both parallel in character to the 'morality of states', the 'international analogue' of old-fashioned liberalism anyway, as noted before, and also provides an intellectual support for state liberty, including its liberty to pursue its development. The point here is that the support of what states and businesses do can come from a theoretical grounding of a universal cosmopolitan kind, one that stresses the value of individual liberty and sees the liberty/autonomy of states and also the liberty of business companies as an expression of that basic liberty.

The different theoretical groundings for libertarianism and the morality of states could lead to a parting of the ways on some issues; for instance, if states were to agree on levels of regulation in the international economy which the libertarian theory would not accept as right. Here the validation within the 'morality of states' conception based on *de facto* agreement would clash with the principled advocacy of liberty. This brings out the point that as a cosmopolitan theory libertarianism is argued for as a universal value framework on theoretical grounds, and does not depend on what happens to be established; it may be opposed to some things that do get established, through whatever laws or conventions are agreed upon within the morality of states.[4]

As for development itself, there will tend to be an acceptance of development as economic growth, on the grounds that most people want to increase their material well-being and exercise their choice wherever possible to do so. The global economy is very much premised on this conception of development, and on the values of the free market and individual liberty, economic and otherwise. Indeed linked to this is a more general, rather materialist and individualist conception of the 'good life'. This libertarian approach then to what constitutes the good life, appropriate development and socio-political order, in being presented as a global ethic, may well be guilty of a kind of 'cultural imperialism' if it is seen as something to be imposed on societies which do not share these values. As such it becomes a variant of idealist–dogmatic cosmopolitanism.

The following criticism may be made of the libertarian position. If the right to liberty is seen as merely a side-constraint on another's actions not to interfere, and there is no implicit duty to further the value of liberty as a value for all, it is difficult to see how even the minimum basis for maintaining social order is possible. If on the other hand we accept that the value of liberty involves promoting that value and opposing what undermines it, it is not clear why we should have a duty to do that if we do not have a duty to promote, and oppose what undermines, the values which liberty enables us to enjoy, values which it cannot do, unless we have adequate resources to do so.

If however a libertarian argues that the value of economic liberty does not merely reside in its intrinsic worth but in its general effects, we have a different kind of argument on our hands, namely that everyone's well-being in the long run will be improved if we allow maximum enterprise and minimum restrictions. In development theory this is often referred to as the 'trickle down' effect. This often goes hand in hand with the common claim that aid does not work, discussed above. Whilst it is plausible to suppose that some benefits often trickle-down to the poor, it is rather unclear whether the poor benefit as much as they would or should if appropriate positive aid is given (and indeed if the global economy is more regulated than libertarians favour – see Section E).

C. SOLIDARISM AND IDEALISM

So far I have not drawn any contrasts between what I have called the solidarist–pluralist and idealist–dogmatic approaches. This is not because there are no differences in this area, but because insofar as there are arguments for positive global responsibility for meeting basic human needs, there is generally not a great amount of difference. We need now to note where there may also be differences in connection with the idea of development, which I discuss in section V.

What I call the idealist approach does assume some fairly specific value system which ought to apply to everyone in the world but is not accepted by some or much of the rest of the world. What is distinctive of this 'dogmatic' view is that it matters a lot that others who do not now hold the theory come to accept it, and that although all human beings according to the theory have an ethical status, there is nevertheless a distinction to be drawn between the community of those who believe and those who do not, between true believer and infidel, between the 'city of God' and the 'earthly city', and so on. We can see this kind of picture in connection both with religious worldviews (though not all of them) and with certain kinds of political views. The antagonism between Christianity and Islam is one case in point, and the cold war opposition between the ideology of the free world and that of the communist bloc another.

The consequences of this for aid, trade and development are significant. Unlike the libertarian approach above, this approach does lay stress on the idea of positive obligation to promote what is valuable, but it will see the promotion of development defined in its own terms as being of central importance. If aid is not merely about meeting the basic needs of people, irrespective of their values and beliefs, then it will make a difference whether there are already people with the requisite values or are people who may be influenced to become so through the aid programme. Aid becomes the instrument of the promotion of wider values. Thus countries and areas may be selected because the strategy makes sense in terms of the promotion of a certain value system in a world which may be resistant to them. What governments ought to do in their more general economic policy in the world and indeed in their foreign policy is to favour those countries where the appropriate forms of development can be supported and strengthened. Development, to be sure, is not merely seen as economic growth, but as desirable social change defined in terms of the value system to be promoted in the world. Thus an Islamic thinker may favour the development of Islam in a society, perhaps the development of a 'theocratic' order, a Christian a society informed more by Christian values, and so on. Many conflicts, including proxy wars in the Third World, have been about the promotion of rival socio-political systems as part of the process of development.

Even modern aid programmes that are based on 'partnership' agreements presuppose that the partners accept the same ethical approach, for instance about good governance. Whether or not this is acceptable depends on particular cases. What it illustrates is that whilst generally conditionalities in aid (tied aid) are condemned either because they promote the donors country's interest unacceptably or project unacceptable values, it is not clear whether all conditionalities are to be rejected, since there maybe some things it is worth insisting on, such as environmental good practice and the protection of workers' and others' rights generally.

The solidarist–pluralist approach agrees with the idealist approach in stressing that development is far more complex than economic growth, and involves a set of values by which to measure desirable social change, and also accepts the general principle that there are positive obligations to promote development anywhere in the world, both by appropriate aid programmes and by general trade policies. However it does not see as an essential objective the promotion of any one particular worldview, rather the development of a set of common elements of well-being valued in almost all the different worldviews which people have and in most of the different cultural formations which exist in different countries. A wide range of ethical theories, secular as well as religious do, I believe, share these characteristics and it is on the basis of convergence of the range of values essential to development that the ethical assessment of aid, trade, economic transactions, as well as development itself, can be based.

D. THE ARGUMENTS FOR AND AGAINST AID

In this section I summarise the various ethical arguments concerning aid. We have already identified three types of argument which may be used by others who question whether we had a duty to give aid, whether as individuals or as governments. Realists, relativists and strong communitarians who restrict community to national bodies may claim that there is no global morality at all, so there are no obligations to the poor across borders. Libertarian cosmopolitans and internationalists may hold that that although there are ethical relations between countries and between individuals in different countries, the general duty of aid is not one of them. What is central is the liberty of individuals and states. Finally there are arguments that say that aid does not or cannot work. These arguments, being empirical ones, are available to various kinds of thinkers, cosmopolitan or otherwise. Often this view is coupled with a view that in the long-run economic growth will percolate down to the least advantaged anyway.

When we turn to the ethical arguments for aid, we need to note that there are two arguments available to the internationalist which any cosmopolitan could support too as supplementing their own arguments. These are the arguments that governments have duties to give aid if they have been democratically mandated to do so by their electorates, and that if countries have entered into international agreements to give aid, then they have obligations in virtue of these agreements, such as the agreement in the UN at the beginning of the 1970s to give 0.7 per cent of GNP in aid, or the commitment to the Millennium Development Goals (MDGs) in 2000.

The remaining arguments are ones that may be used cosmopolitans other than libertarians.

General benevolence: perhaps the most famous single example of an ethical argument used to get the rich to give their money (and no doubt, time, effort and resources generally) is Peter Singer's famous article entitled 'Famine, affluence and morality',[7] reprinted many times because it sets out an argument and replies to objections with a clarity which has hardly been matched since, though many papers have been written. The central argument in this depends upon a simple premise: 'if it is our power to prevent something bad from happening, without thereby sacrificing anything of comparable moral importance, we ought, morally, to do it' (Singer 1972; 1979: ch. 8). Although Singer himself is a utilitarian, he fashions this principle which is the major premise of the argument, in such a way as to include, as he sees it, both consequentialists and any non-consequentialists who include a duty of benevolence as one of their duties.

Human rights: if the right to life (self-preservation) includes both the right not to have it taken away as well as the right to subsistence, what duties correlate with these rights? Shue, as we saw earlier, argued plausibly for three types of correlative duty: the duty not to deprive, the duty to protect from deprivation, and the duty to aid the deprived. Seen on a global scale such duties would provide an impressive basis for action (Shue 1996; Pogge 2003).

Duty to meet basic needs: an example of this kind of argument is O'Neill's Kantian approach. Poverty undermines rational autonomy, so we ought to respect rationality in others by making it possible for their rational agency to be effective, as well as opposing institutions and practices which disempower people through coercion or deception (O'Neill 1979: chs 7 & 8).

Duty of social justice: just as within a society we have a collective duty to ensure through appropriate tax and welfare mechanisms that the needy do not suffer, so we should think of the world as one global society in which the same principles apply. Beitz and others, as we have seen, extend Rawls' ideas on social justice and the difference principle to the world as a whole (Beitz 1979: pt III).

Backward-looking arguments: all the above arguments are essentially forward-looking arguments, in the sense that they do not depend on looking back on the situation and asking 'how did the current level of extreme poverty come to exist?' They are dependent on acknowledging: that it exists, whatever its causes; we in the North (those of us reasonably well-off) have the capacity to give or support (effective) aid; and therefore we ought to do so. Some arguments however for giving aid are backward-looking (to recall Ross's well-known conception in Ross 1930: ch. II) in the sense that they depend on the recognition (which is somewhat controversial) that countries in the North engaged in and continue to be engaged in exploitation of the South through colonialism and neo-colonialism, and therefore ought to make amends/restitution/recompense for the injustice done. If individuals give aid on this basis, they do so as beneficiaries of or as part of larger causal chains of such exploitation, not because they themselves are the active perpetrators of it (e.g. Hayter 1981). Thomas Pogge has developed a version of this argument on the grounds that the current international system violates the rights of the poor. It is not merely the past that is culpable (Pogge 2003).

It will be apparent from the general position adopted in this work that I favour the positive argument (Dower 1983). Although the exploitation argument has some validity, and insofar as it is accepted it requires us to combat others' injustice, it seems more sensible to use less controversial premises and rest the main argument on the positive capacity to help. If we see the whole world as one society and see it as a form of social injustice that the basic needs of many are not met, we will see it as a matter both of justice and of benevolence to help realise the rights of the poor. These rights are not merely to the basic necessities of life but to what assures dignity and the exercise of rational autonomy. Elements of the arguments above can be combined to make a persuasive case. On the other hand I do not think the line taken by Singer can be sustained that we must do all that we can. For reasons given earlier in my criticisms of utilitarianism we need to accept extensive but not exhaustive responsibility.[5]

E. AID AND THE GLOBAL ECONOMY: THE NEED FOR CONSISTENCY

What are the implications of this position for the other areas of concern, like trade, debt cancellation, investment and development itself? First, there must be consistency between aid and what happens generally in economic relations. That is, if we accept that there is a moral argument to give aid to reduce extreme poverty, it would be inconsistent if we accepted, allowed or even supported activities which have the reverse effect; if the effects of business activities directly contributed to poverty, for instance by not paying higher than poverty wages; if debt repayment policies and conditionalities imposed by the IMF exacerbated poverty; if the policies of Southern governments were not properly geared to poverty reduction (to the extent they could, within the limits of their budgets). Likewise it would be inconsistent if the pursuit by business of practices, including the development of new technologies, marginalises those who are not part of it; or if the development of patents and import substitution by rich countries and operations by companies within poorer countries all have indirect impacts which cause economic marginalisation. These processes are particularly well illustrated in the case of biotechnology.

It may be argued that there are many activities which are pursued legitimately but which have unintended indirect negative consequences; these include business activities in a competitive environment, firm measures to get an economy onto its feet, expecting countries to repay debts no less than individuals, and governments pursuing other important objectives. This may be granted. But unless there is a further argument that there are no other ways in which economic well-being for all and other public values can be effectively promoted in the long run (which would be a very pessimistic assessment), the point remains that far more attention could be paid to the general effects of various economic policies. Otherwise aid, even the best aid, is simply giving with one hand what the other hand or rather many other hands are taking away. Businesses operating in poorer countries do not have to pay the lowest wages possible in order to maintain reasonable profitability,[6] most governments could put a lot more effort into poverty-oriented programmes, and so on.

With regard to debt repayment, such debts could and arguably should be reduced or wiped out by rich countries cancelling their own claims and/or compensating private banks if they cancel theirs. The Jubilee 2000 project recommended that this be done at the millennium – with partial success. It is worth noting that typically it is the poor that suffer when austerity measures are in place, though they were not the ones to incur the debt or in many cases to benefit from whatever the loans were used for.

Perhaps the most intractable of issues concerns the indirect effects of competitive economic activity. How far are companies or governments responsible for the indirect effects of their policies? Many economic transactions involve winners and losers. For instance, my getting a job causes you problems if you wanted the job. So we have to distinguish between justified negative effects of actions and unjustified effects. Either the idea of unjustified policies takes us back to more specific canons of fairness and justice discussed earlier (liberty, non-coercion, non-deception),[7] or it points to a principle of not either directly or indirectly causing extreme suffering/poverty, a state of affairs below a minimum level of acceptability, as a basic principle. This cannot be an absolute principle, since there are many other important goals of public policy with which it will clash, but it needs to be seen as an ever pressing consideration.

The cosmopolitan approach which I favour and which neither dismisses the problem in libertarian fashion nor points the finger of blame firmly at businesses themselves in the manner of harsh critics of capitalism, is to suppose that we have a conception of a socially just society. This means a global society, and in the light of the requirements which this conception of global justice generates, we take measures at all levels to ensure as far as possible that the society meets these requirements. Thus if it is part of our conception of a socially just society that everyone's basic needs are met (needs for subsistence, security and basic liberty), then we ought to take measures to ensure as far as possible that basic needs are indeed met. When I say 'we' I mean not only governments, which have arguably a primary task in this regard, but ordinary citizens, who can press for appropriate legislation both to regulate industry and to provide welfare mechanisms, to accept the need for a tax burden to meet these goals, and also where appropriate to help in private ways as well.

What then are the implications of a commitment to a socially just world for the pursuit of development, particularly for richer countries? At the very least it is a commitment to a world in which absolute poverty is brought to a minimum. The reason I have emphasised the alleviation of poverty is both because I see this as having moral priority, and because anyway it is difficult to see how differences between countries are as such morally problematic, except insofar as great differences mean the real difficulties which poorer countries have in meeting basic needs and mean that they do not have proper bargaining power. But there is no more reason for arguing for complete equality between nations (in terms of average standard of living, let alone total wealth) than there is for there being absolute economic equality between individuals (see O'Neill 1993).

It is clear that the development of richer countries will need to be qualified in the light of the kind of cosmopolitan argument above for aid and modified trade practices. Quite apart from any commitments states have entered or will enter into, the cosmopolitan argument (except that of the libertarian) will stress limitations on development, if that conflicts with development elsewhere which meets more immediately urgent human need. Governments need to have more open-door policies on refugees, and there may be a need to accept lower rates of growth through the development of different international agreements designed to establish a fairer world. Many cosmopolitans, though not all, who adopt something like the above approach, also question more radically the whole growth paradigm, partly for environmental reasons (see Chapter 8).

But the following difficulty arises, linked to the considerations to do with the nature of political communities discussed in Part I. Even if one accepts oneself the ethical basis for helping alleviate distant poverty as applied to individuals, is not the situation of governments different? The duties of government are shaped by more complex considerations such as the preference of their electorates on the one hand, and on the other the existing international code of practice and existing agreements. This needs to be accepted, since there are cosmopolitan reasons for supporting both kinds of duty in practice. But it remains open for the cosmopolitan to press the basic arguments for better aid and trade reform as a kind of consideration which governments ought to address (e.g. Dower 1993). In any case, if more people accept this kind of cosmopolitan argument for more vigorous action to combat poverty and to tackle other issues as well, then the conflict between the cosmopolitan argument and the democratic argument reduces, and eventually international agreements will reflect convergence too.

V. DEVELOPMENT

The idea of development has already been invoked several times already, and calls for further consideration, since development is one of the key concepts in world affairs around which ethical issues cluster. First the ethical critique of development as economic growth noted earlier illustrates the increasingly active involvement of cosmopolitan thinking in what is called 'development ethics'.[8] It is also relevant to other issues in that if we are concerned with aid we need to ask: what is it aiding anyway, since aid is only a means to an end. It is also relevant for any proper critique of sustainable development, discussed in the next chapter.

Development has been seen as the standard goal of all countries, rich and poor, for some time, and generally understood as economic growth. Societies have not however always been developing or seen themselves as developing, since societies have sometimes been either static or cyclical in nature and self-conception. One thing that gave rise to a change of perception was the rise of science and thus the control of nature via technology. Rationalism and the Enlightenment also influenced the way people thought about the possibility of deliberately organising human affairs and using the resources of nature to improve the material standard of living generally. The idea of 'progress', linked with 'evolution', from less good to better states became a central concern. In parallel increasingly the role of governments, which had been to secure order and security, became the promotion of economic well-being through general growth and welfare services, and so development became a goal of public policy. The assumption has also been made that the West, whilst still developing, has been achieving this and that poorer countries must do the same to 'catch up', through industrialisation, modernisation and the apparatus of nation-state.

A. THE DOMINANT PARADIGM: ECONOMIC GROWTH

What then dominated thinking and planning were economic growth models. General improvements in the economy of poor countries will lead to reduction in inequalities between countries and reduction of extreme poverty. This is not to deny that there were various rival theories about how best to achieve this, and as the development decades progressed, different theories took precedence. An early approach (still favoured by some) was one according to which general economic growth will benefit everyone including the very poor by a process in which wealth, largely stimulated in the richer sectors, 'spreads' or 'trickles down' to all in society (a modern variant of Adam Smith's 'hidden hand' mechanism).

However others felt that this needed to be modified since it was evident that poverty reduction did not automatically follow from economic growth without some kind of intervention or direction from central institutions such as governments. Modifications (within mainstream development economics/studies) of this economic growth model included 'growth with equity' (growth with mechanisms, generally state-directed ones, to redistribute wealth in favour of the poor), and 'basic needs' theories, again targeting the poor with programmes designed to meet basic needs.

Because the goals (overall growth and poverty alleviation) were seen as self-evidently good and mutually supportive, the mainstream debates about models of development were not usually seen as ethical debates. Rather the various debates about rival models were seen primarily as debates about appropriate means to the same goals, debates about what policies, institutions and so on did as a matter of fact pursue the twin goals most effectively. But the positions adopted were in fact also informed by ethical assumptions, some internationalist, some cosmopolitan, and these were made more explicit as challenges to them emerged.

B. QUESTIONING THE DOMINANT PARADIGM: NORMATIVE ACCOUNTS

By the beginning of the 1980s, both philosophers outside development studies and some within the field such as Amartya Sen (e.g. Sen 1987; 1989; 1999) were self-consciously questioning the ethical foundations of development, both about the appropriate means of pursuing it and about the ends. There were in fact various aspects or phases to this.

Various writers began to stress the humanistic assumptions underlying development discourse – in this respect Denis Goulet, writing books long before the 1980s, was a pioneer (Goulet 1971; 1995). There are two features to what I am calling the humanistic emphasis: first, that in the last analysis it is individual human beings whose lives go well or badly; and second, that an account of human well-being is needed which is considerably richer than an account of increases in economic well-being. In the 1990s, the *Human Development Reports* of the United Nations Development ment Programme have quite explicitly in both title and content stressed the range of criteria for assessing and measuring progress in the good life. Consider also the UN definition in the *Declaration on the Right to Development* (1986):

Development is a comprehensive economic, social, cultural and political process, which aims at the constant improvement of the well-being of the entire population and of all its inhabitants on the basis of their active, free and meaningful participation in development and in the fair distribution of the benefits resulting therefrom. (UN 1986: pa. 2)

This is a rich 'definition' in many ways, though lacking perhaps because it has no reference to the priority of poverty-reduction or to environmental constraints.

Development on this view is about progress in human well-being/flourishing. Economic growth and industrialisation are only means to certain ends, and they are only justified if they achieve those ends. If they do not, as the critics would claim they sometimes do not, then they are not justified, and may even be inappropriate if they frustrate attempts of poor people to achieve well-being. It should be noted that even improvements in indicators such as higher calorie intake, easier access to water or better housing are also means to ends, not ends in themselves.

It is not clear then that development understood in conventional terms does always advance human well-being. Once this has been accepted, various other things held to be self-evident also become questionable. Does the South necessarily have to imitate or catch up with the North? If it is not clear that the image of the good life offered by the model of development in the North – materialism, consumerism, liberal choice – is satisfactory, why should countries with other kinds of values, often religious, seek to imitate the North? Perhaps there are other ways of tackling extreme poverty (bad in almost any value scheme) which do not depend on wholesale commitment to economic growth or liberal markets. All sorts of 'alternative' models of development, based on value and factual premises rather different from those of the economic growth paradigm are offered (many linked to ecological visions or feminist perspectives, as in the writings of Vandana Shiva 1989). At the extreme there is the rejection of 'development' altogether as an appropriate object of pursuit. Thus for instance Sachs and others in *The Development Dictionary* see development discourse as inseparably linked to the global economy which 'homogenises' cultures, and therefore reject it as an important organising concept for identifying desirable social change (Sachs 1992).

These critical responses to the dominant paradigm of development are all based on alternative value systems which have in more recent years led to more sustained philosophical reflection on what the bases of these are. During the last twenty years, mainstream moral philosophy has entered the development stage to a significant degree. Three kinds of questions can be identified: first, if development is about change from a worse state to a better state and this involves centrally the improvement of the lives of human beings, by what criteria do we measure that improvement? What is the good life, human well-being or flourishing? This has been the primary focus of discussion. But two further kinds of question arise: part of what makes a society move from a worse state to a better state is the general nature and quality of its social structure and relations, how human well-being is distributed in the society, what kinds of liberties and rights are in place, what kind of moral culture exists, what values of democratic participation are established, and so on. Third, ethical questions can be raised about the pursuit of development by a country in term of its external relations to at least three things: the environment, future generations and other countries in the world (e.g. Dower 1992).

Here we enter the heartland of ethical theory and the application of the kinds of cosmopolitan theory discussed in Chapter 5: Kantianism, human rights, neo-Aristotelianism, utilitarianism and liberal contract theories (see Aman 1991). Different normative theories will give different accounts of the values (ideas of well-being) and social norms involved; some more extensive (thick), some less extensive (thin) and open to cultural variation. What will generally be accepted (as part of the more meta-ethical or conceptual aspects of development ethics) is that the general idea of development is normative or evaluative. If a formal definition of development is 'a process of socio-economic change which ought to happen', then the challenge is to give an account of what kinds of changes ought to happen and why! (Dower 1988)

What also emerged from these alternative approaches is an important feature: the criticisms of the economic paradigm are not merely criticisms of it as applied to poorer countries in the South. They are in effect (if not in primary focus) criticisms of that paradigm as applied to rich countries as well. In other words development ethics is not really about ethical issues to do with the South, it is about development anywhere. Indeed, much of what motivates philosophical enquiry into the appropriate basis of social change stems from an unease about the priorities and commitments of rich countries themselves. Of course, one source of that unease, already noted, stems precisely from the relationship which rich countries have with poorer countries, both in terms of their aid programmes but also much more significantly in terms of their wider economic relationships. Another source of unease though about the economic growth policies of the North stems from a concern about the way of life in the North, considered in its own right, as being too affluent, too materialistic, too consumerist, and so there is a desire to consider more explicitly the essential values which, the thinker claims, should underlie policy in the North. A third area of concern which invites a re-examination of the basic values underlying development in the North stems of course from concern for the environment, protecting Nature now and the well-being of future generations, and underpins the immense interest in sustainable development.

C. UNIVERSALISM, PARTICULARISM AND RELATIVISM

One kind of consideration, of immense importance in its own right but pertinent to the three cosmopolitan approaches, is the issue of relativism, particularism and universalism. Much of the ethical concern about development has come from an unease that the patterns of development which are dominant in the North are not appropriate to social change in the South, and that in many ways what is happening with the strengthening of the global economy is the destruction of traditional cultures, worldviews and value systems, even though such local or traditional value systems are in fact right for those cultures and the appropriate bases for whatever change needs to take place. In other words, the values which should underlie social change vary from society to society. What is happening in the global economy is but the latest manifestation of European cultural imperialism or 'Eurocentrism'. Most but not all writers in development ethics share this unease, but in varying degrees and with different views of its theoretical significance.

One response, noted earlier, is to see the idea of 'development' as closely tied to the European value system, itself born of the Enlightenment and the idea of 'universal reason', and thus, in the name of celebrating diversity and the need to defend traditional value systems against the encroachment of global capitalism, to reject the idea of development altogether as an appropriate vehicle for articulating desirable social change. (Much of the language of Latin American Liberation Theology reflects this, rejecting development in favour of 'liberation'.) But those within development ethics, who retain a commitment to the central concept but recognise that rival values can be built into it, can also make the point that diversity of cultures and norms within them are to be defended in the name of development, as Goulet does. This is because it can be claimed that the kinds of social change which ought to happen or would be beneficial, will be different in different places, and will, for instance, depend upon the values already accepted by the people in question.

But the recognition that much diversity needs to be accepted and defended (in the face of the 'homogenising' tendency of international economics) can stem from two very different theoretical positions, relativism and universalism incorporating diversity. It is possible of course for a development ethicist to have the first view. There is nothing in the general position of being interested in the ethical issues in development which precludes such a position. On the whole however those interested in development ethics do not adopt this position, but rather the universalist position which incorporates diversity, pluralism and particularism. This stems from both a belief in a universal value core itself and also from a belief in the validity of norms of global responsibility, such as those of the rich to support authentic development in the South, norms which are problematic on a purely relativist position.

Most thinkers interested in development ethics then prefer to identify some kind of universal value framework and then accommodate various kinds of diversity within it. Thus those who advocate a neo-Aristotelian or Kantian or 'rights' approach are generally keen to show that their theories are at a sufficiently high level of generality to allow significant variations in different societies' development: these variations are expressions of or interpretations of the underlying value in different social contexts. It would not be their intention to see their theory as projecting an essentially Western value theory onto other parts of the world, though their critics might argue that, despite their intentions, they are doing just that.

On the other hand, it should be noted that, just as nothing in the idea of development ethics precludes relativism, so nothing in the idea precludes an attachment to a dogmatic idealism of some kind or other which the thinker knows full well is not actually accepted in many of the societies for which it is recommended. Thus a highly specific religious model of appropriate change, a model dominated by an ecological vision, or a model advocated by an avid secular libertarian defender of free choice, might be advocated for all societies, with the quite specific and intended implication that what is dominant and accepted in most countries at present is simply misguided. Whether or not they are to be criticised for this, they are striking examples of a feature present in most development thinking. That is, almost anyone who advocates a model of development advocates one which in some respects is different from what others accept and pursue – and this is true of those that build in respect for cultural diversity as well and fit more my model of solidarist pluralism.

NOTES

1. The issue of the internal mal-distribution of wealth was noted by the World Commission on Development (WCD 1980: ch. 8).
2. For general criticism see Bauer 1984; for arguments linked to environmental constraints see Hardin 1977. Hardin, like other neo-Malthusians, adopts the line that any aid that fuels population increases makes worse the problems aid is intended to solve.
3. There is here a big interpretative issue, not pursued, as to whether agreements between radically unequal parties, whether the weaker party is a Southern government or a worker, are genuinely 'free'. The radical will say such

contracts are formally free, as Marx noted, but really coercive; the libertarian that they are free, because what is chosen is the lesser of two evils.

4. One area where this approach supports some controls, beyond what is assumed traditionally as a necessary backcloth to the proper functioning of markets, is over environmental regulation, to the extent that practices cause harm. See Chapter 8.

5. For a defence of charity not justice as the basis of aid, see Graham 1996: ch. 7.

6. See, for example, Scarrow 1985 and Lehman 1985 on the issue of appropriate levels of wages.

7. Other principles like non-discrimination need to be added. This discussion of business ethics is only concerned with some of the aspects which arise in the international context which illustrate my main themes. For a general survey of business ethics in its global context see Donaldson 1989.

8. Many philosophers and others interested in these value issues belong to the International Development Ethics Association (IDEA) and the Human Development & Capabilities Association (HDCA).

QUESTIONS FOR DISCUSSION

1. How should an internationalist approach the ethics of international aid and trade?

2. Are any of the objections to aid at all convincing?

3. Which ethical basis would you use to make the case for official aid?

4. Are the libertarian accounts of free trade and of development adequate?

THE ENVIRONMENT

I. THE ENVIRONMENTAL CRISIS

Environmental problems have existed in one form or another since time immemorial. Resources were used up or land became degraded, and responses took place. What has converted many smaller problems and crises into the global crisis of the last forty years or so is the increasing recognition of the combined and cumulative effects of what is happening everywhere. This can usefully be summed up in the idea of 'global finiteness'. The crisis stems from the recognition of the finiteness of the planet earth – a feature captured vividly by the image of 'spaceship earth' – and the fact that human practices in the latter half of the twentieth century are coming up against the limits imposed by this finiteness. This finiteness has always been there, of course, but it is now a real constraint on human action. It resolves itself into three areas.

1. *The finiteness of non-renewable resources*: this refers to such resources
   as oil, coal and minerals, with the consequent problem that if these get
   used up too fast before adequate substitutes are found or other necessary adjustments are made, for instance towards using solar power as
   a major input to energy needs, we will not avoid major forms of
   economic dislocation and so on.
2. *The finiteness in the carrying capacity of the world*: this is the finiteness of the world as a whole and of areas of the world to absorb the
   effects of human activity and pollution and/or to tolerate resource-
   extracting practices, without deleterious environmental change,
   damage and degradation. Pollution, largely a product of industrialised countries, degrades our atmosphere and water systems, leading
   to the destruction of forests (as is caused by acid rain), dead lakes
   and rivers and so on. The burning of fossil fuels is, it is now generally recognised, leading to global warming and climate change.
   Over-pressure on land in the Third World through heavy tree-cutting,
   over-grazing and overcropping is leading to land degradation and
   desertification.
3. *The finiteness of areas in the world which produce renewable
   resources*: this relates to resources such as food and timber, and hence
   the problem that there are upper limits to the amount of renewable
   resources that can be produced by the planet on a sustainable basis.

In many ways the IPAT formula, as advanced by the Ehrlichs, is useful in
capturing the nature of the situation (Ehrlich & Ehrlich 1991: 58).

Impact (on the environment) = Population x Affluence x Technology[1]
That is, the impact on an environment (local or global) is a function of the
number of people, the material standard of living enjoyed and the kinds of
technology used to sustain it. No doubt other factors need to be included
(like the time period) but it is useful in that it shows that major adjust-
ment in any of the variables may alter an impact on the environment.
Growing populations in the South are often seen as a key problem to be
tackled, whereas in the industrialised countries the key issue is usually
taken to be the modification of technology – the greening of industry
– and so on. What is not usually challenged is the level of affluence.
Indeed the continued commitment to economic growth assumes that this
can go on growing. Sustainable development, assumed by governments
and industry to be the appropriate way to conceptualise the combination
of environmental protection with development, is taken to be just that,
economic growth so pursued with new technology that the environment
is protected. Many more radical environmental thinkers simply challenge
that assumption as naive, on the grounds that universal growth is simply
not sustainable, even in the North let alone including the South catching

up (see Engel & Engel 1990). Two large countries, China and India, are currently doing just that.

For many concerned about the environment it was concern about the finiteness of non-renewable resources that led to the acknowledgement that there was a crisis, and to the acceptance of the need to check growth in the use of such resources: the Oil Crisis of 1973 was a catalyst in that respect. But since then it has been the second aspect of finiteness – finiteness in the capacity to absorb pollution – that has become of primary concern. The problems of acid rain or ozone layer depletion illustrate this, and the cumulative impacts of CO_2 emissions on the atmosphere with the danger of global warming have now become major preoccupations. The third dimension, the limits of the global system to produce renewable resources, in particular food, has always been a matter of concern to environmentalists, though to varying degrees. Clearly in many parts of the Third World there is pressure on land, due partly to rapidly rising populations, which results in starvation and malnutrition. But this is, it would generally be admitted, not because the world as a whole cannot (and does not) produce enough food for all, but because of poor distribution and the powerlessness of the poor to purchase it, when they cannot produce it. On the other hand, the population explosion is for many a major part of the environmental crisis, perhaps ultimately the crucial part. It must be accepted that there is in some numerical region an upper limit to what level of human population the planet can sustain. Whether or not the global population can stabilise well within those limits without Malthusian mechanisms of war, disease, famine and pestilence operating on a far greater scale than they already operate, is a crucial question.

In 1987 the Brundtland Report was published under the title *Our Common Future*. It was the work that really led to the near universal adoption of the goal of sustainable development. The document called for an international conference on the issues of environment and development and this took place at the Earth Summit in Rio in 1992, twenty years after the landmark conference on the Environment in Stockholm in 1972. The Rio conference adopted an ambitious programme of action called Agenda 21. Numerous agreements have been concluded, but still many people sense that we have not really changed tack in any major way, despite many further international conferences such as the world summits in New York (1997) and Johannesburg (2002).

II. THE ETHICAL FRAMEWORK

In some ways the ethical debates about the environment do not naturally mesh in with the issues concerning international relations which we are discussing, though they are very relevant because environmental problems are nowadays essentially global. This difference of discourse is partly because most who think about the environment have assumed a 'global ethical' framework and sought to go beyond it. The debate within world ethics has been mainly between various theories (cosmopolitan) which say that we do have ethical relations to all currently living human beings on the planet and those which deny that framework, whereas much of the interest in environmental ethics is about whether for instance non-human life counts or whether future generations count. Failure to engage properly with the international relations debate is one reason why, despite so much concern about the environment and about the need to change our ways, so little actually happens. So we need first, as a continuation of setting the context for the international relations debate, to set out the issues which dominate environmental ethics itself.

A. THREE DIMENSIONS OF MORAL RESPONSIBILITY

In fact, we can identify three dimensions to moral responsibility, which environmental ethics brings out. Not all environmentalists would assert all three of these dimensions, but it is in the course of such debates that it becomes clear that it is possible that we have three kinds of responsibility; first to people living in the future, second to kinds of being other than humans, and third globally towards any beings anywhere. The point is that it is possible to deny all three extensions; that is, to deny that we have obligations to any but present generations or those living now, to deny that we have obligations to non-humans, and to deny we have obligations to human beings outside our own society. If one denied all three, one might have an 'us-here-now' conception of morality (my phrase); that is, the scope of moral concern is limited to fellow humans living now in our own society. Although this is hardly a conception of ethics which is advocated in bald form, it does represent how many people think and certainly behave in practice.

B. THE HUMAN-NATURE DIMENSION

Most ethical theories which have been dominant in the Western tradition have been human-oriented or anthropocentric. They have assumed that morality is about the relationships human beings have with each other, and that it is human beings who are the bearers of moral value. Most of the theories we considered in Chapter 5 on cosmopolitanism were anthro-pocentric in character. Natural law theories are concerned primarily with what is essential to the nature of human beings; human rights theories are explicitly about the rights of humans; Kant's theory is as we have seen centrally wedded to the idea of rational agency as the locus of the value of humans as 'persons'; and Marxism shares this human-centred focus since it is human agency which creates the gap between culture and nature. The contractarian theory of Beitz, like contract theories generally, focuses on the contract between human beings as beings who have interests and are capable of contracting. Whatever its defects, utilitarianism has historically been open to wider interpretation, since Bentham well recognised that if the capacity for suffering (and pleasure), not rationality, was the determining characteristic for membership of the moral realm, then non-human higher animals were included.

Communitarianism as a basic ethical approach also tends to be human-oriented precisely because it is the traditions of human beings living together that creates value. Whilst a community can and sometimes does agree to confer certain values on some non-humans such as pets, the general emphasis is still on a community of co-operation between rational agents for mutual benefit. Likewise any theory which based morality on convention and serving mutual interests would see human beings as the bearers of moral value.

Though at least some of these theories can be adapted to 'expand the circle' of direct concern, it remains the case that the tendency of these theories has been to see human beings as special, perhaps because they are rational or are moral agents or possess souls. I stress this aspect of the theories we have considered earlier both to illustrate my claim that many environmentalists have a different framework, and to show how anthropocentric Western thought has been. It is because of this that the development of nature-centred or biocentric theories has been seen as a challenge to the standard assumptions about ethical thought.

What most divides environmentalists is the question of our attitudes towards nature. Granted that environmentalists generally agree on practical measures which are important, such as avoiding pollution, preserving areas of wilderness and species diversity and so on, the question arises: why are these things important? Let us take as an example the preservation of areas of wilderness (see Thompson 1983). Is this important because it contributes to the maintenance of a healthy biosphere which in turn is vital to the continued well-being of human beings? Is it important because areas of the world untamed by human intervention are sources of aesthetic delight and psychological refreshment for human beings? In these cases we clearly still have a human-oriented ethic: nature itself is of no intrinsic value, and in the last analysis the attitude of respect for nature is advocated not because nature is in itself worthy of respect but because this attitude in humans leads to environmentally sound practices and psychologically healthy states of mind.

On the other hand there is, as I have already implied, a nature-oriented ethic, one in which life in general is seen as having a value which ought to be respected and promoted. What is wrong therefore with environmentally damaging practices is not merely that they negatively affect the long-term interests of human beings, but that they damage intrinsically valuable ecosystems, destroy the life and healthy state of plants and animals whose good is quite independent of human interest, reduce intrinsically valuable diversity, destroy objective beauty and so on (see e.g. Rolston 1988). One well-known figure in the ecology movement in the USA, Aldo Leopold, once advocated this principle as his 'land ethic': 'A thing is right when it tends to promote the integrity, stability and beauty of the biotic community. It is wrong when it tends otherwise.' (Leopold 1949: 224) On this view human beings are not at the centre stage of ethics, they are merely plain members amongst others of the biotic community. A related but distinct conception which also emphasises human responsibility for non-human life is the conception of humans as 'stewards' of nature (see Attfield 1983; Brown 2000).

The impression given by the outline in the last paragraph may be of only one overall position, juxtaposed to the human-oriented position. However, as with the latter, there are quite a number of different positions. For instance, one issue centres round the question: is it life itself that has value, or is it some feature or set of features, like sentience or the capacity to feel pleasure and pain, that gives certain forms of life a value which must be respected by human beings? If life itself is the key factor, then things like microbes and trees fall within the category of what has intrinsic value. Another issue, which is analogous to the 'holism versus individualism' issue in social sciences, is whether what has value are individual living things or, in addition or instead, species of living things, whole ecosystems, wilderness areas taken as wholes, the biosphere itself, or the planet, as in the Gaia hypothesis, thought of as a kind of living entity itself (see Clark 1983). Once it has been decided what things in nature have value, or are, to use a phrase sometimes used, 'morally considerable', that is, fall within the sphere of what must be taken into moral consideration, the further question arises as to how they are to be taken into consideration (Goodpaster 1978). Is the life of a butterfly as important as that of a human? Or the life of a microbe as important as that of a bat? If one adopts an egalitarian as opposed to a hierarchical approach, one could be very radical about appropriate human behaviour, unless the right to self-preservation allows humans a fair amount of *de facto* special status (Taylor 1986; Attfield 1983).

There is here a kind of ambiguity about the relationship of human beings to nature. If human beings are morally bound to respect nature and life in it, we seem at the same time to be both part of nature and apart from nature. On the one hand we are just part of the 'biotic community', with no privileged status: our role is to fit in and be part of the wholeness or integrity of nature/creation. On the other hand, the very fact that we have moral obligations makes us different from the rest of nature so far as we can tell, since the morality or ethos of a higher animal is seen as quite different. We are different not merely by virtue of our moral sense, but by virtue of our rationality and our freedom which means that we are not wholly determined by our environment (Matthews 1989). However hard we try to be literally a part of Nature or to abrogate our special status, we undermine the attempt, for the trying is part of what makes us different.

C. THE FUTURE DIMENSION

Let us now turn to the second dimension: How far ought the future to enter our moral thinking? This question is a perplexing one in some ways, and not all environmentalists will handle it in the same way (see Cameron 1989; Partridge 1990). Why are we concerned about the future? Take the case of nuclear power: it is commonly recognised that future generations, existing long after we are dead, will have to cope with contaminated areas associated with dead power stations and dumped nuclear waste. Does the thought that this will be so actually add weight to the moral arguments for winding down our nuclear power programme, given that we already have good reasons for so doing based on the risks and dangers to ourselves and those living now? (Shaw 1989) We can draw a clear distinction between the distant future, that of generations beyond our life-span, and the near future, that of our own life-time and that of those whom we know and love now. It is arguably easier to accommodate the future of present inhabitants of the world into an ethical framework, than to show why the fate of human beings yet unborn should concern us. Certainly, if we accept that the future states of present inhabitants can be of concern through prudence and love and thus through love one can be concerned with the future interests of those whom one loves, a powerful basis for motivation is given. Indeed John Passmore, who was one of the first philosophers to look at environmental issues, saw the chain of love and concern which runs through generations as being the moral basis for concern for the future (Passmore 1974: 88–9).

But there is rather more to our obligations towards distant generations than this. From a logical point of view it may be asked why, if a type of situation is taken to be good like a human being living in an acceptable environment, does the fact that it will occur in the year 2100 make it any less relevant than if it will occur in the year 2000? So if an action now can promote or prevent its realisation, that action ought, other things being equal, to be done or not done.[1] Perhaps it is rare that events or situations in the distant future may hang in the balance so dramatically, but if what we do may have statistically significant effects on the way the distant future turns out for people, then it seems arbitrary not to take account of this. If after all it is said 'Well, it does not make any difference to us – they cannot help us!', the reply must be given, 'Does morality only require of you actions from which you expect some reciprocal benefit?' However there are several lines of resistance here.

Uncertainty about the Future

It may be argued that our efforts might be either redundant or pointless, since we do not know what developments in technology will bring about. Future developments may render what we do unnecessary, and conversely future developments such as catastrophes may render them useless. Such humility about the future is no doubt admirable up to a point, but since we need to work on probabilities, the general response is that we must do what is likely to be relevant to protecting the future. Likewise we need to resist the danger of relying on technology alone to solve our problems.

Sometimes it is argued that we cannot really plan to satisfy the wants of future human people since we do not know what they will want, as people's desires are largely determined by culture which changes radically over time. Again, we need to recognise this but also the fact that people's basic desires and needs for clean air, water, land, health and adequate nutrition are likely to remain constant. What we need to do now, as with development generally, is not make others achieve the good life as we conceive it, but to provide the enabling conditions in which they choose to achieve it as they will conceive it.

Do We Have Duties to Future People?

Other kinds of argument may be given which suggest that we do not have duties towards future people because they do not now exist. Their futurity and potential existence as opposed to actual existence takes them off the moral landscape, either because they do not exist (so they cannot have rights) or because in not being current members of our society and therefore not playing their part in a scheme of co-operation, they have no rights, since rights depend on reciprocity. The difficulties here are more theoretical. It is not clear that being in the future takes away their moral status, if when they exist they will be affected by our actions. If it is correct to say that we now have human rights, then when they exist they will have human rights, and so the duties apply to us now. As to the issue concerning reciprocity, it seems reasonable to argue that obligation does not depend on reciprocity, either actually received or capable of being received. The defence of cosmopolitanism in the book has in part been the defence of a kind of ethical theory which does not make obligation depend on reciprocity.

D. THE INTERNATIONAL DIMENSION

Almost all environmentalists would insist that we adopt a global perspective in facing the problems involved.[2] Although some environmental problems occur entirely within one country as a result of what members of that country do, many of the more serious environmental problems in the world have cause–effect relations which are trans-national in character. Obvious examples are air pollution – acid rain and radiation from a Chernobyl disaster – and river pollution where one country's effluent becomes another country's problem downriver. Other perhaps less obvious examples of environmentally damaging practices are practices in one country which occur in order to satisfy economic demands arising in another country, for instance the cutting down of forests in the Third World in order to supply timber for furniture and newsprint in the First World.

Most thinkers would adopt the following maxim: where the lines of cause and effect run across nation-state borders, so do the lines of moral responsibility. To accept such a maxim is implicitly to endorse a 'global ethic', according to which the whole world is one moral domain, and the network of moral relationships extends in principle across the world. This kind of theory is of course the main preoccupation of the present book, and the implications of adopting it will be considered more fully shortly. The fact is that this area of environmental ethics is much neglected, partly because the global responsibility is assumed by environmentalists as self-evident. (For explicit discussion see Attfield 1999; McGraw & Nickel 1990.) But in fact it comes up against practices, by states and transnational companies, which show that either actors within these institutions are complete hypocrits or powerless victims, or the ethical perspective is certainly not self-evident. The Brundtland Report actually starts one of its chapters with the bald statement: 'The Earth is one but the World is not' (WCED 1989: 27). That is, the planet earth is one vast interconnected ecological whole, but the world as a set of human institutions is not, with fairly poor co-ordination of effort and lack of unity of purpose in responding to environmental problems. This reflects in the last analysis a continuing allegiance to moral values and priorities which are in conflict with the demands of a global ethic.

E. UNINTENDED CONSEQUENCES

Any moral theory that is adequate from an environmentalist point of view must attach importance to the unintended consequences of our actions including our omissions. That is, we must accept responsibility for the unintended (and often unnoticed) consequences of our actions and our failures to act. Whilst it may seem obvious and uncontentious that we are responsible for some unintended harms, what is rather more at issue is how significant this side of moral responsibility is. It is part of the essence of the environmentalist frame of mind to lay stress on this. Equally it has been part of a common approach to morality to think light of this.

It is all too easy to think that what morality really requires of us is to avoid intentionally doing harm to one another, to avoid deceiving, stealing, letting down, assaulting, libelling one another and so on, and that generally what really counts in moral assessment is what one aims at or intends, either as the end of the action, or the means to some other end.[3] That might be all very well, if we lived in a world where the unintended consequences of our actions did not materially affect the conditions under which others pursued their objectives, or where our omissions did not fail to prevent some harm from occurring.

But the world is not like this, and one of the things which precisely brings this out is environmental constraint, which means that we must take very seriously the harm we may do or allow by inaction, without even noticing it. Environmental ethics is if nothing else an ethic of interdependence, and will not countenance the excuse 'I don't intend to help spoil the environment – all I intend to do is get to my meeting ten minutes earlier by private car than by public transport'. Nor is it merely the unintended consequences of particular acts which is important, but as this example shows, the contribution to cumulative impacts of large numbers of similar actions. Environmentalists might well adopt the spirit of Mill's remark in another context that an action may be 'of a class which, if practised generally, would be generally injurious, and this is the grounds of the obligation to abstain from it' (Mill 1962: 270).

III. THE THREE APPROACHES

A. INTERNATIONAL SCEPTICISM/RELATIVISM

It might be thought that environmental problems were the Achilles' heel of realism. After all if the realist is saying that there is no morality in international relations and the relativist likewise denies that we have duties of a global kind, the plain facts of the environmental predicament and our response to it simply falsify the position. Clearly nations have to co-operate and agree to international standards if the environmental problems are to be tackled, and individuals must recognise that they have duties to play their part in protecting a common environment. However such a conclusion would be too quick and fails to appreciate moves that can be made to support the spirit of the sceptical position.

Clearly it would be very difficult to see a realist trying to make the case for the existence of a moral vacuum if that meant there being no rules or laws in operation in international relations. Such rules and laws are clearly there, no more clearly than in the case of the increasing amount of international law to do with protecting the environment. But this has been so for a very long time. There is nothing new in the emergence of co-operation to protect the environment. What the realist can still insist on is that these rules which are accepted by countries are so for prudential reasons. That is, it is in their interests to accept rules and regulations and to get others to accept them and stick by them because it is only in this way that the benefits to that country can come. If a country does not want pollution x to come into it from other countries via the atmosphere, then that means other countries must stop or reduce their production of x. But just as the motive for accepting agreements and doing what one can to get other countries to do what will give one the benefit is national self-interest, so would the motive be if that country no longer perceived there to be a benefit from their continuing to comply, or it decided to engage secretly in a practice in contravention of the regulation. It is rational to be a 'free rider'.

As we saw in the last chapter, from the sceptical realist's point of view the commitment to development in a country is to be seen as part of the pursuit of the national interest. The language and rhetoric of 'sustainable development' is meant to be officially linked to what kinds of develop-ment are sustainable from a global point of view, that is, linked to what kinds of development are to be pursued sustainably compatible with the like efforts for all other countries. However the real concern, according to a realist, with development is a concern for maximal growth for that country itself. If more than a few citizens came to have concerns of a more global kind to do with the environment, that would certainly influence the way sustainable development was pursued, but that would still be the national interest, because it was based on the preferences of its citizens. In the real world any rich country is bound to seek to maintain its economic dominance in the global system and therefore to tolerate a very unequal global order. But he would not regard this as unjust, because at bottom these concepts do not really apply to the global arena. A parallel can be drawn with the way transnational companies operate. Like states they operate to promote their interests, in this case their economic interests, through the 'profit motive'. If the realist analysis applies to states, the same can be equally plausibly applied to such economic institutions.[4]

What about concerns for the distant future or for non-human life which are part of many environmental agendas? Like global ethical concerns, these cannot enter into a realist analysis directly, only via the interests of the country's citizens, as expressed for instance through democratic procedures and preferences.

How can a relativist who says there are no duties to other human beings in other societies handle issues of environmental co-operation? Again he can observe that practices by other countries may affect how things go for his own country, and therefore may have reason to do what will conduce to patterns of activity in the world around him which are of benefit to his country and himself. But what happens elsewhere is of no direct ethical concern to him, since that is no more than part of the backcloth in which the morality in his society functions. He may recognise that other human beings will have similar concerns about having a clean environment and so on, and that they have a conception of 'good' of interest to them, but he will not recognise that ethically he has obligations owing to them, or they to him. Likewise, concern for future generations or for non-human life may or may not be part of in individual's or society's ethic. That is a contingent matter. But even if it is, it cannot be presented as an ethic applicable to all and to be accepted by all, because this is what the relativist denies.

My reasons for rejecting these positions have already been set out in Chapter 3 so I will not go over them again, except to make the following remarks. As elsewhere one has to recognise that the realist analysis at the level of description may be right about the typical motivation of states in their pursuit of environmental protection, their signing up to conventions and so on. But on the deeper issue of whether moral rules apply, the position seems much weaker. Here one needs to note that whatever the motives for compliance, the moral framework may still be valid. Many actions which are morally right are done from self-interested motives, but that does not make the moral description inappropriate. In any case one of the key considerations in the realist's position that there is no enforceability in the international arena needs to be considered carefully. Certainly there is no strict enforceability in the sense of a coercive world government making countries comply, but the procedures whereby international laws are monitored, sanctions applied in various ways and so on, amount to something very like enforcement in many areas, and certainly sufficient to guarantee fairly reliable expectations of compliance.

The relativist argument seems equally implausible, even on its own terms, given the nature of the environmental predicament we are in. Behind the relativist argument must lie some functionalist theory of how the values which are relative to different social groups arise. If one of the sources of agreement about values in a group is a sense that certain things need to be done to protect something which there is a common interest in the group to protect, then the perfect analogue for the development of rules serving common goals is provided by the global environment. The need to protect the environment stems precisely from a common interest all people in all countries have. These common interests may not be fully recognised by all but from the point of view of a relativist who is aware of them, the argument for accepting some kind of common moral framework is surely plausible, give the relativist's own starting point. This of course is compatible with accepting a plurality of values in other areas of life.

B. INTERNATIONALISM/COMMUNITARIANISM

In many ways the internationalist 'morality of states' approach gives both a plausible account of what kinds of action need to be taken and also of the ethical rationale for doing so. In the society of states, each state is committed to maintaining and promoting its interests but within a framework of maintaining a society of states in which other states are enabled to do so. Because the primary emphasis is upon respecting each other's sovereignty and non-interference, states must not harm each other's interests or do what threatens international order. States will therefore have moral reason to take measures to protect the environment for three reasons. First, continued pressures on the environment may threaten international peace and security, like competition for water supplies or other scarce resources. Second, various kinds of action have damaging impacts on other countries like acid rain. Third, their interests which they collectively want to promote via international agreements are shaped increasingly by the interests which their citizens have in the environment in general and in future generations and the natural world. Once of course international agreements are entered into, then the principle of *pacta sunt servanda* applies, which means that states have ethical obligations to keep the agreements which they have accepted. That is, agreements and conventions may come to include international co-operation to protect the environment from ozone layer depletion, to cut back on CO_2 emissions and so on, and once entered into have moral force.

The development of environmental conventions and the increasing tendency for states to have to limit what they do to avoid unacceptable damage to other countries' environments illustrates how the international society of states, originally devoted to the liberal principle of a limited set of moral constraints on one another, has become gradually drawn into something more constraining, and indeed more linked to the common concerns of ordinary citizens. But still it is worth noting that those who support it still see the rationale officially in terms of the interests of states and what states agree to do to protect those interests.

Two further points need to be noted, First, international law, to do with the environment or anything else, acquires its moral force on this view primarily from the fact that it is entered into, rather than the moral arguments or reasons which lie behind them. Indeed the reasons why states may enter into such conventions may be very complex, and may have little to do with moral goals at all. And insofar as they do reflect moral goals, these will be varied. Certainly how states define their interests will reflect in various ways the moral concerns of their citizens. Thus we could see emerging, and many might say this is already partly the case, that the actual thinking of citizens about the reasons for protecting the environment is increasingly global and cosmopolitan, but the way this is reflected is via the interests of states. That is, the content of ethical thought is cosmopolitan, but the form in which it is expressed is internationalist.

Second, the interests of a country, insofar as they are seen genuinely reflecting the interests of people rather than those of governments or rulers, are almost always understood as the interests of current citizens in it. So, insofar as there are ethical concerns which many have about future generations, non-human animals or indeed the rest of humanity, these are only reflected via the interests of those citizens. It is precisely this indirectness which many environmentally minded cosmopolitans object to, because whilst it is good that such perspectives are reflected at all, it is not good that they are seen as only lying in the background of justification rather than the foreground.

Communitarians approach issues to do with the environment in terms of the traditions and shared values and meanings found in the community. The ways the environment, which will tend to be the environment in their own geographical area, is protected and cared for will be understood in terms of how people in that society have responded to the environment. Stress may be placed, taking insights from the phenomenological tradition, on the 'idea' of the environment, not as something out there, but as 'a field of significance', that is something which 'surrounds' people as 'their' environment, their home, place or space which is charged with meaning far in excess of any physical area it is associated with.[5] Clearly the shared norms for responding to the environment will evolve as people learn how to cope with its changing parameters. All this is not to say that the communitarian has no concern about 'the environment' at a global level. Unless a communitarian also accepts a stronger relativist position, already discussed and criticised, there are a number of reasons why he or she can accept responsibility for the global environment and for taking measures to protect the environment elsewhere.

First, unless the communitarian is strongly relativist, he or she can accept a layer of obligations we have as human beings to one another with the values of community being additional to this, albeit often of powerful significance. Second, communities, in recognising that other communities have like concerns about protecting their environments, will accept that ethical norms need to be accepted to allow them to do this as well, and thus to play a part in protecting the common source of different environments (Thompson 2001). This in effect is one of the sources for the morality of states approach which can be seen as protecting the various communities states represent. Third, it is of course entirely possible for the morality of a community to include as part of its own ethos a concern for beings who are not directly human members of the community, whether these be human beings elsewhere in the world, or future generations or non-human life.[6]

My main critical discussion of internationalism and communitarianism has been given elsewhere, but I want to focus on one issue here of relevance to the environmental issues we are considering. This issue has to do with both the contingency and indirectness of concerns for the environment. Yes, the morality of states may come to include many valuable measures to protect the environment through convention and so on, but if the moral obligations are a function of those conventions, this makes it contingent upon those conventions having been entered into. If the arguments given earlier in the chapter are valid, they are only reflected indirectly via people's interests, transmitted through governments to conventions. Yes, the community may well have internal to its traditions concerns for the environment of a wider kind, but communities do not have to have these traditions; it is contingent on those traditions, and if a society does not care much about future generations, animals or the rest of the world, these interests are simply not represented. Most environmental ethics like most cosmopolitanisms see these ways in which interests are represented as altogether too precarious and indirect. It must also be possible to assert these moral claims directly and in such a way that they make a difference to and challenge any conservative arguments of the form: 'This is acceptable because this is accepted', whether at the level of international norms or at the level of community. Apart from any theoretical issues here, there is an urgency about creating much stronger environmental norms both in the cultures of communities and the working practice of states. These cultures and practices are vital, but the arguments for creating them come from, and must come from, elsewhere.

C. COSMOPOLITANISM

The basic idea of cosmopolitanism is of course that of a global framework: all human beings now. Many cosmopolitans would also include non-human well-being into the equation, as well as future generations. But neither of these extensions is strictly required. That is, a cosmopolitan could be strictly anthropocentric, on the grounds that only humans are the source of value – with possible extension to higher animals as bearers of sentience – or take a view, considered earlier, that future generations do not, either in theory or in practice, enter the moral arena for current decision-making. Is the converse possible? That is, is it possible for someone to have a nature-centred approach or a future-centred but not a global approach? This is possible but seems less plausible for the following reason. As noted earlier concern for future people in one's own country or for non-humans could be derived from the attachments, perhaps shared in the community, of current people (and this is consistent with a lack of interest in the rest of the world). But if future generations or non-human life are seen as having intrinsic value which we ought to respect (whether we feel attachment to them or not), then the kind of moral theory that makes them objects of moral concern must in consistency make present humans elsewhere objects of moral concern.

Does a cosmopolitan need to advocate extensive action to protect the environment and need to push people and governments to do a lot more than is generally being done to protect the environment? The answer is that a cosmopolitan need not do so, for two kinds of reason, one to do with a radically different reading of the 'facts' about the environment, the other a more moral-theoretical point.

First, any cosmopolitan could have a very optimistic view of the human prospect. An example of this is Julian Simon who in a number of works has argued that our situation is nothing like as dire as the doomsters make out and that by adjusting our practices and technologies we will find solutions to the problems which arise (Simon 1981; 1995). Part of this line of argument is to stress that in some sense humans are the 'ultimate resource' in that we can adapt and be 'resourceful' in responding to pressure on the environment. Such an argument does not deny that we need to make lots of particular adjustments, since clearly pollution does occur, resources do go short, animals do suffer, wildernesses are being reduced, and if we do not want these things to happen we need to take measures, but what we do not need are wholesale adjustments to the way we live or challenges to growth.[7] Sustainable development is indeed to be seen as sustainable economic growth. There is no reason to challenge the conception of quality of life and material abundance, now achieved largely in the North and sought after by the South. Technology can take care of the problems and create the conditions for producing future abundance.

Second, coupled with the more optimistic scenario, there is also a more theoretical position of an ethical kind linked to what I have earlier called the libertarian–minimalist approach. On this view what morality requires of us is primarily that we respect other people's liberties, including economic liberties, and that we do not adopt an interventionist pro-activist approach. Yes, we need to avoid actively harming the environment for ourselves or others where clearly the chain of responsibility lies with us as significant cause, but there is no general duty of extensive co-opera-tion to protect and enhance other people's environments. On the whole the libertarian thinker will want to downplay the negative indirect conse-quences of economic activity in affirming economic liberty, whereas other thinkers will see these indirect and contributory factors as being of central importance to the development of environmental responsibility.

Most cosmopolitans interested in the environment will however incline to a less optimistic reading of the human prospects and advocate a rather stronger claim about environmental responsibility. As such they will be highly critical of state practices and the general patterns of accepted values in many societies, especially affluent ones. The idea that develop-ment is to be seen as essentially growth will be challenged, both because it is unsustainable and because it involves a misguided understanding of well-being anyway. The point about sustainability needs to be stressed. From a cosmopolitan point of view, the sustainability of a country has to be seen in its global context: can a country's policies be sustained within a framework of other countries doing the same? It is not enough to ask: can my country's policies be sustained taken in isolation? We need to ask: ought it to be pursued consistent with the wider ethical framework? Generally a cosmopolitan view will require us to look very hard at policies with a view to answering the question: does this contribute to or avoid not impeding the overall global good *vis-à-vis* the environment?

Even if we retain the discourse of sustainable development, we have to ask just what conception of development we are assuming. Any talk of sustainability presupposes a set of things valued – material wealth, quality of life, the natural world, democracy or cultural diversity – which are worth sustaining or ought to be sustained (see e.g. Dobson 1988: ch. 1). Sustainability does not itself confer a value on anything, rather it presupposes a value or a set of values which, once the issue is made explicit, reveals disagreements and contestation (see e.g. Jacobs 1989; Lee, Holland & McNeill 2000).

There is not space here to develop these arguments further. The purpose of this book is not to spell out the full story which an acceptable cosmo-politanism would provide, but to chart the different positions and outline the main moves to be made. But it would be helpful to illustrate the kinds of international issues I have raised with one complex case.

IV. THE RAIN FOREST, OIL RESOURCES AND THE OCEAN BED: ENVIRONMENTAL SOVEREIGNTY OR COMMON HERITAGE OF MANKIND?

A cornerstone of the dominant paradigm of international relations is sovereignty. One aspect of sovereignty often claimed is something called environmental sovereignty, the right of a nation state to control the use of the natural resources within its territorial borders. The UN *Declaration on the Right to Development* (1986) asserts that all peoples have a right to self-determination which includes 'the exercise of their inalienable right to full sovereignty over all their natural wealth and resources' (UN 1986: art. 1.2). Since much of the natural wealth of the world is in the South, this may be a useful check in practice on attempts by those operating from the North to control it. But from a theoretical point of view, particularly one informed by ecological values, it is troubling. It is not at all clear if we adopt a global ethic, that morally, whatever its standing in international law, a country has a right to do just what it wants with its resources, if for instance its misuse of them had bad consequences for others outside that country.

Take for instance a tropical rain forest. Does a country like Brazil morally have a right to do what it will with it? There are many things to be said against the destruction of a rain forest from an environmental point of view. First let us look at typically human-centred concerns, like concern about the loss of genetic information through the relentless loss of species, or concern about the disturbance to global weather systems that destruction of much of it would cause, or regrets that we lose a significant arena of aesthetic appreciation of nature. Do these considerations over-ride the rights of states and people to their own resources? In suggesting that they do, in principle, one must be careful to put the argument in context, otherwise it will seem like a Northern argument directed against the South, which it is not intended to be.

First, by the same token, it must stressed, the argument shows that resources like oil which a country like the USA comes to possess because they were bought on the international market would also be subject to the same proviso. Climate change, it is now generally recognised, will have serious negative effects globally, in rising sea levels, violent weather, desertification etc. The manner and extent of our use of oil seriously affects the global common good. Arguably the extensive use of fossil fuels by countries in the North, especially the USA, is far more damaging to the environment overall than what is done in the South. Indeed any resource taken from nature is subject to the question: is the use of this resource consistent with protecting the global environment (or indeed any other values accepted)? The rain forest simply stands out as an example, because it is such a conspicuous example of a global resource.

Second, any argument directed at a country like Brazil to check a use of the environment, has to address the goals associated with that use like economic development, and, if appropriate, has to provide co-operation and assistance. The North cannot assert its rights in saying 'Stop' and not exercise its duties by helping in the stopping. Likewise if a country like China wants lots of fridges for its people, can we who have plenty of them simply say 'Stop' if that means using cheap CFC-emitting devices, without doing anything else?

What the two cases about the rainforest and oil illustrate is that, apart from the propriety of a global ethical standpoint from which to make judgements of appropriate or inappropriate use, the idea of ownership, whether by a person, an organisation, a people or a state, does not establish absolute rights of use and disposal. In what ways and how far environmental factors should restrict the rights to property is another issue that needs and receives attention. Linked to this is another: was Locke right to suppose that in 'mixing our labour' with natural materials we added 99 per cent of their value? (Locke 1960: ch. 5). From an ecological perspective this is highly questionable for a variety of reasons. But if Locke is wrong, then the right of property theory partly founded on it is also partly questioned.

Should then the Brazilian rainforest be seen, ethically, as on all fours with the resources of the deep-sea bed, the 'common heritage of mankind', to use the language of the UN Convention on the Law of the Sea of 1982 (UNCLOS)? Much effort was expended in the 1970s and early 1980s by the international community to agree on a convention on the use of the largest resource of the world – the oceans – to determine agreed territorial zones (the EEZs or exclusive economic zones), policies on quotas for husbanding and thus protecting the renewable resources of the ocean, but perhaps most critically future policies to do with the mineral wealth of the ocean bed. The concept of the 'common heritage of mankind' captured a certain global conception, and might in the future, if the conventions are followed with regard to future extensive mining operations, lead to an international fund being set up to hold the revenues from mineral extraction activities and to be used to help land-locked states with their development.

There is however an interesting paradox at the heart of this. In seeing the ocean bed and its stock as 'common heritage' there is an implied contrast in law to the non-common heritage, namely what each country has a right to in the way of natural resources geographically associated with it. But from a cosmopolitan point of view, at least one that is not libertarian in conception, this is deeply troubling because it seems a contingent matter, in the sense of being morally irrelevant, what resources happen to be within and what outside conventionally agreed geographical areas, and what matters at bottom is that the resources of the world are there for the common good of all. Clearly property regimes are needed, but they have to be seen in context, as noted above.

However, this line of thought fails to take on board a deeper problem. Let us return for a moment to the tropical rain forest. What is wrong about destroying it? There are, as I implied earlier, biocentric reasons as well as human-centred reasons: the destruction of animal and plant life, the destruction of species and the wrecking of areas of wilderness of signifi-cance and thus failing to respect the integrity of the 'biotic community' are all ethically problematic, quite apart from human interests.

So we can restate our problem in this way: even if we think of the tropical rain forest as the 'common heritage of mankind' as opposed to, say, Brazil's exclusive resource, it still suggests that the natural world as a whole is there for the use of humankind as a whole. It repeats in different language the conception of nature as a bundle of resources for human use, or as Heidegger criticised it in his perceptive essay, *The Question concerning Technology*, a 'standing reserve' (Heidegger 1977: 17). Of course we cannot avoid altogether thinking of the natural world as the supplier of the resources we all need, but the idea of common heritage/resources is for many environmentalists questionable, unless there is a proper corrective to the one-sidedness of it in terms of the importance of other kinds of relationship which we have towards the natural world. This illustrates a key general point. It is not enough to have a global ethic. It has to be the right kind.

NOTES

1. For a subtle discussion about the relevance of the future and about the rational structure of prudence, see Nagel 1970: pt II.
2. See, for example, Magraw & Nickel 1990 for an interesting discussion of the realist approach. The international dimension is also explored in Dower 1983.
3. Cf. the doctrine of 'double effect' discussed in Chapter 6.
4. The issue of transnationals has been discussed more fully in Chapter 7.
5. See, for example, Cooper 1992, and reply by Dower 1994.
6. Many animals, particularly farm animals and domestic animals, enter more strongly into community anyway.
7. See Graham 1996: ch. 8 for a mildly sceptical account of many of the usual arguments for a radical response.

QUESTIONS FOR DISCUSSION

1. In what ways are environmental problems global problems?
2. Would you defend the 'us, here now' conception of morality? If not, in what respects would you reject it?
3. Compare the ways in which an internationalist and a cosmopolitan might defend the claim that states ought to co-operate in protecting the environment.
4. Does either of the conceptions of environmental sovereignty and the common heritage of mankind adequately capture how a country ought to regard the natural resources within its territorial boundaries?

CHAPTER 9

WHICH WAY FORWARD? GLOBALISATION, GLOBAL GOVERNANCE AND GLOBAL ETHICS

I. GLOBALISATION

In the course of this book I have argued that we need to accept a global ethic and to see ourselves as world citizens, and that for such an ethic to be realised and such citizenship to find proper expression, we need the development of a global civic culture, of institutions, practices, and codes of conduct in which these values are embedded. It might be thought that what I have been arguing ought to happen is in fact happening anyway. That process is called globalisation. We need therefore to look at the trends indicated by the idea of globalisation, and consider in what ways it is an appropriate expression of a global ethic and in what ways it is not, and therefore since ethics is about choice, decide what to work for and what to resist.

A. THE TRENDS

The first thing we tend to think of about globalisation is the development of the global economy, particularly since the Second World War, of the world becoming one big market of goods and services, dominated by transnational companies and a certain 'free market' culture. All this is made possible in part through developments in global communications, information technologies, transport systems and technologies generally.

But there are at least two other important areas in which globalisation occurs, one to do with the spread of more informal global linkages between people, the other the development of the international system itself (see e.g. Scholte 2000; Held & McGrew 2000a; 2000b). Changes in technology have facilitated other changes, particularly in the way people 'think' beyond the boundaries of their own societies, whether through the Internet, mass communications, or INGOs (international non-governmental organisations). Alongside this the international system (in the precise sense of 'international' meaning 'inter-nation-state') has developed too, with the proliferation of international institutions, and the strengthening of international law, which, though not technically enforceable, makes it more and more difficult for nation-states not to respond to the background mechanisms of compliance.

Increasingly actors, whether 'princes' (nation-states), 'merchants' (economic agents) or 'citizens' (all of us in the variety of ways we interact), have as their remit, and take into account, the 'global stage' beyond our country or society (Nerfin 1987). Although of course we can, and many do, consider what we do in a global context but still with a view to what will benefit our own country or society (or benefit ourselves as members of it), increasingly, and as part of the process of globalisation, loyalties go beyond the nation-state and identities broaden beyond membership of our 'own' society, so that a person's interests may include what benefits wider wholes (or what benefits oneself as a member of wider wholes, such as a transnational, an INGO, or simply as a 'world citizen') (see e.g. Tomlinson 1999).

Globalisation is expressed through the development of global institutions in all three areas, and it is because these institutions necessarily have certain norms internal to their operation which are global too, that we see how globalisation contributes towards the spread of world ethics of various kinds. What are these kinds of international institutions?

B. INTER-STATE ORGANISATIONS

Organisations are international in a full sense or a partial sense depending on whether all countries or only some countries are members of them.

Fully International Organisations

Many organisations are fully international in the sense that they are bodies whose membership is worldwide and whose members are nation-states. They are world organisations in the sense that any country in principle could be a member, provided certain conditions are met. The more important of these are the United Nations and its associated bodies.

The UN was founded in the aftermath of the Second World War. The preamble of its charter reads: 'to save succeeding generations from the scourge of war'. Its main purpose was to preserve peace and security. It had other aims too, to do with enlarging rights and freedoms, and providing economic advancement to all people. Its main organs include the General Assembly, in which all nations, large or small, have one vote; the Security Council, with power to respond to emergencies rapidly, composed of five permanent members (USA, UK, Russia, France and China) with the power of veto, and a number of other members, based on rotation, representing the rest of the world; and the Secretariat headed by the Secretary-General.

Apart from its other formal organs like the Economic and Social Council (ECOSOC), it has developed a very large range of specialised agencies such as the International Labour Organisation (ILO), the World Health Organisation (WHO), the Food and Agriculture Organisation (FAO), the United Nations Development Programme (UNDP) and the United Nations Environment Programme (UNEP), largely dealing with issues of development in all its aspects and increasingly with environmental issues. The World Bank and the International Monetary Fund (IMF) act as its global lending institutions. The International Court of Justice in The Hague, which predated the UN, acts as the final global court of appeal in question to do with violations of international law. The range of international laws, including both declaratory documents with moral force rather than legally binding force such as the *Universal Declaration of Human Rights*, and legally binding covenants and protocols, has increased enormously under the aegis of the UN since the Second World War.

Over the years the UN has played its part in containing violent conflict, whether through the often unnoticed 'good offices' of the Secretary-General and his colleagues, or through the intervention of peace-keeping forces. Some of the latter operations have been successful but some in recent years have not, as in Somalia. It has presided over and facilitated the immensely complex and far-reaching change in the last fifty years of decolonisation, so that whereas there were 52 nation-states in 1945 signing up to the Charter we now have over 180 nation-states in membership. It also had a significant role in co-ordinating the international pressure in support of the crucial internal struggle against the South African Government to get rid of apartheid and this finally occurred in 1994.

The UN is not however a world government, though it can be argued that if it had acquired a standing military force, as envisaged in the early days but rendered impossible by the cold war, it might have become more like a world government, with coercive power to make nations comply with its decisions. But in terms of its rationale as an international institution, that is an institution through which autonomous and sovereign states co-operate, it was not conceived of as a world government, though it might have become one as things evolved. Whether a move towards world government would be desirable will be discussed later in the chapter.

Other Inter-State Bodies
Other bodies are international in the more limited sense that they are bodies made up of some but not all nation-states. These may be regional organisations such as the North Atlantic Treaty Organisation (NATO), which is a military alliance, the Organisation for Security and Co-operation in Europe (OSCE) with a rather different agenda for security and co-operation in Europe, or the European Community, a group of countries bound together by a complex bureaucratic and legal structure with the potential of becoming itself a super-state. They may be inter-state organisations based on similar economic interests, such as the powerful Organisation for Economic Development and Co-operation (OECD), the grouping of economically advanced states in the so-called North. They may be based on historical factors such as the Commonwealth, founded on little else than the historical accident that the countries were once part of the British Empire. Such limited inter-state bodies may support global goals, as was advocated by functionalists like Mittrany (Mittrany 1970), but equally they may assert their collective interests against the interests of other countries in the world.

C. INTERNATIONAL NON-STATE BODIES

There are also international organisations in a rather different sense of 'international', that is organisations whose operations occur in many parts of the world. What is common to a diverse range of institutions is the fact that the nation-state is not the unit in terms of which the organisation is defined. Although the term 'non-governmental organisation' (NGO) is in practice restricted to a sub-class of these, all these organisations are in effect 'non-governmental' organisations which are international if their operations occur in a number of different countries, if not worldwide.

Transnational Companies

Business corporations, such as Nestlé, Ford, Shell and Mitsubishi, often called transnational or multinational companies, operate in many different countries, and often have subsidiary operations and investments in different countries. Such corporate entities are immensely successful because each is overall a single entity with a remit of making profit; also because they are only answerable in a formal sense to their shareholders, largely of course people or other organisations in the North.

INGOs

There are also a large number of increasingly influential NGOs, many of the international kind, hence the phrase 'INGO', either acting as pressure groups on governments, such as Amnesty, Oxfam, Greenpeace, or promoting co-operation amongst individuals and groups with similar ideals and aspirations, such as the Catholic Church or the Boy Scout movement. Such bodies, especially those with expertise on issues such as environmental protection, disarmament, development or human rights observance, can act in a very influential way, for instance as advisers at international conferences.[1]

Collectively, they constitute what is often called 'Global Civil Society'. Mary Robinson, former President of Ireland, was quoted in 2002 as saying 'There are two superpowers in the world today – the USA and Global Civil Society' (and a similar thing has been said about the USA and world public opinion (Wikipedia 2006)). Others may more sceptically question its significance or even its existence as a single 'society'. The term clearly does not cover all international non-governmental organisations – at least they need to have global ethical goals and be committed to democracy and non-violence too (see Keane 2003; Eade & O'Byrne 2005).

II. ETHICAL APPROACHES

A. VALUES INTERNAL TO ORGANISATIONS

Two things need initially to be said about all these kinds of organisations. First, like other organisations, they exist to pursue certain goals, whether it be common defence, economic growth, the spread of or support for religious truth, or the reduction of human rights violations. These goals represent agreed values in some sense. Second, in order for co-operation to occur there needs to be a normative framework within which the organisation functions, that is agreed procedures, ranging from a more general agreed moral culture to specific rules about how decisions are taken in meetings. The presence of values, both goals and rules, in any organisation can hardly be disputed, so that if there do exist international organisations (in the various senses indicated), then on the face of it values in these two forms exist at the international or global level. What we make of this fact that values are present is another matter.

B. INTERNATIONAL SCEPTICISM

It may be thought that the sceptic will have a hard time fitting the existence of the United Nations and inter-state institutions into his framework, since the very existence of such institutions presupposes a normative framework. But this is misleading. First, the UN is to be supported and used as an instrument of foreign policy, according to the sceptic, ignored or flouted when it is contrary to national interests, and the moral values associated with it are illusory but to be manipulated to advantage. Thus, the motive for co-operation may be self-interested. This will apply not merely to individual acts of co-operation but also to standing arrangements for co-operation, such as being a member of institutions. Second, the use of moral language both to support the institution and to promote policies within its chambers may simply be an instrument of power, one amongst a number of strategies for getting one's way in the international arena.[2]

As for world government, the position of a realist will be ambiguous. On the one hand, insofar as the world is seen as a system of co-operating nation-states each bent on preserving or enlarging its power and influence, there would be no motive for any nation-states voluntarily to accept any arrangement which undermined its autonomy or power. On the other hand, if a really powerful nation-state thought that it could in effect seize power at a global level and impose its power on the rest of the world, then world government would come into existence, not by the voluntary agreement of states, but by force. This would be the global analogue of what Hobbes called 'commonwealth by acquisition' (Hobbes 1991: ch. 20).

What can a realist say about other organisations? Does the presence of values in organisations whose members and operations straddle many nation-states show that there are global values after all which states ought to observe? Not at all. Take first a world organisation such as a transnational company. It may well be that the development of its corporate identity with its own goals and ethos has an internal set of values, including moral values, just as within organised societies there are moral values. The point is that *vis-à-vis* what lies outside it – other transnationals, governments, and people – it need not stand in any moral relations. There still is no common moral framework from which to assess its operations *vis-à-vis* others. Such bodies co-operate with other bodies, and adapt their behaviour to the laws and culture of places where they operate, but all this is driven by the profit motive.

If we turn to other kinds of international NGO, such as a church or Amnesty International, again the analysis will be that, although members of these bodies may indeed co-operate within them because they believe that there is a universal religious or moral truth about God or human rights, this does not show that there are such universal truths, or even if there are, that they apply to the behaviour of states. There may not be universal moral values to be accepted by all. The truth of relativism, which as we have seen partly sustains realism, is not merely a truth about moral values being relative to discrete geographically separate communities. It can be extended to accept that other groupings, such as a worldwide religious body or a pressure group inspired by a socio-political agenda, may also come to have shared particular values. But this in no way shows that there are universal values.

C. INTERNATIONALIST/COMMUNITARIAN PERSPECTIVE

The approach of the internationalist will be rather different from that of a realist towards existing international institutions but like the realist he will be very sceptical of world government. On the one hand he will, in being an internationalist, see the present world order of states as a value worth preserving. The society of states is itself of vital importance, both for the preservation of nation-states within it and because such a system of states is the only realistic way of organising human affairs in such a way that well-being can be generally maintained. It is important that the society of states retains the monopoly of legitimate violence, for to allow it to other actors would be to allow far greater chaos into the world. Conversely the development of one superstate into becoming a world government, either by force or by a voluntary giving up of sovereign powers to form a world government, would lead to global tyranny, if not initially at least eventually.

So on an internationalist reading, the UN is primarily an instrument for the maintenance of world order, peace and security. Its essential role is to preserve international peace. Aggression is the key modern international sin. The UN is not merely an international body because it is made up of nation-states as members, it is essentially a statist organisation, dedicated to preserving the state-system. Another aspect of the system, apart from the emphasis upon outlawing aggression, is the emphasis upon the principle of non-intervention or non-interference in the internal affairs of other states (see for example article 2.7).

So far as other institutions are concerned, the internationalist will have a complex set of responses. On the one hand, given the internationalist's normative position that the system of nation-states is central to world order, that nation-states are the key international actors and that its 'morality of states' is essentially the global ethic to be accepted, the growth of other kinds of international body will be viewed with some caution. It is clear that the power of transnational companies, the budgets of many of the larger ones exceeding the budgets of many poor countries in the South, represents a significant challenge to the all-important role of nation-states. Indeed some are concerned that nation-states, even though they co-operate and promulgate international laws, are hardly co-ordinated effectively enough to counter the economic power of many companies which are of course organised as single corporate entities with a single will.

What about NGOs? NGOs increasingly act as lobby groups and as providers of expert information and advice, not merely to individual governments but also at international conferences and in international institutions. Characteristic of their perspective is an emphasis upon the status of individual human beings and in particular on their rights, and thus insofar as the pressure from such bodies constitutes a kind of interference in the internal affairs of nation-states, there is an implicit challenge to one of the cornerstones of internationalism, namely the immunity of states from external criticism *vis-à-vis* their internal affairs.

The internationalist is however unlikely to have any theoretical objection to the development of other kinds of international institutions. If after all the moral norms appropriate to a body are those which have emerged from co-operation, shared traditions and so on, the development of other kinds of bodies, with their own goals and rules, is to be expected and accepted. Of course different bodies will develop different mores, often in conflict with one another. Greenpeace is unlikely to have the same agenda or values as Rio Tinto Zinc, or the Campaign Against the Arms Trade as an arms manufacturer. The internationalist insofar as his position is partly shaped by communitarian considerations, needs to recognise the 'validity' of any of these ethical consensuses. Thus as we discussed earlier, there may emerge a number of different 'world ethics'. In practice these will all interact with one another. This will certainly affect the way decisions are taken by governments in the pursuit of what they take to be legitimate interests, but it may also of course shape the kinds of rules which states accept in their general dealings with one another and the sort of laws and covenants which they see their way to accepting.

As an example of this we can take the development, in the 1980s and 1990s in particular, of environmental law, which has centrally transformed the way legitimate foreign policy is pursued. The idea that an economic activity, for instance burning fossil fuels in power stations, could be seen as infringing the rights of other countries would have seemed strange before the last thirty years, but now that kind of contribution to a negative global impact such as climate change are seen as something countries have a duty to refrain from.[3]

D. COSMOPOLITAN PERSPECTIVE

As has been noted many times, the cosmopolitan position comes in many forms, but the essential core of the position is a belief that in the last analysis all human beings live in one 'moral community' and that any form of organisation at any level has to be assessed in terms of how well it allows or enables human beings to achieve well-being and moral agency. So a cosmopolitan will support the development of international institutions insofar as they contribute to these goals.

For most cosmopolitans the UN is the embodiment of global values such as the values of peace, justice, human rights and basic well-being for all human beings, and ought to be seen as a vehicle of the effective promotion of these. Insofar as it falls short of this, it ought to be reformed and subject to criticism in a spirit of critical loyalty. The idealism of the charter's preamble is significant, stressing the value of freedom and economic progress for all, as well as that of security, and many of the subsequent documents which have come out of the UN system, such as the *Universal Declaration of Human Rights*, presuppose a framework of global ideals to be promoted though the UN as effectively as possible.

If the UN can be changed to be more effective towards realising these goals, then it should be changed. If in changing the UN to become more effective the freedom of action of member states becomes more limited because of the strengthening of international law, then that is to be accepted even if it shows clearly that the 'sovereignty' of states is even more an illusion than before, at least in the original sense envisaged by Bodin and early writers. And if there comes to be a point in the development of world affairs where the well-being and moral agency of human being are better achieved through having something called world government, then that is what we ought to accept and welcome.

Of course whether any particular cosmopolitan would argue for a changed or strengthened role of the UN or argue for world government, depends upon many factors, some to do with the basic values which the theory advocates, and some to do with what the theorist sees as the facts about the world with regard to what the general effects of institutional change would be. For instance, a cosmopolitan who was strongly libertarian in his or her value system and believed that the central value to be facilitated in the world was personal and group choice would have reason to check the tendencies to strengthen or centralise power. More generally, any cosmopolitan who believed that a world government, however democratic and liberal it might be in its inception, would inevitably become dictatorial and undemocratic over time, would have strong reason not to favour such developments. (My own cosmopolitan line on the UN is given later in the chapter.)

What about other kinds of institutions? Here a cosmopolitan, whatever her or his views, will adopt a radically different strategy from that of an internationalist. For, given the claim that there are universal principles and global obligations which are applicable to all people, including all corporate agents as well, he or she is unlikely to endorse the goals and rules internal to all international organisations, precisely because the goals and rules of many of these organisations will run counter to the very values which his or her theory proposes. For instance, if one's cosmopolitan values are partly founded on the 'right to life', interpreted as pro-life groups interpret it to be an absolute injunction against taking innocent life (including the unborn child), then one will simply think an organisation committed to population limitation is wrong. The latter commitment might of course itself be founded on a rather different understanding of a right to life as a right to a quality of life enjoyed by persons. If an organisation is founded on a cosmopolitan conception of the good life based on the centrality of human relationships and harmony with nature, members of it will be opposed to the activities and philosophy of multinationals, both because of their conception of the good life and because, even in terms of that conception, the effects of the global economy often impoverish poor people and nature. If conversely one's cosmopolitanism is informed by a belief in centrality of economic liberty and choice as universal values, one will welcome the development of the global economy, and by and large the part played by transnationals in this process, and one will reject philosophies of life which may inform NGOs devoted to opposing it.

The general point about the cosmopolitan approach towards assessing international institutions such as the UN and also other kinds of non-state organisations, is that it is necessarily an appraisal in critical mode. That is, it is bound to assess institutions, not in terms of the values internally accepted by the institution, but in terms of some wider or broader standard which the thinker takes to have some kind of universal validity. Since not all institutions are indeed guided by the same goals or values, it follows that the cosmopolitan, whatever his or her colours, will necessarily be critical of some, partly because of rival theories, but mainly because of different prescriptions about what ought to be done in the world as it is. What a cosmopolitan argues for will be a function partly of the basic ethical approach he or she adopts, like one of the three approaches I have highlighted, and partly of how he or she understands the 'facts' of the world.

I have argued for solidarist-pluralism, and it will be clear from the above discussion that I see such a cosmopolitanism as pushing at existing inter-state institutions including the UN to be more effective in promoting commonly shared human values; pushing international economic actors to behave in ways that really promote economic well-being, and thus challenging the power of the transnationals insofar as they tend to cause poverty or promote inappropriate forms of development; supporting NGOs generally to the extent that they are not themselves contributing by their message to divisiveness; but equally stressing the value of peace and consensus-building as important, both theoretically as valuable in itself and pragmatically as a means to these other values.

By contrast, the libertarians will effectively support the internationalist status quo and also the relatively free operation of the global market and trans-national economic institutions, and the idealists will have more of an eye to supporting or not supporting international bodies, governmental as well as non-governmental, if these bodies advance or do not advance the values held dear. Thus, whilst generally committed to peace and mutual co-existence, they may be willing to sacrifice these values to some extent in the promotion of their ideals.

E. GLOBALISATION AND WORLD ETHICS

Does then the process of globalisation make a difference to what needs to be said about world ethics? The answer is that it both does and does not make a difference, depending on whether, to invoke the distinction I have already indicated several times, a world ethic is seen as a theory or seen as a global social reality. However, even before we examine what may be called the 'globalisation of ethics', we should note that there is a sense in which of course globalisation gives rise to a whole host of ethical issues which did not exist before or were not as important before. Even if one does not think that globalisation affects the basic moral principles one holds or how one thinks of morality, one may say that it affects greatly the applications of ethics. Singer for instance has made much of the 'ethics of globalisation' (Singer 2002).

In the sense in which a world ethic is an established ethic, shared by a significant number of actors acting in different part of the world and having a global ethical content, clearly globalisation contributes significantly to the existence of such world ethics, that is, many world ethics in the plural. Apart from the specific norms of many different organisations, like the norms of the Catholic church or the norms of Amnesty International, there are the well established norms of the morality of states and the well established free market norms of the global economy. It will be apparent that from the point of view of any thinker, not all these norms can be supported, partly because they are in mutual conflict with each other. So the question one has to ask is whether globalisation is helping to develop the appropriate kinds of ethical culture which one's own theory supports. The answer is: in some ways it does and in some ways it does not. What however is clear is that the development of international institutions and practices, which globalisation as a process reflects, is absolutely essential to the embodying of any ethic which is seen as a world ethic. The challenge is: what institutions should we support and what values should inform them? There are many aspects and levels to meeting this challenge, partly to do with global governance (see next section), partly to do with global citizenship (discussed at the end of Chapter 5), and partly to do with human rights. The following remarks supplement what has already been said about human rights in Chapter 4.

For many cosmopolitans the existence of a strong human rights culture is at least one hopeful sign of what globalisation can achieve. The case of human rights is worth considering precisely because human rights readily serves two functions, that of being something already established in the world, and that of providing an ethical theory. Does then globalisation establish human rights or not? (cf. Bull 1979)

My thesis is this. First, globalisation, including the development of certain international institutions, is crucially relevant to the claim 'do human rights exist?', if we take the assertion that human rights exist to be an assertion about certain features of global social reality. If the claim that human rights exist is a claim that there is a trans-societal culture in which there is a shared recognition that all human beings have certain rights along correlative obligations, and that these human rights are embedded in law, along with correlative duties, domestic and international, then the facts of globalisation are very relevant to whether human rights exist, and if so, what they are.

But, second, globalisation is completely irrelevant, if we take the claim 'human rights exist' to be a moral claim, based on a moral theory, about the moral status of human beings, as discussed in Chapter 4. That human beings possess these rights does not depend on whether, as a matter of fact, these rights are accepted by others generally, embedded in law, custom or convention. If human rights do not depend for their existence on such facts of social reality, then, *a fortiori*, they do not depend on facts about global social reality. If human rights discourse has not only become a firmly established part of our international law (declarations, covenants and so on) but also the public culture of statesmen, diplomats and the media, and the internalised moral thinking or habits of moral thought of very large numbers of people, then these changes are no doubt important for the greater realisation of human rights, but they are neither here nor there so far as the theory of human rights is concerned. The existence of human rights predates processes of globalisation and expression in law, and is unaffected by whatever processes are taking place.

In both senses the claim 'human rights exist' may be correct, and both senses are legitimate and important ways of taking the claim.[4] The theoretical claim about human rights is vital, not least because without such a commitment as a moral thinker, most of the interest in human rights as part of global social reality evaporates. Nevertheless the existence of human rights in institutions, practices and habits of thought and action on a global scale is of great significance to any theorist of human rights who has any interest in seeing what he advocates being practised in the world.

III. GLOBAL GOVERNANCE

In terms of the approach I have adopted, what attitude should we take towards the idea of global governance? Should we advocate world government? Should we support the United Nations, and if so, is this because we see it, however much it may change, as remaining an alternative to world government or because we think that eventually it will turn into world government? The Commission on Global Governance, in its 1995 report, *Our Global Neighbourhood*, defined governance as 'the sum of the many ways individuals and institutions manage their common affairs' and contrasted this strongly with government, where the latter implied a central authority with the power to enforce its decisions (CGG 1995: 2; see also Halliday 2000; Rosenau 2000).

At the moment we have various structures reflecting global governance, but we do not have world government. We do order our public affairs at a global level, however imperfectly, through state interactions, bilateral and multilateral, in particular through the UN system but also through myriads of other more informal international bodies and associations. Given the extent of global problems – massive poverty, environmental degradation, violence, human rights abuses, refugee displacements – it is hard to resist the impression that we are not ordering our global public affairs terribly well. Of course the problem partly reflects how we do not order our public affairs very well within countries, but since many of the problems are partly caused by lack of concern or restraint *vis-à-vis* other states and peoples, the issue of how to order our global affairs better is a real and pressing one. Would a move as quickly as possible towards world government be the answer?

A. WORLD GOVERNMENT

What arguments are there for world government?

1. As Nielsen argues, we need a world government as a global *Leviathan* to give us peace. Only then with a world coercive power capable of enforcing compliance to rules will states have the security we need (Nielson 1988). Traditionally the horrors of inter-state war have provided a strong impulse to seek world government.

2. Although international law already contains many of the appropriate laws to do with human rights, the environment and so on, it remains ineffective and largely unimplemented (where it conflicts with national interests) because, as Cohen argues, it lacks the authority which comes from decisions being enforceable (Cohen 1954: ch. 5).

3. Only with world government ensuring that others co-operate in self-denying behaviour, will we get over the compliance problem of international relations, particularly in the modern world over effective environmental restraint, where compliance seems to require coercion on a global scale.

4. As Nielsen again argues, social justice *vis-à-vis* meeting the needs of the poor could be effectively implemented, both because the bureaucracy to deliver global 'welfare state' measures would be in place and because the measures could be financed through international taxation.

5. If we are world citizens, then we need the corresponding political institutions to give proper expression to our citizenship.

The arguments against world government proceed by answering the arguments above and by showing that world government is not necessary to achieve these objectives, and also that it is inappropriate because of the dangers it contains.

1. World government would not guarantee universal peace, any more than national governments guarantee peace within their borders. Wars would become global civil wars, all the more ghastly because of the divided loyalties involved. But more fundamentally the challenge for us is to counter the Hobbesian assumption that peace can only be maintained by fear and coercion, and argue that in various other ways the habits of peace can be developed (Jenkins 1971).

2. The effective implementation of international law is indeed vital, but its authority need not depend on a coercive power to enforce implementation. The compliance problem needs to be tackled, but through the strengthening of the range of social sanctions, world public opinion and so on.

3. The danger of world government is that it would become a global

tyranny, with no effective countervailing force, which could become oppressive of human rights without redress. Many advocates of world government such as Nielsen, are keen to stress the compatibility of world government with democratic institutions, and argue for some form of world federalism, in which semi-autonomous regions (no longer sovereign of course in the traditional sense) each contribute in a democratic way to the decisions made at a global level (Nielsen 1988). But it is difficult to see how this could be guaranteed. Likewise although a plurality of values could be maintained, as Cohen argues (Cohen 1954: ch. 5), as it does within modern pluralistic societies, there is a danger that it might not, partly because the analogy is not exact. As it is now other states can apply pressures and there are 'other places to escape to'.

4. Adequate measures to tackle evils such as world poverty will only come about if sufficient people believe in the arguments for greater aid, trade reform and so on, and therefore influence governments into taking more action. A radical conception of social justice such as Nielsen's would either have to be imposed if not generally accepted, or would not need to be imposed if it was generally accepted.

5. Still, does not the sense of world citizenship, with the appropriate perceptions to influence governments, require world government to give it embodiment? I would argue that it does not, since world citizenship need not be on all fours with citizenship within a state. Of course it needs embodiment, both via international institutions, and through national and international NGOs, that is an array of public institutions through which citizens can participate with a view to influencing global public affairs. To be sure, there is an argument for enabling 'we the peoples' of the UN to have more say in a more democratic UN, through for instance elected representatives in an organ not composed of state representatives.[5] But this would be part of a modified global institutional arrangement in which the state system continues to exist, albeit with increasing limitations on what sovereignty implied.

This discussion then points to the need for a truly international body at the heart of a matrix of other global institutions and associations, not a world government. Does the UN match up to this?

B. SHOULD WE SUPPORT THE UNITED NATIONS?

First, it seems that whatever normative position we adopt, there are reasons for supporting the UN. Even the realist will generally have prudential reason to do so, whilst the internationalist and most cosmopolitans will have moral reason to support it.[6] Second, in terms of the kind of cosmopolitanism which I have been advocating, there are both the general reasons for doing so, and also specific considerations, some in favour and some mildly sceptical.

But before we look at these reasons we need to make a distinction between on the one hand support for a truly international organisation of some kind and support for the UN as it currently operates. It is important to point out that whilst there may be various reasons for wanting the UN to be reformed, these considerations are somewhat separate from the question whether we need an international body as such in which representatives of counties can meet on matters of common interests, represent their interests and come to collective decisions.

Both the internationalist and the cosmopolitan, whatever his hue, will recognise the general desirability of peace and co-operation: that 'jaw-jaw' is better than 'war-war' (to quote Churchill); that international affairs are better regulated by international law than without it; that common threats to humanity such as the cumulative impacts of environmental damage need to have co-ordinated decisions; and that conditions of extreme poverty, regarded as bad in any society, need to be addressed in an internationally co-ordinated and co-operative way. It is almost inconceivable to suppose that any of these things could be achieved with anything like the same degree of success in the absence of a truly universal organisation than in the presence of it. Whether or not the UN could do better, for instance in improving its efficiency or structure, is another matter. That we could do without it or something very like it is quite implausible. Although it could certainly benefit from improvements in efficiency and structure, it is also worth remembering that it is like states themselves a human institution, exposed to the same weaknesses and inadequacies that states are, and therefore as Luard once remarked, it is only because people have unrealistic and utopian expectations of the UN that we 'condemn ... inadequacies which elsewhere they would accept as inescapable' (Luard 1981: 3).

Furthermore, however much a cosmopolitan will insist that what is right is not to be equated with what is thought to be right or what is established in custom and practice (since these could be mistaken), nevertheless there is little doubt that unless moral values are embedded in public culture, in laws and in institutions, they will not be effective or generally acted on. This is not merely the practical and mundane point that if values are not publicly embodied in practices then fewer people believe them, so fewer people will act on these beliefs, it is rather the point, recognised long ago in a different context by Bradley, that a morality in its entirety requires both body and soul, the body being the public culture, and the soul being the individuals' moral will breathing life into the body.[16] So the UN and related institutions represent part of the public embodiment of shared values which at least many actors agree upon. Even if a cosmopolitan had reason to be sceptical about some of the values reflected in the UN and international institutions and could wish for others to be in place, nevertheless he or she would have reason to support the UN as the embodiment of a world ethic, just so long as he or she felt that by and large the values embodied were to be accepted and supported. Only someone who really was totally disillusioned with virtually all the values it represented would have reason not to support the UN in principle. In this case, his or her position would be that although there was a world ethic embodied in the UN, it was a world ethic which he or she could not support, given his or her own cosmopolitan values and assessment of the global situation and what was needed to be done in the world.

From the point of view of the solidarist–pluralist cosmopolitanism which I have advocated, all this is to be accepted. Certainly the commitment to peace, to dialogue and consensus building, to co-operation to protect the environment, to upholding cultural diversity, to eradicating poverty and so on, are all to be commended. On the other hand, there are several weaknesses. First, although it is firmly committed to the promotion of democratic values, it is hardly very democratic itself, as I noted above, certainly in the sense of giving proper expression to the will of 'we the peoples'. In this connection we should note the advocacy by writers like Held and Archibugi of 'cosmopolitan democracy', for instance wanting to make the UN more democratic, wanting trans-societal law to be more cosmopolitan law than internationalist law, and generally advocating institutions and practices which correct the 'democratic deficit'. This is the fact that citizens within countries – even democratic countries with responsible governments – do not control many of the factors which affect their life prospects because these are determined or influenced by international factors beyond their countries' control (see Archibugi & Held 1995; Dower 2003: ch. 8 for further discussion).

Second, because of its being an organisation premised on the nation-state, it is perhaps too cautious about the issue of intervention, in many forms not merely or primarily military intervention, for the sake of human rights elsewhere. A consistent cosmopolitanism which is not so cautious as merely to endorse the internationalist order must be prepared to take a firm line on this issue of sovereignty. Third, it is arguable that the consensus within the UN system, particularly its development/economic institutions, on what development is and how it can be pursued consistently with environmental objectives is open to question, as I discussed earlier. What is being pursued in the name of sustainable development may be neither possible nor desirable.

But that said, the UN is to be strongly supported for the reasons given above, although there may also be reasons for wanting to see it modified in certain ways. But a judgement in the spirit of 'critical loyalty' is very different from a negative condemnation of it. It is the same critical loyalty which we need to bring to our nation-states as well. What a cosmopolitan global ethic provides us with are the tools of constructive criticism.

IV. THE NEW AGENDA

The world has major global problems, such as extensive conflicts, mass poverty, serious pressures on the environment. These require global solutions. The world has also become a 'global neighbourhood', and whether we like it or not, we have become thoroughly interdependent. For both reasons, the need to address problems and the challenges of living together in the 'global village', we need an ethic which is global in an upbeat form. The present state of the world provides global ethics with a new and pressing agenda. As I indicated at the beginning, the idea of a global ethic is not new and does not depend on modern conditions for it to be accepted in principle. But the modern world does require us to rethink our role as citizens of the world and to rethink the way we see the society of states and the norms which have governed them. The newness of the agenda however can be understood in two ways. First, it can be seen as a claim that we need a new way of thinking about the role of states and the identity of individuals, and this I think would be accepted by thinkers of a wide variety of persuasions. Second, it can be seen as a more specific claim about the particular content or priorities of this agenda.

A. A NEW WAY OF THINKING ABOUT THE STATE AND THE INDIVIDUAL

The processes of globalisation have led to increases in the levels of knowledge which people have about the world, to changed identities as members of bodies outwith the state, and generally to an increase in the capacity to act at a distance, whether this be by governments, corporations or NGOs. The need to pursue common goals (and not merely to pursue the national interests) is in turn grounded in an increasing consensus about certain norms and values, as witnessed by human rights instruments and many other attempts to formulate shared values.[8] These things are happening whether we like it or not, and the ethical categories of people's thinking are changing.

Thus the freedom of manoeuvre of states is, compared with the past, distinctly limited by what their electorates, now better informed and concerned about the world, may want; by a greater amount of international law and regulation, and by a general perception of what is needed by way of restraint to pursue common goals of environmental protection, peace and development. As Ramphal once put it concerning the reality of the human society we have become:

> I do not speak of world government; but as the concept of one world comes to signify more clearly a single human entity than that of an aggregation of states, we shall understand better the need to trim the edges of sovereignty and merge our national loyalties into our global responsibilities. (Ramphal 1981: 28)

But if one is also a cosmopolitan, and accepts for oneself an ethical theory in which these goals are seen as ones to be pursued, then one will have one's own reasons for endorsing the development of this framework – both the reshaping of state priorities and the development of a culture in which one's identity as a world citizen is recognised and nurtured. There may be much disagreement about how much emphasis should be put on developing this level of identity, through cosmopolitan education and so on, but the existence of the level of active concern will be endorsed by a wide variety of thinkers, for which the development of an appropriate global ethic as a social reality will be an important part of the process of promoting what one values.

B. A RADICAL AGENDA

But the new agenda as a reordering of priorities can go beyond the acceptance of the new framework indicated above. Here I collect together themes, especially in Part II, and summarise the case for a new agenda which would not generally be accepted, but which is required, I would argue, if we combine a certain factual understanding of the world with the ethical framework I have presented. It has only been sketched in at various points in the discussion. This is partly because my main tasks in this book have been, in descending order of importance: to outline the general lines of approach, to make a general case for an active cosmopolitanism, and to make a case for solidarist–pluralism as a general approach. It is also partly because my own views have been expressed elsewhere in various papers.[9]

We live on a planet with a finite carrying capacity. Human populations are set to grow significantly even though they may level off by 2030. We seek through development to increase the level of material well-being for all. We need to live at peace with one another if we are to achieve well-being. There are deep tensions here. Achieving high levels of material affluence for all in our world will be impossible. Even maintaining it for the rich parts of the world may be impossible in the long run. Long before that intense conflicts over competition for resources, including resources like water, will develop. If peace is not just the absence of war, but a condition in which there are not the seeds of future conflicts, we simply do not have peace in the world now, quite apart from all the overt wars which occur. In any case it is surely intolerable that a fifth of the world's population exists in extreme poverty alongside the conspicuous affluence of most in the North. The right to subsistence surely takes precedence over the right to maintain our affluence at the highest level.

This is not an argument that those of us who enjoy materially affluent life-styles should give them up. But it is an argument that we weaken our relentless pursuit of it and attachment to it. So we need to re-evaluate our commitment to material affluence, for the sake of the environment, for the sake of peace and for the sake of the poor. We also need fundamentally to re-evaluate our idea of well-being and thus the idea of development. Well-being has at least two levels: the common core of health, nutrition, a clean and resource-full environment, basic security, community, personal autonomy, knowledge and the exercise of skills, and also the variable elements defined by different cultures, religions, traditions and so on. To affirm these in their variety is to endorse the way of peace, and to act in solidarity with the rest of the world is to accept our global responsibility. This more radical agenda is not a call for self-sacrifice, though it may involve a re-evaluation of what is important in our lives. Part of my moral optimism in the face of a world that invites pessimism resides in the view that doing what we ought can be self-affirming rather than self-denying.

Nor is this more radical agenda a call for world government. Of course the more its principles or indeed cosmopolitan principles generally are adopted, the more states will be constrained and directed towards greater levels of co-operation. The United Nations will become a more genuine and effective expression of global goals rather than the arena it tends to be at present for accommodating conflicting state interests. We need global governance, not world government. To the extent that citizens accept a level of identity as world citizens, to that extent their states will be directed to the global common good anyway. World government would only be acceptable when it became unnecessary. So let us be good world citizens instead.

NOTES

1. There are also hybrid cases, such as the World Conservation Union (IUCN) which is made up of representatives from other NGOs and from governments.
2. See my discussion in Chapter 2 of Carr on idealism and Zolo on the Gulf War.
3. Likewise the development of international law to do with economic cooperation. See Chapter 7.

4. There is a parallel here with claims about a 'global ethic' or 'world ethic'. The assertion that 'there is a global/world ethic' contains just the same ambiguity.
5. CAMDUN, the Campaign for a More Democratic UN, works on this issue.
6. For a useful examination of different ways of looking at international institutions, see Goodwin 1970.
7. Bradley 187: Essay V, 177–81. Bradley would not necessarily have approved of this radical use of his idea!
8 See for instance the Commission on Global Governance 1995: 48–54, for its list of 'neighbourhood values': respect for life; liberty; justice and equity; mutual respect; caring; integrity.
9. Some of these are indicated in the bibliography. For a fuller list, please contact the author.

QUESTIONS FOR DISCUSSION

1. In what respects might a cosmopolitan favour globalisation and in what respects might she criticise it?
2. How big a role do international non-state bodies play in global affairs? How a bigger role should they play?
3. Granted that a realist, an internationalist and a cosmopolitan could all support United Nations, how different would their reasons be for doing so? Would there be any reason for wanting it to evolve into a world government?
4. In what respects is world ethics a new agenda and in what respects is it not?

BIBLIOGRAPHY

(Note: where several chapters are given which appear in the same book, full bibliographical details are given in the book entry. Where square brackets are used, they indicate the original publication date, and the date in round brackets indicates a modern edition.)

Aiken, W. & LaFollette, H. (eds) (1977), *World Hunger and Moral Obligation*, Englewood Cliffs, NJ: Prentice-Hall.

Almond, B. (1990), 'Alasdair MacIntyre: the virtue of tradition', *Journal of Applied Philosophy*, Vol. 7, No. 1.

Aman, K. (ed.) (1991), *Ethical Principles for Development: Needs, Capacities and Rights*, Upper Montclair, NJ: Institute for Critical Thinking, Montclair State University.

Anscombe, G. E. M. (1970), 'War and murder', in Wasserstrom, R. (ed.), *War and Morality*.

Apel, K.-O. (1992), 'The moral imperative', *UNESCO Courier*, July/August.

Appiah, K. (2006), *Cosmopolitanism – Ethics in a World of Strangers*, New York: W. W. Norton & Co.

Aquinas, Th. (1953 [c. 1270]), *Summa Theologiae*, e.g. excerpts in Bigongiari, D. (ed.), *The Political Ideas of St Thomas Aquinas*, New York: Hafner.

Archibugi, D. & Held, D. (eds) (1995), *Cosmopolitan Democracy – An Agenda for a New World Order*, Cambridge: Polity Press.

Aristotle (1988 [c. 350 BC]), *The Politics*, e.g. in Everson, S. (ed.), Cambridge: Cambridge University Press.

Atack, I. (2005), *The Ethics of Peace and War*, Edinburgh: Edinburgh University Press.

Attfield, R. (1983), *The Ethics of Environmental Concern*, New York: Columbia University Press.

Attfield, R. (1999), *The Ethics of the Global Environment*, Edinburgh: Edinburgh University Press.

Augustine (1947 [c. 412]), *City of God*, e.g. Healey, J. (tr.), London: Dent.

Austin, J. (1995 [1832]), *The Province of Jurisprudence Determined*, Cambridge: Cambridge University Press.

Axelrod, R. (1984), *The Evolution of Co-operation*, New York: Basic Books.

Barnaby, F. (ed.) (1988), *The Gaia Peace Atlas*, London: Pan Books.

212

Barry, B. (1986), 'Can states be moral? International morality and the compliance problem', in Ellis, *Ethics and International Relations*.

Bauer, P. (1984), *Rhetoric and Reality*, London: Weidenfeld and Nicolson.

Beitz, C. R. (1979), *Political Theory and International Relations*, Princeton, NJ: Princeton University Press.

Beitz, C. R. (1992), 'International justice: conflict', in Becker, L. C. and Becker, C. B. (eds), *Encyclopaedia of Ethics*, Chicago, IL: St James Press.

Beitz, C. R. (1999), *Political Theory and International Relations*, 2nd Edition, Princeton, NJ: Princeton University Press.

Beitz, C. R. et al. (eds) (1985), *International Ethics*, Princeton, NJ: Princeton University Press.

Benedict, R. (1935), *Patterns of Culture*, London: Routledge.

Bodin, J. (1962 [1576]), *Six Books of a Commonwealth*, e.g. McKnee, K. D. (ed.), Cambridge, MA: Harvard University Press.

Borchert D. M. & Stewart, D. (1986), *Explaining Ethics*, London: Macmillan.

Boulding, E. (1990), *Building a Global Civic Culture – Education for an Interdependent World*, Syracuse, NY: Syracuse University Press.

Boutros Ghali, B. (1992), *Agenda for Peace*, New York: United Nations.

Bradley, F. H. (1878), *Ethical Studies*, Oxford: Oxford University Press.

Brandt, R. B. (1967), 'Ethical relativism', in Edwards, P. (ed.), *Encyclopaedia of Philosophy*, New York: Macmillan.

Brandt, R. B. (1974), 'Utilitarianism and the rules of war', in Cohen, *War and Moral Responsibility*.

Britain Yearly Meeting (1995), *Quaker Faith and Practice*, London: Warwick Printing Co.

Brown, C. (1992), *International Relations Theory: New Normative Approaches*, New York: Harvester Wheatsheaf.

Brown, P. G. (2000), *Ethics, Economics and International Relations*, Edinburgh: Edinburgh University Press.

Brown, E. & Kleingeld, P. (2003), 'Cosmopolitanism', *Stanford University Encyclopaedia*, accessed 7/11/06 on http://plato.stanford.edu/entries/cosmopolitanism/.

Bull, H. (1966), 'The Grotian conception of international society', in Butterfield, H. & Wight, M. (eds), *Diplomatic Investigations*, London: Allen and Unwin.

Bull, H. (1979), 'Human rights and world politics', in Pettman, R. (ed.), *Moral Claims in World Affairs*, New York: St Martin's Press.

Bull, H. (1985), *The Anarchical Society*, 2nd edn, London: Macmillan.

Cameron, J. R. (1989), 'Do future generations matter?', in Dower, *Ethics and Environmental Responsibility*.

Carnegie Council on Ethics and International Relations, *Ethics and International Affairs*.

Carr, E. H. (1939), *The Twenty Years' Crisis: 1919–1939*, London: Macmillan.

Carter, A. (2001), *The Political Theory of Global Citizenship*, London: Routledge.

Ceadel, M. (1987), *Thinking about Peace and War*, Oxford: Oxford University Press.

Clark, R. (1983), 'Gaia and the forms of life', in Elliot & Gare, *Environmental Philosophy*.

Clausewitz, von, C. (1968 [1832]), *On War*, in e.g. Rappoport, A. (ed.), Harmondsworth: Penguin Books.

Cohen, J. (1954), *The Principles of World Citizenship*, Oxford: Blackwell.

Cohen, J. (1985), 'Moral Skepticism and International Relations', in Beitz, *International Ethics*.

Cohen J. (ed.) (1996), *For Love of Country: Debating the Limits of Patriotism*, Boston, MA: Beacon Books.

Cohen, M. et al. (eds) (1974), *War and Moral Responsibility*, Princeton, NJ: Princeton University Press.

Commission on Global Governance (CGG) (1995), *Our Global Neighbourhood*, Oxford: Oxford University Press.

Cooper, D. E. (1992), 'The idea of environment', in Cooper, D. E. & Palmer, J. A. (eds), *The Environment in Question*, London: Routledge.

Crocker, D. (1991), 'Towards Development Ethics', *World Development*, Vol. 19, No. 5.

Crocker, D. (1992), 'Functioning and Capability: the foundations of Sen's and Nussbaum's development ethics' *Political Theory*, Vol. 20, No. 4.

Crocker, D. (1995), 'Functioning and capability: the foundations of Sen's and Nussbaum's development ethics', in Nussbaum, M. & Glover, J. (eds), *Women, Community and Development*, Oxford: Clarendon Press.

Crocker, D. A. (1991), 'Towards Development Ethics', *World Development*, Vol. 19, No. 5.

Curle, A. (1981), *True Justice*, London: Quaker Home Service.

de Vattel, E. (1811 [1755]), *The Law of Nations*, London: Clarke.

de Vitoria, F. (1991 [1532]), *De jure belli Hispanorum in barbaros*, e.g. in *Political Writings*, Pagden, A. & Lawrance, J. (tr.), Cambridge: Cambridge University Press.

Dobson, A. (1998), *Justice and the Environment: Conceptions of Environmental Sustainability and Theories of Distributive Justice*, Oxford: Oxford University Press.

Dobson, A. (ed.) (1999), *Fairness and Futurity*, Oxford: Oxford University Press.

Donaldson, T. (1989), *The Ethics of International Business*, Oxford: Oxford University Press.

Donaldson, T. (1992), 'Kant's Global Rationalism', in Nardin & Mapel, *Traditions of International Ethics*.

Donelan, M. (1990), *Elements of International Political Theory*, Oxford: Clarendon Press.

Dower, N. (1983), 'Ethics and environmental futures', *International Journal of Environmental Studies*, Vol. 21.

Dower, N. (1983), *World Poverty – Challenge and Response*, York: Ebor Press.

Dower, N. (1988), *What is Development? A Philosopher's Answer*, Glasgow: Centre for Development Studies, University of Glasgow.

Dower, N. (ed.) (1989), *Ethics and Environmental Responsibility*, Aldershot: Gower.

Dower, N. (1991), 'World poverty', in Singer, P. (ed.), *Companion to Ethics*, Oxford: Blackwell.

Dower, N. (1992), 'Sustainability and the right to development', in Attfield, R. A. & Wilkins, B. (eds), *International Justice and the Third World*, London: Routledge.

Dower, N. (1993), 'Are official aid and private charity ethically on a par?', in Carty, A. & Singer, H. (eds), *Conflict and Change in the 1990s*, London: Macmillan.

Dower, N. (1994), 'The idea of the environment', in Attfield, R. A. & Belsey, A. (eds), *Philosophy and the Natural Environment*, Cambridge: Cambridge University Press.

Dower, N. (1995), 'Peace and security: some conceptual notes', in Salla, M. et al. (eds), *Essays on Peace*, Rockhampton: Central Queensland University Press.

Dower, N., (2002), 'Against War as a Response to Terrorism', *Philosophy and Geography*, Vol. 5, No. 1.

Dower, N. (2003), *Introduction to Global Citizenship*, Edinburgh: Edinburgh University Press.

Dower, N. (2005), 'The Nature and Scope of Global Ethics and the Relevance of the Earth Charter', *Journal of Global Ethics*, Vol. 1, No. 1.

Dower, N. & Williams, J. (2002), *Global Citizenship: A Critical Reader*, Edinburgh: Edinburgh University Press.

Drydyk, J. & Penz, P. (eds) (1997), *Global Justice, Global Democracy; Prospects for a New Internationalism*, Halifax: Fernwood.

Drydyk, J. (2003), 'How to make global ethics credible: beyond minimalism', Ottawa: Department of Philosophy, Carleton University.

Eade, J. & O'Byrne, D. (eds) (2005), *Global Ethics & Civil Society*, Aldershot: Ashgate.

Earth Charter (2002), www.earthcharter.org/, March 2002.

Ehrlich, P. & Ehrlich, A. (1991), *The Population Explosion*, London: Hutcheson.

Ekins, P. (ed.) (1986), *The Living Economy*, London: Routledge.

Elfstrom, D. (1990), *Ethics in a Shrinking World*, London: Macmillan.

Elliot, R. & Gare, A. (eds) (1983), *Environmental Philosophy*, Milton Keynes: Open University.

Ellis, A. (ed.) (1985), *Ethics and International Relations*, Manchester: Manchester University Press.

Engel, J. R. & Engel, J. B. (eds) (1990), *Ethics of Environment and Development: Global Challenges and International Responsibilities*, London: Belhaven Press.

Falk, R. (1975), *A Study of Future Worlds*, New York: Free Press.

Feinberg, J. (1973), *Social Philosophy*, Englewood Hills, NJ: Prentice-Hall.

Fichte, J. G. (2000) [1796]), *Foundations of Natural Right*, Neuhouser, F. (ed.) & Baur, M. (tr.), Cambridge: Cambridge University Press.

Finnis, J. (1990), *Natural Law and Natural Rights*, Oxford: Oxford University Press.

Fishkin, J. (1985), 'The theory of justice and international relations: the limits of liberal theory', in Ellis, *Ethics and International Relations*.

Frank, A. G. (1975), *On Capitalist Underdevelopment*, Bombay: Oxford University Press.

Frankena, W. K. (1973), *Ethics*, 2nd edn, Englewood Cliffs, NJ: Prentice-Hall.

Frost, M. (1996), *Ethics in International Relations: A Constitutive Theory*, Cambridge: Cambridge University Press.

Fukuyama, F. (1992), *The End of History and the Last Man*, London: Penguin Books.

Fullinwider, R. K. (1984), 'War and innocence', in Beitz, *International Ethics*.

Fullinwider, R. K. (1988), 'Understanding terrorism', in Luper-Foy, *Problems of International Justice*.

Gasper, D. (2003), *The Ethics of Development*, Edinburgh: Edinburgh University Press.

Gerle, E. (1995), *In Search of a Global Ethics*, Lund: Lund University Press.

Gewirth, A. (1978), *Reason and Morality*, Chicago, IL: Chicago University Press.

Glover, J. (1977), *Causing Death and Saving Lives*, Harmondsworth: Penguin Books.

Godwin, W. (1946 [1793]), *Enquiry Concerning Political Justice*, Priestley, F. E. L. (ed.), Toronto: University of Toronto Press.

Goodpaster, K. (1978), 'On being morally considerable', *Journal of Philosophy*, Vol. 75, No. 6.

Goodwin, G. L. (1970), 'World institutions and world order', in Cosgrove, A. & Twitchett, K. J. (eds), *The New International Actors: the UN and the EEC*, London: Macmillan.

Goulet, D. (1971), *The Cruel Choice – a New Concept in the Theory of Development*, Lanham: University Press of America.

Goulet, D. (1995), *Development Ethics – Theory and Practice*, London: Zed Books.

Graham, G. (1996), *Ethics and International Relations*, Oxford: Oxford University Press.

Grotius, H. (1925 [1625]), *De Iure Belli ac Pacis (On the Law of War and Peace)*, Kelsey, F. W. (tr.), Oxford: Clarendon Press.

Halliday, F. (2000), 'Global Governance: Prospects and Problems', in Held & McGrew, *The Global Transformations Reader*.

Hardin, G. (1977), 'Lifeboat ethics: the case against helping the poor', in Aiken & LaFollette, *World Hunger and Moral Obligation*.

Hare, J. E. & Joynt, C. B. (1982), *Ethics and International Affairs*, London: Macmillan.

Hare, R. M. (1963), *Freedom and Reason*, Oxford: Oxford University Press.

Hare, R. M. (1972), 'Peace', *Applications of Moral Philosophy*, London: Macmillan.

Hare, R. M. (1974), 'The rules of war and moral reasoning', in Cohen, *War and Moral Responsibility*.

Hare, R. M. (1981), *Moral Thinking*, Oxford: Oxford University Press.

Harman, G. (1977), *The Nature of Morality*, New York: Oxford University Press.

Harris, J. (1980), *Violence and Responsibility*, London: Routledge.

Hayter, T. (1981), *The Creation of World Poverty*, London: Pluto Press.

Heater, D. (2002), *World Citizenship*, London: Continuum.

Hegel, G. (1942 [1821]), *The Philosophy of Right*, e.g. Knox, T. M. (tr.), Oxford: Clarendon Press.

Heidegger, M. (1977 [1952]), *The Question concerning Technology*, e.g. in Lowitt, W. (tr.), *The Question concerning Technology and Other Essays*, New York: Harper & Row.

Held, D. & McGrew, A. (eds) (2000a), *The Global Transformations Reader*, Cambridge: Polity Press.

Held, D. & McGrew, A. (2000b), 'The Great Globalization Debate', in Held & McGrew, *The Global Transformations Reader*.

Hobbes, Th. (1991 [1651]), *Leviathan*, e.g. Tuck, R. (ed.), Cambridge: Cambridge University Press.

Hockaday, A. (1982), 'In defence of deterrence', in Goodwin, G. (ed.), *Ethics and Nuclear Deterrence*, London: Croom Helm.

Holmes, R. (ed.) (1990), *Non-Violence in Theory and Practice*, Belmont, CA: Wadsworth Publishing Co.

Honderich, T. (2003), *After the Terror*, Edinburgh: Edinburgh University Press.

Hume, D. (1888 [1742]), *A Treatise of Human Nature*, e.g. in Selby-Bigge, L. A. (ed.), Oxford: Oxford University Press.

Huntington, S. P. (1996), *The Clash of Civilizations and the Remaking of World Order*, New York: Simon and Schuster.

Hutchings, K. & Dannreuther, R. (eds) (1999), *Cosmopolitan Citizenship*, Basingstoke: Macmillan.

Ihara, C. (1978), 'A defence of pacifism', *Ethics*, Vol. 88.

Jacobs, M. (1999), 'Sustainable Development as a Contested Concept', in Dobson, *Fairness and Futurity*.

Jenkins, I. (1973), 'The conditions of peace', *The Monist*, Vol. 57, No. 4.

Jones, Ch. (1999), *Global Justice – Defending Cosmopolitanism*, Oxford: Oxford University Press.

Jubilee Debt Campaign (2006), accessed on 10/11/06 at www.jubileedebtcampaign.org.uk/.

Kaldor, M. (2001), *New & Old Wars*, Cambridge: Polity Press.

Kant, I. (1970 [1784]), 'The idea of a universal history with a cosmopolitan intent', e.g. in Reiss, H. (tr.), *Kant's Political Writings*, Cambridge: Cambridge University Press.

Kant, I. (1949 [1785]), *The Groundwork of the Metaphysic of Morals*, in Paton, H. (tr.), *The Moral Law*, London: Hutcheson.

Kant, I. (1970 [1795]), *Perpetual Peace*, e.g. in Reiss, H. (tr.), *Kant's Political Writings*, Cambridge: Cambridge University Press.

Kavka, G. (1974), 'Doubts about unilateral nuclear disarmament', in Beitz, *International Ethics*.

Keane, J, (2003), *Global Civil Society?*, Cambridge: Cambridge University Press.

Kekes, J. (1993), *The Morality of Pluralism*, Princeton, NJ: Princeton University Press.

Kenny, A. J. P. (1985), *The Logic of Deterrence*, London: Firethorn Press.

Kidder, R. (1995), *How Good People Make Tough Choices*, New York: Simon & Schuster.

Kim, Y. (1999), *A Common Framework for the Ethics of the 21st Century*, Paris: Unesco.

Küng, H. (1990), *Global Responsibility – In Search of a New World Ethic*, London: SCM Press.

Küng, H. & Kuschel, K.-J. (1993), *A Global Ethic: The Declaration of the Parliament of the World's Religions*, London: SCM Press.

Lackey, D. (1989), *Ethics of War and Peace*, Englewood Cliffs, NJ: Prentice-Hall.

Lackey, D. (1974), 'Missiles and morals', in Beitz, *International Ethics*.

Laszlo, E. (ed.) (1993), *The Multicultural Planet* (UNESCO Report), Oxford: Oneworld.

Lee, K., Holland, A. & McNeill, D. (eds) (2000), *Global Sustainable Development in the 21st Century*, Edinburgh: Edinburgh University Press.

Lehman, H. (1986), 'Equal pay for equal work in the Third World', *Ethics and International Relations*.

Leopold, A. (1949), *A Sand County Almanac*, Oxford: Oxford University Press.

Linklater, A. (1992), 'What is a Good International Citizen?', in P. Keal (ed.), *Ethics and Foreign Policy*, London: Allen and Unwin.

Locke, J. (1960 [1689]), *Second Treatise of Government*, e.g. in Laslett, P (ed.), Cambridge: Cambridge University Press.

Luard, E. (1979), *The United Nations*, London: Macmillan.

Luard, E. (1981), *Human Rights and Foreign Policy*, London: Pergamon Press.

Luban, D. (1974), ' Just war and human rights', in Beitz, *International Ethics*.

Luper-Foy, S. (ed.) (1988), *Problems of International Justice*, London: Westview Press.

Machiavelli, N. (1988 [1513]), *The Prince*, e.g. in Skinner, Q. (ed.), Cambridge: Cambridge University Press.

Machiavelli, N. (1979 [1531]), *Discourses*, e.g. in Bondanelli, P. & Musa, M. (eds), *The Portable Machiavelli*, Harmondsworth: Penguin Books.

MacIntyre, A. (1967), *A Short History of Ethics*, London: Routledge & Kegan Paul.

MacIntyre, A. (1981), *After Virtue: A Study in Moral Theory*, London: Duckworth.

Mackie, J. L. (1984), 'Can there be a right-based morality?', in Waldron, J. (ed.), *Theories of Rights*, Oxford: Oxford University Press.

Macquarrie, J. (1973), *The Concept of Peace*, New York: Harper & Row.

Magraw, D. B. & Nickel, J. W. (1990), 'Can today's system handle transboundary problems?', in Scherer, *Upstream Downstream – Issues in Environmental Ethics*.

Matthews, E. H. (1989), 'The metaphysics of environmentalism', in Dower, *Ethics and Environmental Responsibility*.

Mavrodes, G. I. (1985), 'Conventions and the morality of war', in Beitz, *International Ethics*.

Maxwell, M. (1990), *Morality among Nations – An Evolutionary View*, Albany, NY: State University of New York Press.

Mazzini, G. (2004 [1844]), *The Duties of Man*, Kessinger Publishing.

McGrew, A. (2000), 'Democracy beyond Borders?', in Held & McGrew, *Global Transformations Reader*.

Midgley, E. B. F. (1975), *The Natural Law Tradition and the Theory of International Relations*, London: Paul Elek.

Mill, J. S. (1962 [1861]), *Utilitarianism*, e.g. Warnock, M. (ed.), London: Fontana.

Miller, J. D. B. (1979), 'Morality, interests and rationalisation', in Pettman, R. (ed.), *Moral Claims in World Affairs*, New York: St Martin's Press.

Miller, L. H. (1990), *Global Order: Values and Power in International Politics*, London: Westview Press.

Mittrany, D. (1970), 'The Functionalist approach to World Organisations', in Cosgrove, C. & Twitchett, K. J. (eds), *The New International Actors: The UN and the EU*, London: Macmillan.

Morgenthau, H. (1954), *Politics among Nations*, New York: Albert Knopf.

Mothersson, K. (1992), *From Hiroshima to The Hague: A Guide to the World Court Project*, Geneva: International Peace Bureau.

Moynihan, D. P. (1993), *Pandemonium – Ethnicity in International Politics*, Oxford: Oxford University Press.

Naess, A. (1989), *Ecology, Community and Life-style: Outline of an Ecosophy*, Rothenberg, D. (tr.), Cambridge: Cambridge University Press.

Nagel, Th. (1970), *The Possibility of Altruism*, Oxford: Clarendon Press.

Nagel, Th. (1974), 'War and massacre', in Beitz, *International Ethics*.

Nagel, Th. (1979), 'Ethics without biology', in *Mortal Questions*, Cambridge, Cambridge University Press.

Nagel, Th. (2005), 'The Problem of Global Justice', *Philosophy & Public Affairs*, Vol. 33.

Nardin, T. (1983), *Law, Morality, and the Relations of States*, Princeton, NJ: Princeton University Press.

Nardin, T. and Mapel, D. (eds) (1992), *Traditions of International Ethics*, Cambridge: Cambridge University Press.

Narveson, J. (1970), 'Pacifism: a philosophical analysis', in Wasserstrom, *War and Morality*.

Nerfin, M. (1987), 'Neither Prince nor Merchant: Citizen', *Development Dialogue*, Vol. 1.

Niebuhr, R. (1932), *Moral Man and Immoral Society*, New York: Charles Scribner.

Nielsen, K. (1988), 'World government, security and social justice', in Luper-Foy, *Problems of International Justice*.

Nozick, R. (1974), *Anarchy, State and Utopia*, Oxford: Blackwell.

Nussbaum, M. (1992), 'Human functioning and social justice: in defence of Aristotelian essentialism', *Political Theory*, Vol. 20.

Nussbaum, M. (1994), 'Patriotism and cosmopolitanism', *The Boston Review*, October.

Nussbaum, M. (2000), *Women and Human Development*, Cambridge: Cambridge University Press.

O'Neill, O. (1989), *Faces of Hunger – An Essay on Poverty, Justice and Development*, London: Allen & Unwin.

O'Neill, O. (1993), 'International justice: distribution', in Becker, L. C. & Becker, C. B. (eds), *Encyclopaedia of Ethics*, Chicago: St James Press.

Parekh, B. (2002), 'Cosmopolitanism and Global Citizenship', *Review of International Studies*, Vol. 31, No. 2.

Parekh, B. (2005), 'Principles of a Global Ethic', in Eade & O'Byrne, *Global Ethics and Civil Society*.

Partridge, E. (1990), 'On the rights of future generations', in Scherer, *Upstream Downstream – Issues in Environmental Ethics*.

Passmore, J. (1974), *Man's Responsibility for Nature*, London: Duckworth.

Peffer, R. G. (1990), *Marxism, Morality and Social Justice*, Princeton, NJ: Princeton University Press.

Penn, W. (1993 [1693]), 'An essay towards the present and future peace of Europe, by the establishment of an European dyet, parliament, or estates', in Bronner, E. B. (ed.), *The Peace of Europe, The Fruits of Solitude and other writings*, London: Dent.

Peterson, V. S. (ed.) (1992), *Gendered States: Feminist (Re)Visions of International Relations Theory*, London: Lynne Rienner.

Pogge, Th. (1989), *Realising Rawls*, New York: Cornell University Press.

Pogge, Th. (1992), 'Cosmopolitanism and Sovereignty', *Ethics*, Vol. 103.

Pogge. Th. (1995), 'An egalitarian law of peoples', *Philosophy & Public Affairs*.

Pogge, Th. (ed.) (2001), *Global Justice*, Oxford: Blackwell.

Pogge, Th. (2003), *World Poverty and Human Rights*, Cambridge: Cambridge University Press.

Ramphal, S. S. (1981), *Sovereignty or Solidarity* (T. Callendar Memorial Lectures), Aberdeen: University of Aberdeen.

Rawls, J. (1971), *A Theory of Justice*, Oxford: Oxford University Press.

Rawls, J. (1993), *Political Liberalism*, New York: Columbia University Press.

Rawls, J. (1993), 'The law of peoples', Shute, S. & Hurley, S. (eds), *On Human Rights*, New York: Basic Books.

Rawls, J. (1999), *The Law of Peoples*, Cambridge, MA: Harvard University Press.

Reiss, H. (tr.) (1970), *Kant's Political Writings*, Cambridge: Cambridge University Press.

Riddell, R. (1987), *Foreign Aid Reconsidered*, London: James Currey.

Robertson, R. (1992), *Globalisation: Social Theory and Global Culture*, London: Sage.

Robinson, F. (1999), *Globalizing Care: Ethics, Feminist Theory, and International Relations*, Boulder, CO: Westview Press.

Robinson, M. (1985), BBC Talk, Autumn.

Robinson, M. (2002), Lecture (reported).

Rolston, H. (1988), *Environmental Ethics*, Philadelphia, PA: Temple University Press.

Rosenau, J. (2000), 'Governance in a Globalizing World', in Held & McGrew, *The Global Transformations Reader*.

Ross, W. D. (1930), *The Right and the Good*, Oxford: Oxford University Press.

Rousseau, J.-J. (1966 [1762]), *The Social Contract*, e.g. in Cole, G. D. (tr.), London: Dent.

Sachs, W. (ed.) (1992), *The Development Dictionary*, London: Zed Books.

Sandel, M. (1982), *Liberalism and the Limits of Justice*, Cambridge: Cambridge University Press.

Scarrow, D. S. (1985), 'Institutional rights and international duties', in Ellis, *Ethics and International Relations*.

Scheffler, S. (1999), 'Conceptions of Cosmopolitanism', *Utilitas*, Vol. 11, No. 3.

Scherer, D. (ed.) (1990), *Upstream Downstream – Issues in Environmental Ethics*, Philadelphia, PA: Temple University Press.

Scholte, J.-A. (2000), *Globalization: A Critical Introduction*, Basingstoke: Palgrave.

Sen, A. (1987), *On Ethics and Economics*, Oxford: Blackwell.

Sen, A. (1989), *Inequality Re-examined*, Cambridge, MA: Harvard University Press.

Sen. A. (1999), *Development as Freedom*, Oxford: Oxford University Press.

Sen, A. (2006), *Identity and Violence – The Illusion of Destiny*, London: Allen Lane.

Shaw, D. (1989), 'After Chernobyl: the ethics of risk taking', in Dower, *Ethics and Environmental Responsibility*.

Shiva, V. (1989), *Staying Alive – Women, Ecology and Development*, London: Zed Books.

Shue, H. (1996), *Basic Rights: Subsistence, Affluence and US Foreign Policy*, 2nd edition, Princeton, NJ: Princeton University Press.

Sidgwick, H. (1919 [1877]), *Elements of Politics*, London: Macmillan.

Simon, J. (1995), *The State of Humanity*, Oxford: Blackwell.

Simon, J. (1981), *The Ultimate Resource*, Oxford: Robertson.

Singer, P. (1972) 'Famine, affluence and morality', *Philosophy & Public Affairs*, Vol. I, and, extended (1979), 'Rich and poor', in Singer, P., *Practical Ethics*, Cambridge: Cambridge University Press.

Singer, P. (2002), *One World – The Ethics of Globalisation*, London: Yale University Press.

Smart, J. J. C. & Williams, B. A. O. (1973), *Utilitarianism For and Against*, Cambridge: Cambridge University Press.

Smith, J. B. D. (1979), 'Morality, interests and rationalisation', in Pettman, R. (ed.), *Moral Claims in World Affairs*, New York: St Martin's Press.

Smith, R. (1961), 'The witness of the church', in Stein, *Nuclear Weapons and Christian Conscience*.

Smith, R. K. M. & van den Anker, Ch. (eds) (2005), *The Essentials of Human Rights*, London: Hodder and Stoughton.

Stace, W. (1937), *The Concept of Morals*, London: Macmillan.

Stein, W. (ed.) (1961), *Nuclear Weapons and Christian Conscience*, London: Merlin Press.

Streeten, P. (1999), 'Components of a Future Development Strategy – The Importance of Human Development', *Finance and Development*, Vol. 36.

Suarez, F. (1866 [1597]), *Disputationes Metaphysicae*, in *Opera Omnia*, Berton, C. (ed.), Vols 25–6, Paris: Vives.

Tamir, Y. (1993), *Liberal Nationalism*, Princeton NJ: Princeton University Press.

Tan, K.-Ch. (2004), *Justice without Borders Cosmopolitanism, Nationalism, and Patriotism*, Cambridge: Cambridge University Press.

Taylor, Ch. (1989), *Sources of the Self: the Making of Modern Identity*, Cambridge MA: Harvard University Press.

Taylor, P. W. (1986), *Respect for Nature*, Princeton, NJ: Princeton University Press.

The Boston Review (1994), 'Patriotism or cosmopolitanism?', October.

Thompson, J. (1983), 'The preservation of wildernesses', in Elliot & Gare, *Environmental Philosophy*.

Thompson, J. (1992), *Justice and World Order*, London: Routledge.

Thompson, J. (2001), 'Planetary citizenship: the definition and defence of an ideal', in Gleeson, B. & Low, N. (eds), *Governing for the Environment*, Basingstoke: Palgrave.

Tomlinson, J. (1999), *Globalization and Culture*, Cambridge: Polity Press.

Toulmin, S. (1992), *Cosmopolis – The Hidden Agenda of Modernity*, New York: Free Press.

Tuck, R. (1989), *Hobbes*, Oxford: Oxford University Press.

UNESCO (1992), 'Universality – A European Dream?', Paris: UNESCO.

UNHCR (2006), accessed on 10/11/06 at www.unhcr.ch/

United Nations (UN) (1986), *Declaration on the Right to Development*, New York: United Nations, 4 December, 41/128.

United Nations (UN) (2000), *Millennium Development Goals*, accessed on 9/11/06 at http://www.un.org/millenniumgoals/.

United Nations Development Programme (UNDP) (1990–1997), *Human Development Reports*, New York: United Nations.

Van den Anker, C. (2002), 'Global Justice, Global Institutions and Global Citizenship', in Dower & Williams, *Global Citizenship: A Critical Reader*.

Vincent, R. J. (1986), *Human Rights and International Relations*, Cambridge: Cambridge University Press.

Walzer, M. (1974), 'World War II: why was this war different?', in Cohen, *War and Moral Responsibility*.

Walzer, M. (1977), *Just and Unjust Wars*, New York: Basic Books.

Walzer, M. (1985), 'The rights of political communities' & 'The moral standing of states', in Beitz, *International Ethics*.

Wasserstrom, R. (1970), 'On the morality of war: a preliminary enquiry', in Wasserstrom, *War and Morality*.

Wasserstrom, R. (ed.) (1970), *War and Morality*, Belmont, CA: Wadsworth Publishing Co.

Westermarck, E. (1932), *Ethical Relativity*, New York: Harcourt.

Wheeler, N. J. & Dunne, T. (1998), 'Good International Citizenship: A Third Way for British Foreign Policy', *International Affairs*, Vol. 74, No. 4.

Widdows, H. (2005), 'Why Global Ethics?', in Eade & O'Byrne, *Global Ethics and Civil Society*.

Wight, M. (1991), *International Theory – The Three Traditions*, London: Leicester University Press.

Wikipedia (2006), entry on 'Second Superpower', accessed 7/11/06 on http://en.wikipedia.org/wiki/Second_Superpower.

Wilkinson, P. (1986), *Terrorism and the Liberal State*, 2nd ed., New York: New York University Press.

Williams, B. A. O. (1972), *Morality – An Introduction to Ethics*, New York: Harper.

Williams, H., Wright, M. & Evans, T. (eds) (1993), *International Relations and Political Theory*, Buckingham: Open University Press.

Williams, J. (2002), 'Good International Citizenship', in Dower & Williams, *Global Citizenship: A Critical Reader*.

Wong, D. (1984), *Moral Relativity*, Berkeley, CA: University of California Press.

Wong, D. (1992), 'Moral relativism', in Becker, L. C. & Becker C. B. (eds), *Encyclopaedia of Ethics*, Chicago, IL: St James Press.

Woolman, J. (1963), *The Journal and Essays*, Gummere, A. M. (ed.) (1922), London: Macmillan.

World Commission on Development (WCD) (1980), *North South – A Strategy for Survival (The Brandt Report)*, London: Pan Books.

World Commission on Environment and Development (WCED) (1987), *Our Common Future (The Brundtland Report)*, Oxford: Oxford University Press.

World Court (1996), *Advisory Judgement*, General List No. 95, 8 July.

Zolo, D. (1997), *Cosmopolis – Prospects for World Government*, Cambridge: Polity Press.

INDEX

ABMs, 138
absence of war, peace as, 143, 209
absolute poverty, 7, 162; *see also* poverty
absolutism in ethics, 128, 130
aesthetic appreciation of nature, 174, 187
affluence, 11, 159, 171, 209–10
African National Congress, 127
Agenda for Peace, 73
aggression, 7, 44, 48, 61, 125, 127, 197
aid, 1, 8, 22, 27, 81, 84, 88–90, 105, 118,
    148–63, 204–5
    as global income tax, 97
allegiance, 77, 134, 178
alleviation of poverty, 162; *see also* aid
alliances of convergence, 107
America
    South America, 135, 167
    see also USA
Amnesty International, 108, 195, 197, 201
anarchical society, 39–41, 57
anarchism, 20, 38, 39
anarchy, 20, 31, 39, 44
animals, 37, 80, 95, 130, 141, 174–5, 183,
    184, 185, 189
Anscombe, G. E. M., 100, 127
anthropocentrism, 104, 173–4, 185
apartheid, 2, 67, 108, 141, 194
applied ethics, 5–6
Aquinas, 9, 55
arguments for aid, 158–60
articles of peace, 39, 83
artificial persons, states as, 21, 65
Augustine, 143
authority
    legitimate, 127–8
    political, 35, 54–6, 203, 204
autonomy, 27, 33, 45, 59, 61, 74, 84, 88,

102, 106, 155, 159, 160, 196, 210
    of international relations, 9
    rational, 159, 160
Aztecs, 48

balance of power, 57, 133
basic needs, 97, 117, 157–64
Beitz, C. R., 19, 24, 39–40, 41, 50n, 59,
    69, 74, 77, 79, 88, 89, 92, 97, 159,
    174
benevolence, 102, 158–60
Bentham, J., 59, 82, 98, 174
biocentrism, 91, 174–5, 189
biosphere, 138, 174–5
biotechnology, 160
biotic community, 175–6, 189
Boutros Ghali, 73
Bradley, F. H., 72, 118, 206
Brandt Report, 149, 168
brotherhood of humankind, 6, 43, 91
Brown, C., 9, 19, 25, 77, 81, 90
Brundtland Report *see Our Common
    Future*
Bull, H., 19, 23, 39, 46, 57–8, 65, 69, 88,
    123, 124, 128, 202

CAMDUN, 211n
capabilities approach, 85, 164–7
capitalism, global, 161, 167
Carr, E. H., 35, 36, 48
categorical imperative, 83; *see also* Kant,
    Kantianism
Catholic church, 55, 195, 207
Catholic theology, 95
Chernobyl, 178
China, 137, 172, 188, 193
Christianity, 37, 55, 104, 157

225